FUN WITH THE FAMILY

D0591397

Maryland

Hundreds OF Ideas FOR Day Trips WITH THE Kids

SECOND EDITION

Karen Nitkin

travel

Guilford, Connecticut

All the information in this guidebook is subject to change. We recommend that you call ahead to obtain current information before traveling.

To buy books in quantity for corporate use or incentives, call **(800) 962-0973** or e-mail **premiums@GlobePequot.com**.

Text design: Nancy Freeborn and Linda R. Loiewski
Maps: Rusty Nelson © Morris Book Publishing, LLC
Spot photography throughout © Photodisc and Rubberball Productions

ISSN 1548-4203
ISBN 978-0-7627-5068-9

Printed in the United States of America
10 9 8 7 6 5 4 3 2 1

To my family

Contents

Acknowledgments

My wonderful husband, David, has given me unstinting support and encouragement. I could not have written this book without his good humor and understanding—not to mention the many hours he spent entertaining, feeding, and otherwise parenting the children solo while I sat in front of the computer, attempting to put my observations into words.

My two terrific children, Ronnie and Sammy, never complained (well, not much) as I dragged them from one end of the state to the other. They have probably seen more living history museums, farm animals, art exhibits, and state parks than any other children in Maryland, yet they approached each new place with enthusiasm and a sense of adventure.

My wonderful friends were eager accomplices on this project, turning even short road trips into grand adventures. In particular, I want to thank Laura, Cheri and Lynne, who brought their own children along on several outings and made every experience fun.

My parents, Barbara and Gary, always give me tremendous love and support. Thanks, guys.

Introduction

From the cheerful boardwalk charm of Ocean City to the rustic pleasures of Deep Creek Lake, Maryland is a great place for families. Although the state is only 10,460 square miles, ranking it No. 42 in size, it is often called America in Miniature because it packs in mountains, beaches, amusement parks, a major city, many charming towns, and a wealth of history. It is particularly well suited for families with children, since there is so much to do within a short distance.

First settled in the 1600s, Maryland is a treasure trove for history buffs. The state played key roles in the American Revolution, the War of 1812, and the Civil War. In Annapolis, lawmakers conduct business in the state capitol building where the Continental Congress once mulled over the future of the young nation.

Take your kids to Fort McHenry in Baltimore, where the flag still waved during the War of 1812, inspiring Francis Scott Key to pen the poem that became "The Star-Spangled Banner."

Visit the Antietam National Battlefield in Sharpsburg, site of one of the bloodiest battles in the Civil War.

If your youngsters are interested in trains, Maryland boasts one of the finest train histories in the nation, which can be explored at the excellent Baltimore & Ohio Railroad Museum in Baltimore, and its sibling, the B&O Railroad Station Museum in Ellicott City. The 13 miles of tracks between these two stations were the first commercial rail lines in the nation.

Many museums in Baltimore are **free,** so there's no reason not to introduce your youngsters to the mummies and other exhibits at the Walters Art Gallery, or the Matisses and Picassos at the Baltimore Museum of Art.

When you're ready to tackle the great outdoors, there's skiing at Wisp Resort, boating on the Chesapeake Bay, and hiking and biking in state parks everywhere. Maryland has nearly 4,000 miles of shoreline, more than any other state in the nation. It also has about four hundred lakes, all man-made.

Animal lovers can see wild ponies on the beaches at Assateague Island, or let butterflies land on their fingertips and shoulders at Brookside Gardens.

Everyone knows Maryland is famous for crab cakes, but there are plenty of other local taste treats, too. In the summer, snowball stands offer this icy regional treat in dozens of flavors. Check out Fisher's Popcorn in Ocean City and Berger's Cookies in Baltimore for two distinctly local delights that are hard to find elsewhere.

Baltimore has a wealth of attractions specifically for children, including Port Discovery, the Maryland Science Center, and the National Aquarium. The Baltimore Zoo and National Aquarium are among the best of their kind in the nation. The Inner Harbor, with its restaurants and retail stores, is a popular family destination.

Traveling in Maryland is easy. The state is generally divided into five regions: Central Maryland, which includes Baltimore and Annapolis; the Capital Region, which includes the tony suburbs close to Washington, D.C.; Western Maryland, which includes the year-round resort of Deep Creek Lake; Southern Maryland, a sparsely populated region with a slow-paced charm of its own; and the Eastern Shore, home to Ocean City and several small towns worth visiting. In this book, I have given Baltimore and Annapolis their own chapters but have otherwise organized sights and attractions into the five regions.

The state is carved almost in two by the Chesapeake Bay, which divides the Eastern Shore from the rest of the state. To get to the Eastern Shore, you'll probably cross the 4-mile-long Bay Bridge.

A good place to gather information about traveling in Maryland is the state's Office of Tourism Development (800-719-5900, www.mdisfun.org). If you will be driving through large chunks of Maryland, you might want to purchase an E-ZPass, which cuts time at tolls by automatically deducting the amount from a prepaid card affixed to your car. Since many surrounding states also use E-ZPass, it can save a lot of time when driving through the region. To get one, call (888) 288-6865 or go to www.EZPass.com.

Wearing seat belts is mandatory in the state, so buckle up before you begin, and make sure young ones are securely fastened in their car seats. For more information about car travel and regulations, including up-to-date reports on road closings or delays, check with the state's transportation administration at (410) 539-5000 or www.mtamaryland.org.

LODGING, RESTAURANT, AND ATTRACTION FEES

In the "Where to Eat" and "Where to Stay" sections, dollar signs indicate general price ranges or averages. For meals, the prices are generally for individual adult entrees. Be aware that lunch is often a better value than dinner.

For lodging, the rates are generally for a double room for a family of three or more. Rates may be higher during peak vacation seasons and holidays.

Rates for attractions are per person; these ratings appear at the end of the italicized information in the heading for each attraction and represent admission costs for both adults and children.

Rates for Attractions

$	up to $5
$$	$5 to $10
$$$	$11 to $20
$$$$	more than $20

Rates for Lodging

$	up to $50
$$	$51 to $100
$$$	$101 to $150
$$$$	more than $150

Rates for Restaurants

$	entrees less than $10
$$	entrees $10 to $15
$$$	entrees $16 to $20
$$$$	entrees more than $20

Attractions Key

The following is a key to the icons found throughout the text.

SWIMMING		**FOOD**	
BOATING/BOAT TOUR		**LODGING**	
HISTORIC SITE		**CAMPING**	
HIKING/WALKING		**MUSEUMS**	
FISHING		**PERFORMING ARTS**	
BIKING		**SPORTS/ATHLETIC**	
AMUSEMENT PARK		**PICNICKING**	
HORSEBACK RIDING		**PLAYGROUND**	
SKIING/WINTER SPORTS		**SHOPPING**	
PARK		**PLANTS/GARDENS/NATURE TRAILS**	
ANIMAL VIEWING		**FARMS**	

Baltimore

From its pre-Revolutionary roots to its modern industries and attractions, Baltimore is a city with a rich history and lots of things to do with the kids. Like animals? Don't miss the excellent aquarium and zoo. Is history your thing? Check out Fort McHenry, where the flag still waved in 1814, inspiring Frances Scott Key to write "The Star-Spangled Banner." For sports fans, there's the Babe Ruth Birthplace and Museum, the Sports Legend Museum, the Lacrosse Museum and National Hall of Fame, and of course Camden Yards for the beloved Orioles and M & T Stadium for Ravens fans. If your kids are looking for hands-on activities, Port Discovery and the Maryland Science Center are perfect places to spend a few hours or the whole day.

Baltimore is sometimes known as Charm City, and there's no doubt it does have a quirky charm all its own. Where else would a person find a kid-friendly museum devoted to dentistry (the Dr. Samuel D. Harris National Museum of Dentistry), or another that explores plumbing, road construction, and other aspects of public works (Baltimore Public Works Museum)?

Many of Baltimore's attractions are clustered around the Inner Harbor. Others are just a short drive away.

This chapter begins with an exploration of the Inner Harbor. From there, we proceed east to the neighborhoods of Fells Point and Canton, head north up Charles Street to the Mount Vernon section of town, and then hit Interstate 83 to continue north for a visit to the Maryland Zoo in Baltimore, the colorful community of Hampden, and other attractions.

Baltimore can be reached by train, airplane (Baltimore-Washington International Airport is about 10 miles away), and of course automobile. Driving around the city is easy, and there are parking garages everywhere. The Maryland Transit Administration (MTA) operates buses and trains throughout the city and surrounding counties. For more information on those services, call the MTA at (410) 539-5000 or (866) RIDE-MTA or visit its Web site at www.mtamaryland.com.

The beautiful 8,000-square-foot Baltimore Visitor Center, which opened in 2004, is a good first stop. It's located right in the Inner Harbor, between Harborplace and the

BALTIMORE

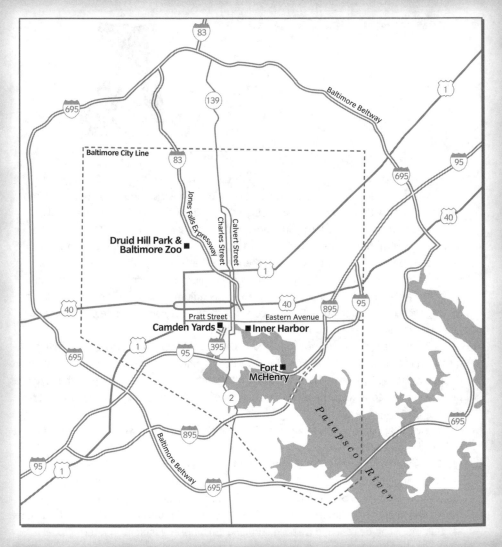

Science Center, and it's where you can buy tickets for attractions and shows or make reservations for lodging or restaurants. The center has loads of pamphlets and brochures, plus touch-screen kiosks for information, and of course, local experts eager to answer your questions.

The Inner Harbor and Southwest

For most Baltimore visitors, the first stop is the Inner Harbor, a cluster of museums, shops, restaurants, and attractions that forms a half-circle around Baltimore's historic harbor.

From I-95, take the I-395 exit and turn right on Pratt Street. In a few minutes, you'll see the boats and water on your left. There's a small parking lot in front of the Science Center, and many garages are located on the streets to the right. In our tour of the Inner Harbor, we'll cover the north side of the harbor and one of the state's most popular attractions, the National Aquarium in Baltimore, to the Museum of Industry, which anchors the other side.

We'll also head west of the Inner Harbor and south of Route 40 to explore Baltimore's baseball heritage and see where our national anthem was created.

American Visionary Art Museum (ages 3 and up)
800 Key Hwy, Baltimore 21230; (410) 244-1900, www.avam.org. Open Tuesday through Sunday 10 a.m. to 6 p.m. $, children under 4 free.

This totally unique and exuberant museum features artwork only by self-taught artists. Kids will be inspired to see what can be created by retirees, disabled people, housewives,

Karen's
TopPicks for fun in Baltimore

1. National Aquarium

2. USS *Constellation*

3. Maryland Science Center

4. Baltimore Museum of Industry

5. Oriole Park at Camden Yards and Babe Ruth Birthplace Museum

6. Fort McHenry

7. Port Discovery

8. Baltimore Public Works Museum

9. Walters Art Gallery

10. The Maryland Zoo in Baltimore

farmers, and others, and they will love the sculpture garden, with its enormous and fantastic creations.

Babe Ruth Birthplace Museum (ages 4 and up)

216 Emory St., Baltimore 21230; (410) 727-1539, www.baberuthmuseum.com. April through October open 10 a.m. to 5 p.m. daily and 7 p.m. when Orioles have a home game; November through March open 10 a.m. to 4 p.m. $, children under 5 free. The museum is 2 blocks northwest of Oriole Park at Camden Yards.

Young sports enthusiasts won't want to miss this museum, housed right in Babe Ruth's childhood home.

Before Ruth was the Sultan of Swat, he was George Herman Ruth Jr. of Baltimore. Born February 6, 1895, in his grandfather's modest home, Ruth attended St. Mary's Industrial School for Boys, a place for orphans and delinquent boys. In 1906, the family moved to 406 West Conway St., now short centerfield at Oriole Park. He played for the Orioles in 1914, then the Boston Red Sox and, most famously, the New York Yankees. He went on to become one of the greatest ballplayers of all time, known forever as the Home Run King for his 1927 single-season home run total of sixty.

Though that record has since been broken, Babe Ruth remains a legend.

Baltimore Maritime Museum (ages 4 and up)

Piers 3 and 5, Inner Harbor, Baltimore 21202; (410) 396-3453, www.baltomaritimemuseum .org. In winter, Friday through Sunday 10:30 a.m. to 5 p.m., in spring and summer, Sunday through Thursday 10 a.m. to 5:30 p.m., Friday and Saturday 10 a.m. to 6:30 p.m. Ticket booth closes a half hour before ships. $.

Here's a place where kids can see boats—lots of boats. The Baltimore Maritime Museum includes ships and a lighthouse that tell the story of U.S. naval history from 1930 to 1986.

Each ticket gives you access to the U.S. Submarine *Torsk,* the Lightship *Chesapeake,* the U.S. Coast Guard Cutter *Taney,* and the Seven Foot Knoll Lighthouse—all fun for kids to explore, and maybe they'll learn a little history while they're at it. My kids love to admire the *Torsk,* which is painted to look like a shark, with huge, scary teeth. Tickets to all these attractions are available at the ticket booth on Pier 3, in front of the National Aquarium.

Baltimore Museum of Industry (ages 3 and up)

1415 Key Hwy, Inner Harbor South, Baltimore 21230; (410) 727-4808, www.thebmi.org. Open Monday through Saturday 10 a.m. to 4 p.m. $.

Known as the "museum that works," the Museum of Industry, housed in an 1865 building that used to be an oyster cannery, explores Baltimore's industrial heritage with plenty of hands-on activities for children, including a Motorworks Assembly Line and a Cannery Children's Activity Center. Re-created workshops let kids touch and explore the nineteenth-century worlds of printing, metalworking, and garment making. Outside is the only operating steam tugboat on the East Coast, the coal-fired SS *Baltimore.* A gift shop open during museum hours sells puzzles, knickknacks, and books.

Amazing
Maryland Facts

Doc Holliday, best known for his gunfighting antics in the American West, was a student at the Baltimore College of Dental Surgery in the 1870s. The school was the world's first dental college when it was founded in 1840.

B and O Railroad Museum (all ages)

901 W. Pratt St., Baltimore 21223; (410) 752-2490; www.borail.org; Monday through Saturday 10 a.m. to 4 p.m., Sunday 11 a.m. to 4 p.m. $$$.

With real trains—not replicas—inside a gorgeous wheelhouse, the B and O is a place where youngsters can run and climb while learning about railroading history or just enjoying the majesty of the old Iron Horses. The first commercial long-distance track was laid right at the museum site in 1829, and the museum, restored after a 2003 snowstorm caused the roof to cave in, retains a strong sense of its history. Exhibits include actual trains as well as small items like pocket watches, lanterns, and dining car china. Train rides are offered Wednesday through Sunday in April through December, and on weekends in January. Other child-friendly events include a fantastic G-scale garden layout over the holiday season, and frequent visits from Thomas the Tank Engine.

Clipper City (all ages)

Departs from the Harborplace piers in front of the Science Center, Baltimore 21202; (410) 931-6777, www.sailingship.com. The ship departs at noon and 3 p.m. Monday through Saturday, and at 3 and 6 p.m. on Sunday. $$.

You and your kids can hear the sails billowing in the wind and feel the salty spray when you take a cruise on this tall ship, a replica of one that carried lumber to East Coast ports between 1854 and 1892. The ship can accommodate as many as 140 passengers for daily cruises and private charters. The two-hour daily cruises start at the Inner Harbor and continue up the Patapsco River. Instead of having a set itinerary, the captain chooses his course depending on the wind and tide.

The Dr. Samuel D. Harris National Museum of Dentistry (ages 3 and up)

31 South Greene St., Baltimore 21201; (410) 706-0600, www.dentalmuseum.org. Open Wednesday through Saturday 10 a.m. to 4 p.m., Sunday 1 to 4 p.m. $, children 6 and under free. From I-95, take Route 395 toward downtown Baltimore and exit onto Martin Luther King Jr. Boulevard. Remain in the right lane. At the fourth traffic light, turn right onto Baltimore Street. Turn right at the next traffic light onto Greene Street. The museum is on the left.

This one-of-a-kind museum, created in association with the Smithsonian Institution, has fun, interactive exhibits on dentists in history, toothbrushes through time, and the importance of good tooth care. Though there are lessons here, the museum is far from serious.

Kids will probably love the world's only mouth-shaped jukebox, which plays old tooth-related advertisements. The museum's collection includes a set of George Washington's dentures, as well as dental instruments used to treat Queen Victoria. You'll come out smiling!

ESPN Zone (ages 6 and up)

601 East Pratt St., Baltimore 21201; (410) 685-ESPN; www.espnzone.com. Open daily 11:30 a.m. to midnight. $$.

You and your kids can easily spend hours at this sports entertainment complex. You don't even have to leave to eat, since there's a restaurant on-site with burgers, chili, and other kid-friendly fare. State-of-the-art interactive games make that round of golf, boxing match, or NASCAR race seem real. Your kids can shoot baskets, go bowling, play hockey against a computerized goalie, or just do a little (simulated) fishing. This place is popular with young adults, and the noise level can be quite high, especially on the weekends.

The France-Merrick Performing Arts Center (all ages)

12 N. Eutaw St., Baltimore, 21201, (410) 837-7400, www.france-merrickpac.com. $$$$.

This venue, better known as the Hippodrome, is Baltimore's answer to Broadway, the place to see such crowd-pleasing kid-friendly extravaganzas as *The Lion King, Annie, Cats,* and *Riverdance.* While most performances are in the evenings, and too late for young sleepyheads, matinees are offered on weekends. Special events like a Dora the Explorer show are frequent. The Hipp Café inside the center serves flat-bread pizzas, soups, sandwiches, and salads.

Fort McHenry National Monument and Historic Shrine
(all ages)

East Fort Avenue, Baltimore 21230-5393; (410) 962-4290, www.nps.gov/fomc. Open daily 8 a.m. to 4:45 p.m. $, children 17 and under free. The park is about 3 miles from the Inner

Amazing
Maryland Facts

Among the many inventions created in Baltimore, the Ouija board may be the most bizarre. This board, patented by a group of Baltimoreans in 1890, consists of letters and numbers, as well as the words "yes" and "no." A pointer that glides across the board supposedly allows users to communicate with the dead.

Junior **Rangers**

Kids ages eight to fourteen can take part in Fort McHenry's Junior Ranger program. Ask for an activity sheet at the visitor center, then explore the fort and grounds to answer questions about its history. Return the activity worksheet to earn a Junior Ranger certificate and badge.

Harbor. From I-95 take exit 55, Key Highway, and follow the Fort McHenry signs to Lawrence Street. Turn left on Lawrence Street and then left on Fort Avenue. Proceed 1 mile to the park. From the Inner Harbor, take Light Street south to Key Highway. Turn left and follow the Fort McHenry signs to Lawrence Street. Turn right on Lawrence Street and then left on Fort Avenue to the park.

Do your kids know the story behind "The Star-Spangled Banner"? It took place at Fort McHenry, during the War of 1812, which pitted the United States against England. English troops attacked Fort McHenry, but after twenty-five hours of fighting, the American flag still flew high over the fort, and the British were defeated.

Marylander Francis Scott Key, who saw the flag from a nearby ship, was inspired to write a poem that began with the words, "O say can you see." In 1931, Congress made it official, and "The Star-Spangled Banner," written by a thirty-five-year-old poet and lawyer, became our national anthem.

Today, the site's visitor center shows a free fifteen-minute movie about the battle and offers plenty of photographs and displays about the fort and its place in history.

The movie is a little complicated for young viewers, but it has no gore. There is also a wonderful park with a walking trail, a great place to observe harbor activity. Visits to the park and visitor center are free; admission is charged only to explore the fort.

Harborplace (all ages)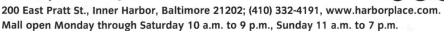

200 East Pratt St., Inner Harbor, Baltimore 21202; (410) 332-4191, www.harborplace.com. Mall open Monday through Saturday 10 a.m. to 9 p.m., Sunday 11 a.m. to 7 p.m.

With its dozens of shops and restaurants, Harborplace is a bustling centerpiece to the Inner Harbor and a great place to shop or get something to eat while visiting the area. Harborplace consists of two pavilions, the Light Street Pavilion and Pratt Street Pavilion,

Save Money

Every year in early December, Harborplace hosts Dollar Days, in which participating attractions offer admission for a dollar and Inner Harbor shops have special deals. Year-round in Mount Vernon, participating shops and attractions offer special deals and extended hours on First Thursday, the first Thursday of each month.

and a fancy shopping mall called the Gallery. The city's largest tourist attraction, it lures about ten million visitors a year.

In the summer, musicians and magicians perform in the Harborplace Amphitheater. Kids will also enjoy riding the carousel near the Science Center.

Lexington Market (all ages)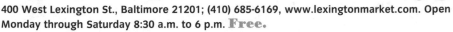

400 West Lexington St., Baltimore 21201; (410) 685-6169, www.lexingtonmarket.com. Open Monday through Saturday 8:30 a.m. to 6 p.m. Free.

From Utz potato chips to Konstant's Candy, there's plenty here to make a child's mouth water. Built in 1782, Lexington Market bills itself as the world's largest continually running market, with stalls of vendors selling seafood, produce, sandwiches, chocolates, baked goods, and nearly any other food you can imagine. Live music is often a part of the experience.

The crab cakes at the J.W. Faidley stall are considered by many to be the best in Baltimore, which means they are quite possibly the best in the world. And even the most finicky eater can't resist a cookie from the Berger's bakery stall.

Maryland Science Center (all ages)

601 Light St., Baltimore 21230; (410) 685-5225, www.mdsci.org. Open Monday through Friday 10 a.m. to 5 p.m., Saturday 10 a.m. to 6 p.m., and Sunday noon to 5 p.m. $$$, children under 3 free.

The Maryland Science Center is packed with room after room of hands-on science-related activities specifically for kids. Though the focus is educational, my kids, ages three and five, have so much fun here they don't realize all they are learning. The new Kids Room, for example, lets children age eight and younger examine X-rays, play with magnets, build with blocks, dress up, learn about gravity, and more. Note that the Kids Room closes an hour before the museum does, and children must be accompanied by an adult.

The exhibits are always changing, but recent ones have included the world's largest collection of authentic Chinese fossils, and an exhibit on cells with a time-lapse movie about human fetal development and that let kids try to match cell shapes with their function. Permanent exhibits give kids the opportunity to learn through play about archaeology, outer space, and the Chesapeake Bay. There is a five-story IMAX theater, which has shown films such as *Beauty and the Beast*—though other movies may be too much for sensitive types. The Davis Planetarium, also part of the center, is a 50-foot dome that uses images and special effects for an experience that is literally out of this world.

The museum has elevators and is wheelchair accessible, but if you can leave the stroller behind or check it in the coatroom, you're better off. Kid-friendly meals and snacks can be found at the MSC Café on the first floor.

National Aquarium (all ages)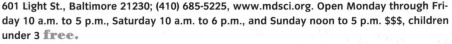

501 East Pratt St., Baltimore 21202; (410) 576-3800, www.aqua.org. In July and August, open Sunday through Thursday 9 a.m. to 6 p.m., Friday and Saturday 9 a.m. to 10 p.m. In March, April, May, June, September, and October, open daily 9 a.m. to 5 p.m., till 10 p.m.

on Friday. In November, December, January, and February, open daily 10 a.m. to 6:30 p.m., till 9:30 p.m. on Friday. $$$.

You'll find sea life ranging from tiny seahorses to enormous flat stingrays in the National Aquarium's beautiful five-story building on Pier 3 of the Inner Harbor. The aquarium now has an Immersion Theater which combines a 3D movie experience with wind and mist effects to make it even more realistic. (Tickets cost extra.) The layout is designed so you ascend from floor to floor as you check out the displays. On the top floor, the Australia exhibit, called Animal Planet Australia: Wild Extremes, gives the impression that you are really there.

There are no cages or tanks, so it feels like you're actually in an Australian river gorge, complete with a 35-foot waterfall. Kids are sure to spot plenty of birds, lizards, and even crocodiles and the pretty bird known as the laughing kookaburra. A long, spiraling ramp takes you back down to the first floor.

My kids always get a kick out of the dolphin show, where these amazing mammals show off their aquatic skills, and audience members close to the tank are sure to get wet. The aquarium is often crowded, so it's a good idea to reserve tickets for the popular show in advance.

Oriole Park at Camden Yards (ages 4 and up)

333 West Camden St., Baltimore 21201; (410) 685-9800, (410) 547-6234 for updated and off-season tour schedule, www.ballparks.com/baseball/american/oriole.htm. Tours offered April through September 11 a.m., noon, 1 and 2 p.m. Monday through Saturday, 12:30, 1, 2, and 3 p.m. Sunday. $.

There's no guarantee your kids will meet a famous ballplayer, but they'll learn about Babe Ruth and check out the dugout and pressroom in a seventy-five-minute tour of the famous ballpark, which set a new standard for urban baseball stadiums when it opened in 1992.

The tour includes a history of the park.

More Games, Less Money

Orioles fans old enough to sit through the games might want to sign up for the **Junior Orioles Dugout Club,** a kid-size season ticket for youngsters ages two through fourteen. The $15 package includes an official ball, hat, and membership card, as well as general admission for one to each of the ten Dugout Club games. For more information, call (410) 685-9800.

A Nitkin Family **Adventure**

After several weeks of bitter winter weather, the temperature finally rose to forty degrees one Sunday in February. The sun was out, the wind was blowing, and we could almost smell spring in the air. My husband and I decided to take our kids to Fort McHenry. We figured they could run around the grounds and explore the fort, while we would learn a little about the battle that inspired "The Star-Spangled Banner."

The outing was better than expected. At the visitor center, my five-year-old daughter seemed to like the short film about the defense of Fort McHenry, and it had enough action to hold the attention of my two-year-old son. Then we walked around the old fort, which overlooks the harbor. The kids were fascinated by the boats on the water and the cranes in the port, and they were equally interested in the indoor displays of old uniforms and weapons.

All in all, it was a much-needed day outdoors, one that gave us a new appreciation for Baltimore history.

Reginald F. Lewis Museum of Maryland African-American History and Culture (ages 7 and up)

830 E. Pratt St., Baltimore, 21202; (443) 263-1800, www.africanamericanculture.org. Open Tuesday through Saturday, 10 a.m. to 5 p.m., Sunday noon to 5 p.m. $$.

This stunning museum, with its beautiful red and yellow inflected façade, is both ambitious and beautiful. Named for Reginald F. Lewis, a Baltimore native who established the first African-American law firm on Wall Street and who died in 1993 at the age of 50, it seeks to do nothing less than document the African-American experience in Maryland.

The permanent collection has three galleries, focusing on family life, labor, and black art and intellect. Through the stories of real families and with the help of artifacts, photos, and interactive displays, children can see how African Americans lived in slavery and in freedom in Maryland for more than two centuries.

Performance footage from Baltimore notables including Cab Calloway, Billie Holiday, and Eubie Blake are sure to enchant.

Ride the Ducks (all ages)

25 Light St., Baltimore 21202; (410) 727-DUCK, www.baltimoreducks.com. Open daily from April to October, limited hours in November; ticket office open 9 a.m. to 6 p.m. $$–$$$, children under 3 free.

Your kids (and you!) will shriek in delight when the tour bus they are riding suddenly heads for the harbor, splashes in, and becomes a boat. This amphibious vehicle travels on both land and water during its eighty-minute narrated tour of the Baltimore area, including Edgar Allan Poe's grave, Fells Point, and Camden Yards. In Fells Point, your bus hits the water and paddles for about twenty minutes past Federal Hill and the aquarium. Kids are encouraged to use their Wacky Quackers, bill-shaped plastic horns that sound like ducks, throughout the narrated tour.

Seaport Taxi and Water Taxi (all ages)

Seaport Taxi: various Inner Harbor locations; (410) 675-2900, www.nathistoricseaport.org. Operates daily 6:55 a.m. to 8:25 p.m. $. Water Taxi: various locations; (410) 563-3901 or (800) 658-8947, www.thewatertaxi.com. Operates November 1 through March 31, 11 a.m. to 6 p.m.; April, 9 a.m. to 6 p.m.; May 1 through September 3, 9 a.m. to 11 p.m.; September 4 through October 31, 9 a.m. to 8 p.m. $.

These boats, which travel throughout the harbor with stops at local attractions, are used by both commuters and tourists. Both taxis offer all-day tickets that are a great and inexpensive way for families to get from one place to another or just enjoy being out on the water. The Water Taxi also rents colorful paddleboats for those who prefer to travel by their own steam.

Sports Legends Museum (ages 4 and up)

301 W. Camden St., Baltimore 21201, open October through March, Tuesday through Sunday 10 a.m. to 5 p.m., April through September daily, 10 a.m. to 6 p.m., and 7 p.m. on game days. $$

The museum includes exhibits about Johnny Unitas, the Baltimore Colts star who is considered the "Babe Ruth of the NFL." Unitas, who was born May 7, 1933, and died September, 11, 2002, quarterbacked for the Colts for seventeen years starting in 1956. The football memorabilia he donated to the museum includes photos, trophies, and the football he threw for his last touchdown as a Colt. Another exhibit tells of what many consider the "greatest game ever played," the 1958 NFL championship game between the Baltimore Colts and the New York Giants, which the Colts, led by Unitas, won in overtime. Other exhibits celebrate Baltimore's soccer, amateur baseball, and college sports highlights. A "kid discovery zone" lets youngsters try on uniforms and compare their stances to those of real players outlined in a facing mirror.

USS *Constellation* (ages 4 and up)

Pier 1, Inner Harbor, Baltimore 21202; (410) 539-1797; www.constellation.org. Open May 1 through October 14, 10 a.m. to 6 p.m.; October 15 through April 30, 10 a.m. to 4 p.m. $$, children 5 and under free.

Kids can turn the steering wheel and pull the ropes as they explore the only Civil War vessel that's still afloat. The USS *Constellation* was built in 1854 as the last all-sail ship commissioned by the U.S. Navy. Today, the interior looks much as it did during the Civil War, except that photographs and explanatory exhibits have been added. You'll receive an audiotape that takes you on a self-guided tour of the boat, or you can opt for a tour from a staffer in Civil War–era uniform. Kids ten and older can participate in a special hands-on tour that shows them what life was like for boys eleven to eighteen years old who served in the navy during the Civil War.

Amazing
Maryland Facts

In 1831, a train with the B&O Railroad in Baltimore set a speed record by traveling at the now wholly unremarkable speed of 30 mph.

World Trade Center (all ages)

401 East Pratt St., Baltimore 21202; (410) 837-VIEW, www.Baltimore.to/TopofWorld. Open Wednesday through Sunday 10 a.m. to 6 p.m. $, children 2 and under free.

For a panoramic view of the city, take the kids up the elevator to the twenty-seventh floor and the Top of the World, the observation level of the city's World Trade Center. The beautiful building, designed by renowned architect I. M. Pei, is the tallest pentagonal building in the world. Exhibits give some history of Baltimore and help explain what you are seeing.

Westminster Cemetery, Grave of Edgar Allan Poe (ages 7 and up)

509 West Fayette St., Baltimore 21201; (410) 706-2072. Open daily 8 a.m. to dusk. Free.

If your kids have read the "Telltale Heart" or other Edgar Allan Poe stories, or if they just like cemeteries, they may get a kick out of visiting Westminster Cemetery, the city's oldest burial ground and the site of Poe's grave, as well as the graves of many Revolutionary War and World War I generals. For an especially Baltimore experience, sit your kids down for a reading of "The Raven" before attending. Baltimore's football team is named for the poem.

Where to Eat

Five Guys Burgers and Fries. 201 E. Pratt St., Baltimore 21202; (410) 244-7175, www.fiveguys.com. This beloved chain has developed almost a cult following for its meaty burgers and fabulous fries. $

Hard Rock Café. 601 East Pratt St., Baltimore; (410) 347-7625, www.hardrockcafe.com. With all the noise and activity in this cavernous chain restaurant, nobody will notice if your kids have a temper tantrum. But they probably won't, because there's so much to see, including music videos, Elton John's shoes, and a 1960 teal Caddy hanging over the bar. Crayons are provided, and a kid-friendly menu leans toward burgers and sandwiches. $$

Matthew's Pizza. 3131 Eastern Ave., Baltimore 21224; (410) 276-8755, www.matthewspizza.com. The very definition of a family-friendly neighborhood pizza shop, Matthew's has been wowing customers young and old since it opened in 1943. The restaurant is known for its classic pies, but also serves up near-perfect subs and pasta dishes. $

Papermoon Diner. 227 W. 29th St., Baltimore 21211; (410) 889-4444, www.papermoondiner24.com. From the shelves lined with toys to meals ranging from classic meat loaf to tofu stir-fries, this is a diner to top all diners. The colorful walls and even more colorful characters will have your youngster staring, but those delicious sweet potato fries should snap her back to attention. $

Where to Stay

Baltimore Marriott Waterfront. 700 Aliceanna St., Baltimore, 21202; (410) 385-3000, www.marriott.com/hotels/travel/bwiwf-baltimore-marriott-waterfront. This stunning new hotel is right on the water and on the edge of the Inner Harbor. Rooms are smoke-free, have great views and high-speed Internet. The hotel has a pool. $$$$

Sheraton Inner Harbor Hotel. 300 S. Charles St., Baltimore, 21201; (410) 962-8300, www.starwoodhotels.com. Connected to the Convention Center and just a short walk to the Inner Harbor, this hotel combines convenience and luxury. All rooms are nonsmoking and have high-speed Internet access. $$$

For More Information

Baltimore Area Convention and Visitors Association. 100 Light St., Twelfth Floor, Baltimore 21202; (877) BALTIMORE, www.baltimore.org.

Harborplace. 200 East Pratt St., Fourth Floor, Baltimore 21202; (410) 332-4191, www.harborplace.com.

Office of Promotion and the Arts. 7 Redwood St., Suite 500, Baltimore 21202; (877) BALTIMORE, www.promotionandarts.com.

Fells Point and Canton

To the east of the Inner Harbor are the historic neighborhoods of Fells Point and Canton, all crammed with locally owned shops and restaurants. The cobblestoned streets of Fells Point were laid out by Edward Fell in 1761, and many still have English names like Thames and Shakespeare. Youngsters may enjoy window-shopping in these neighborhoods, and you and the kids won't want to miss aMuse, a great locally owned toy store at 1623 Thames St. in Fells Point (410-342-5000).

Fells Point is only a short drive away from the Inner Harbor. Just turn right on South President Street and left on Eastern Avenue. To get to Canton from that point, go east on Thames Street, then right on Aliceanna Street and right on Boston Street.

Baltimore City Fire Museum (ages 6 and up)
414 Gay St., Baltimore 21202. Open by appointment, call (410) 327-3380. Free.

If your child wants to be a firefighter when he or she grows up, you'll want to make an appointment to visit this fascinating museum, which shows youngsters how Baltimore firefighting evolved over the years.

They will be intrigued by exhibits that include a hand pumper from the 1800s, a 1960 square-box ambulance, and displays of old badges and fire extinguishers. The museum is housed in an 1853 former watchtower, and tour guides explain how fire alarms were sounded in the days before the development of 911. Kids will also be awed by photos of the Great Fire of 1904, which destroyed about 70 blocks of Baltimore's business district. Note: Some of the images of devastation may be disturbing.

Read All about It

Several local publications offer up-to-date listings of things to do. Check out the *Live* section of the *Baltimore Sun*, which appears every Thursday, or look for free copies of the monthly *Baltimore's Child*, available in super-markets, libraries, and boxes on the street. *CityPaper*, a free weekly geared more toward adults, also lists some children's activities. It is available in boxes on the street and at some restaurants and shops.

Baltimore Civil War Museum (ages 5 and up)

601 President St., Baltimore 21202; (410) 268-7601, www.mdhs.org/explore/baltcivilwar .html. Open daily 10 a.m. to 5 p.m. $, children 12 and under free.

Even children who know very little about the Civil War will enjoy visiting this small museum, housed in the brick 1849 train station where the first blood of the conflict was shed. Operated by the Maryland Historical Society, the museum mainly consists of photographs with descriptions and some audiotapes that highlight Maryland's ambivalent role in the war, as a state just south of the Mason-Dixon Line. Kids will learn about the state's railroad history, about the station's role in the Underground Railroad that helped slaves escape to the north, and about how and why Confederate sympathizers attacked a Massachusetts regiment that was passing through this very station. Four soldiers and twelve Baltimore citizens died during that skirmish on April 19, 1861. A gift shop is also on the premises.

Baltimore Public Works Museum (ages 3 and up)

751 Eastern Ave., Baltimore 21202; (410) 396-5565, www.ci.baltimore.md.us/government/ dpw/museum. Open Wednesday through Sunday 10 a.m. to 4 p.m. $, children under 6 free.

Any child with an interest in bathrooms, garbage removal, or construction will get a kick out of this unusual place. This small museum, housed in a 1911 former pumping station

Amazing
Maryland Facts

The state's official song, "Maryland, My Maryland," was written in 1861 by a twenty-two-year-old schoolteacher named James Ryder Randall after federal troops were attacked in Baltimore. The song expresses his eagerness for Baltimore to join the Confederate cause. With lines like "Avenge the patriotic gore/that flecked the streets of Baltimore," it's not exactly peace loving.

(ew!), explores the history of the city's public works department and the technology behind its work, all presented in kid-friendly terms. Kids can play in the "construction site," admire a Lego city, or laugh over a newspaper-style fact sheet headlined HISTORY OF THE BATHROOM, which explains that Queen Elizabeth I, who had a water closet installed in 1598, wrote in her diary that she bathed once a month whether she needed it or not.

For the price of admission, your young ones can also climb on the "cityscape" that's outside next to the museum. This is a full-scale model of a street corner, raised so that the utility pipes and drains underneath are at street level. It's educational, but it also makes a great playground.

Local art for sale in the gift shop has a public works theme and recently included art made from recycled materials.

Baltimore Ice Rink at Harbor Point (ages 3 and up)

At the intersection of South Caroline, Thames, and Block Streets, Baltimore 21231; (410) 522-3213. Open daily in the winter months, weather permitting. $ for rentals and time on the rink.

Outdoor skating in a waterfront location right in Fells Point can warm the hearts of even the most winter-grumpy kids. Special events include Tykes on Ice, Saturday-morning skate sessions with kid-friendly music and costumed characters, and skating with Santa in the days before Christmas. You and your kids are sure to meet the rink's friendly mascot, Perky the Penguin, as he glides around the ice.

Dominic "Mimi" Dipietro Family Skating Center (all ages)

200 South Linwood Ave., Canton 21224; (410) 396-9392. Open from mid-October to mid-April. Public ice-skating sessions are scheduled Tuesday noon to 2 p.m. and 7 to 9 p.m., Thursday noon to 2 p.m., Friday 7 to 9 p.m., Saturday and Sunday 3 to 5 p.m. and 7 to 9 p.m. $.

Located within Patterson Park, this indoor rink offers lessons for all ages, ice hockey clinics for kids as young as five, and public skating sessions.

Movie Night

On Friday nights in July and August, thousands of movie lovers attend the Italian-theme movies that are shown outdoors at the intersection of High and Stile Streets, in Baltimore's Little Italy neighborhood. The movies start at 9 p.m., but not all films are rated G. To find out what's playing, check local newspapers or go to www.marylandnightlife.com/LittleItaly.htm.

The Fells Point Maritime Museum (ages 6 and up)

1724 Thames St., Baltimore 21231; (410) 732-0278, www.mdhs.org. Open Thursday through Monday, 10 a.m. to 5 p.m. $, children 12 and under and members of the Maryland Historical Society free.

This museum opened in June 2003 to explore the people, ships, and history of Fells Point, mostly through artifacts, models, and paintings.

Your children can learn how the clipper schooners built in Fells Point were used to carry everything from spices and tobacco to heroin and slaves. The museum is housed in a block-long nineteenth-century building that was once a barn for the city's horse-drawn trolley service.

Jewish Museum of Maryland (ages 3 and up)

15 Lloyd St., Baltimore 21202; (410) 732-6400, www.jhsm.org. Open Sunday, Tuesday, Wednesday, and Thursday noon to 4 p.m., with tours offered at 1 and 2:30 p.m. $.

Children can learn about Jewish culture in an engaging environment at this museum, the nation's largest repository of regional Jewish-American history. The museum maintains two synagogues on its campus: the Lloyd Street Synagogue, built in 1845, and the B'Nai Israel Synagogue, built the following year. The Lloyd Street Synagogue has a family learning place for children in kindergarten through third grade, where they can learn about Baltimore's immigrant Jewish population at the dawn of the twentieth century through photographs and exhibits.

The museum hosts many family programs throughout the year, including a Christmas Day party with music and puppet shows. Many of the changing exhibits are appropriate for young children, such as a recent one called *From Tent to Temple: Life in the Ancient Near East,* on loan from the Jewish Children's Learning Lab in New York. Call or check the Web site for exhibits and programs geared specifically for kids.

Patterson Park (all ages)

200 South Linwood Ave., Canton 21231; (410) 276-3676, www.patterson park.com. Open year-round. Free.

Sometimes called the "best backyard in Baltimore," the 155-acre Patterson Park, with its lake, trails, ballfields, playgrounds, and historic buildings, is a great place for families to run off some steam in the great outdoors. The four-story "pagoda," built in 1891 and open Sundays from May to October, offers fine views of the city for young ones willing to make the climb. An outdoor pool is open daily in the summer months. A large playground with slides and climbing structures is a magnet for children—and it provides shaded benches for adults.

The Can **Company**

This mix of stores and restaurants at 2400 Boston St. in a former Canton cannery is a fun place to visit, and it has lots of special events throughout the year, including free outdoor music from 6 to 9 p.m. the last Friday of the month during the summer. In October, kids will get a kick out of seeing dogs in costume at the annual "Howl-a-ween" Fancy Dress Dog Competition. In early December, kids will enjoy the lighting of the tin-can tree, complete with seasonal music and free holiday treats. For more Can Company information, call (410) 558-0525 or go to www.thecancompany.com.

Port Discovery (all ages)

35 Market Place, Baltimore, 21202; (410) 727-8120, www.portdiscovery.org. Open Sunday noon to 5 p.m., Tuesday through Saturday 10 a.m. to 5 p.m. $$, children under 3 free. From the Inner Harbor, take Pratt Street past the National Aquarium and get into the far left lane to make a left onto Market Place. After crossing Lombard Street, Port Discovery will be on the right.

Located near the Inner Harbor, this "kid-powered" museum was recently ranked by *Child* magazine as one of the top five children's museums in the country. So it's no wonder that my kids, at ages five and three, love this museum, with its giant indoor climbing structure, a Kid Karaoke room, computers, costumes, crafts, and more. There are enough hands-on exhibits and activities to keep them busy for at least a couple of hours. When you get tired of standing, a kid room with seats has plenty of things for them to touch, climb, and explore.

Robert Long House Museum and Garden (ages 6 and up)

812 South Ann St., Baltimore 21231; (410) 675-6750, www.preservationsociety.com. Open daily year-round noon to 4 p.m., with tours several times daily. $.

At this museum, kids always seem fascinated by the garden that's used to grow plants for medicine and by the porcelain chamber pots under the bed, commonplace in the days before indoor plumbing. The brick-front house, built around 1765, is the state's oldest surviving suburban residence and has been restored to show how the family of a merchant in the eighteenth century might have lived. Tour guides make an effort to tailor the information to young audiences.

Star-Spangled Banner Museum (ages 3 and up)

844 East Pratt St., Baltimore 21202; (410) 837-1793, www.flaghouse.org. Open Tuesday through Saturday 10 a.m. to 4 p.m. $, children 18 and under free. Metered and street parking is available on nearby streets.

The awe-inspiring Great Flag Window on this recently expanded museum is 30 feet by 42 feet, the same size as the flag created by Mary Pickersgill that flew over Fort McHenry and inspired Francis Scott Key in 1814 to write the song that became the national anthem. And like that flag, the window has fifteen stars and fifteen stripes.

The museum, within walking distance of the Inner Harbor, is located at Pickersgill's 1793 home. Inside the house, kids can peer at furniture and artwork from the era, including some toys, and learn how Pickersgill, a widowed mother, made the flag. A museum attached to the house shows a video about the war, the flag, and Mary Pickersgill. You'll also find a gift shop. Outside, the Flag House Garden has a unique stone map of the United States, with each state cut from stone native to that state.

Where to Eat

Bo Brooks Crab House. 2701 Boston St., Canton; (410) 558-0202, www.bobrooks .com. Famous seafood restaurant with a kids' menu. $$$

Brick Oven Pizza. 800 South Broadway, Fells Point; (410) 563-1600. Kids can peer at the brick oven behind the counter or admire colorful wall murals while waiting for their pies. This corner eatery boasts more than fifty pizza toppings, plus pasta dishes, wrap sandwiches, a gyro platter, and salads. For dessert, there's ice cream or a specialty of the house—a dessert pie made with raspberry preserves and chocolate. But the best thing about eating here is walking around Fells Point after the meal. $

Broadway Market. Broadway and Thames Street, Fells Point; (410) 396-3100. This indoor food market has been in operation since 1776. $

Jimmy's Restaurant. 801 South Broadway, Fells Point; (410) 327-3273. This Fells Point diner is known for its huge portions and low prices. $

Petticoat Tea Room. 814 South Broadway, Fells Point; (410) 342-7884. This rose-festooned and teacup-crowded room inside the Admiral Fell Inn is an old-fashioned setting for an old-fashioned spot of tea. A Tinkerbell tea, for children ages five to eleven, includes child-appropriate treats like gummy bears, chicken noodle soup, and peanut-butter-and-jelly sandwiches. $$

Where to Stay

Admiral Fell Inn. 888 South Broadway, Fells Point; (410) 522-7377, www.AdmiralFell .com. The eighty-room inn in the heart of Fells Point has served as a YMCA and vinegar factory. Now it is registered as a Historic Hotel of America. Services include complimentary continental breakfast and free shuttles to area attractions. $$$

For More Information

Fells Point Visitor Center. 1724–26 Thames Street, Baltimore; (410) 675-6751, www.preservationsociety.com.

Central Baltimore and to the North

While many of Baltimore's attractions are located near the Inner Harbor, there are plenty of things to see and do north of Baltimore Street. From the Inner Harbor, Charles Street is the main north–south route through the heart of the city. Charles Street starts in the Mount Vernon Cultural District, then connects with I-83 (the Jones Falls Expressway) to take visitors to Hampden and the Baltimore Zoo.

Antique Toy Museum (ages 3 and up)

222 West Read St., Baltimore 21201; (410) 230-0580. Open Thursday through Saturday 11 a.m. to 4 p.m. and by appointment. $, children 12 and under free.

Nineteenth- and twentieth-century dollhouses, games, toys, and other items pertaining to childhood are on display in this museum. There's even an antique apothecary. Don't worry about your kids damaging the antiques—they're all behind glass. The museum, near Mount Vernon's Antique Row, also has an antiques shop and gallery.

Taking Kids to Museums

I like taking my kids to museums, and I've learned a few tricks for making the experience enjoyable.

- Kids will enjoy art museums more if they know what to expect. Before I took my youngsters to visit the mummy at the Walters, we read a few books about mummies, then talked about what we might find.

- Kids can get more out of their museum experience if you take the time to talk to them about what they see. Get their opinions and observations. Are the people in the painting happy or sad?

- Find out ahead of time what will be on exhibit. That way, you can choose what you will do, since it is difficult to take in a whole museum with young children. And be sure to select something appropriate. I learned this from experience. On one visit to the Science Center, we decided to check out an exhibit on the *Titanic*. That turned out to be a bad idea, because my daughter, who was four at the time, was rattled by the story of so many people dying. If we had done a little research before we went, we would have stayed away from that part of the museum.

Baltimore Museum of Art (ages 3 and up)

10 Art Museum Dr., Baltimore 21218; (410) 396-7100, www.artbma.org. Open Wednesday through Friday 11 a.m. to 5 p.m., Saturday and Sunday 11 a.m. to 6 p.m., first Thursday of each month 11 a.m. to 8 p.m. Free.

With its family programs (for example, Matisse for Kids) and its lush sculpture garden, the Baltimore Museum of Art is a great place for kids to explore art. Adults will be happy, too. This acclaimed museum has thousands of important works from such artists as Renoir, Cézanne, Manet, and Dürer, as well as collections of African, American, European, and Asian art. Call or visit the Web site to get on a mailing list of family programs.

Baltimore Streetcar Museum (ages 4 and up)

1901 Falls Rd., Baltimore 21211; (410) 547-0264, www.baltimorestreetcar.org. Open year-round on Sunday noon to 5 p.m. and on Saturday from June to October, noon to 5 p.m. $$, children under 4 free.

Admission to this fun museum offers you unlimited rides on original Baltimore streetcars (on an outdoor track), including several built in the late 1800s, as well as a guided tour of the car house and a film on the history of streetcars in Baltimore. All aboard!

Carrie Murray Nature Center (all ages)

1901 Ridetop Rd., Baltimore 21207; (410) 396-0808. Open Monday through Friday 8:30 a.m. to 4:30 p.m., Saturday 10 a.m. to 4 p.m., Sunday 10 a.m. to 3 p.m. Free.

Located within Gwynns Falls Park, the nature center entices children with an Insect Zoo, with hundreds of local and exotic species, a rehabilitation center for injured birds of prey, and a display of reptiles and amphibians. Call for information about children's camps and programs.

A Nitkin Family **Adventure**

For some reason comprehensible only to a five-year-old, my daughter, Veronica, has become obsessed with bugs. She wants to learn everything she can about them. We bought her a magnifying glass and a book about insects, then we took her to the Insect Zoo at the Carrie Murray Nature Center.

There we saw giant cockroaches, beetles, millipedes, and tarantulas, as well as stick insects and crickets. I was a little creeped out, but my daughter was fascinated. A park employee named Lloyd spent a half hour with us, discussing the different creatures and holding them so my daughter could get a close look. She didn't flinch once, and she even stroked the wings of a cockroach.

Elsewhere in the nature center, we saw enormous snakes and lizards, furry bunnies and gerbils, and an American eagle, among other birds of prey.

Mount Vernon Cultural District

This residential urban area within 3 blocks of the Washington Monument is rich in museums, theaters, libraries, and more. In the summer, activities for preschoolers are offered under the tent in West Park on Tuesday mornings at 10:30. Activities might include Opera for Kids by the Baltimore Opera Company or History for Kids by the Maryland Historical Society. On summer Sundays from 12:30 to 2 p.m., musicians perform live. For more information, check out www.mcvd.org.

Clyburn Arboretum (all ages)

4915 Greenspring Ave., Baltimore 21209; (410) 367-2217. Mansion is open Monday through Friday 8:30 a.m. to 3:30 p.m.; grounds open dawn to dusk year-round. Free.

Kids who like nature will enjoy a visit to this beautiful place. Attractions in this 176-acre park include a "garden of the senses," designed for disabled visitors, and a mansion built by Baltimore businessman Jesse Tyson in 1863. Inside the mansion is a nature museum and the Baltimore Bird Club Museum, with a collection of mounted Maryland birds.

Druid Hill Park (all ages)

2600 Madison Ave. and Druid Hill Park Drive, Baltimore 21201; (410) 396-6106. Open daily dawn to dusk. Free.

This 744-acre park, home to the Baltimore Zoo, boasts miles of paths for walking, running, or pushing a stroller. Take your kids to see the Baltimore Conservatory and Botanic Gardens, featuring the 1888 Victorian Palm House, three greenhouses, and 1.5 acres of gardens.

If you and your kids like Easter egg hunts and weren't invited to the White House hunt, come take part in Baltimore's largest egg hunt in the Botanic Gardens.

The Eubie Blake National Jazz Institute and Cultural Center
(ages 5 and up)

847 North Howard St., Baltimore 21201; (410) 225-3130, www.mvcd.org/members/eubie .html. Open Tuesday through Friday 10 a.m. to 5 p.m., Saturday 10 a.m. to 8 p.m. $ donation.

Jazz fans both young and old will be enchanted with the museum's exhibits on Baltimore's jazz greats, including Eubie Blake (1883–1983), Billie Holiday (1915–1959), and the Hi De Ho man, Cab Calloway (1907–1994). The center also serves to educate local youngsters through educational programs in dance, drama, music, and art, and it provides exhibit space for local artists. Call or check the Web site for a schedule of programs and exhibits geared to children.

Story Time

For a fun—and free—way to spend an afternoon, check out the story times and activities at the **Enoch Pratt Free Library,** one of the oldest library systems in the country. The central library, which opened on Mulberry Street in 1883 thanks to funding from Mr. Pratt, is located at 400 Cathedral St.

Branches are found throughout the city. The central library has an amazing collection of Edgar Allan Poe artifacts and memorabilia. For more information on specific kid-friendly events, call the library at (410) 396-5430 or visit www.pratt.lib.md.us/kids/events.html.

Lacrosse Museum and National Hall of Fame Museum

(ages 7 and up)

113 West University Parkway, Baltimore 21210; (410) 235-6882. Open February through May, Tuesday through Friday 10 a.m. to 3 p.m.; June through January, Monday through Friday 10 a.m. to 3 p.m. $, children 5 and under and U.S. Lacrosse members free.

This museum on the north side of the Johns Hopkins University campus pays tribute to one of Maryland's most popular sports. Exhibits trace the history of lacrosse from its Native-American origins to modern times, with photos, uniforms, memorabilia, and a multimedia show.

Leakin Park and Gwynns Falls Park   (all ages)

Windsor Mill and Franklinton Road, Baltimore 21216; (410) 396-7931. Open daily dawn to dusk. Free.

Gwynns Falls Park, which is run by the city, features hiking and biking trails and habitats for owl, deer, red fox, raccoon, and other animals. Leakin Park, a separate facility within the borders of Gwynns Falls, has tennis courts, running tracks, and other athletic facilities that are open to the public year-round.

Maryland Historic Society Museum   (ages 5 and up)

201 West Monument St., Baltimore 21201; (410) 685-3750, www.mdhs.org. Open Wednesday through Friday 10 a.m. to 5 p.m., Saturday 9 a.m. to 5 p.m., Sunday 11 a.m. to 5 p.m. $, children 12 and under free, on Sunday free to all.

A hands-on history center here lets kids try on costumes, play with toys, and hold utensils from earlier eras. The recently expanded and renovated museum is brimming with cool stuff, including the actual manuscript of "The Star-Spangled Banner," collections of nineteenth-century American silver, and other Baltimore and Maryland artifacts. But kids may prefer spending time at the exhibit of children's games, toys, and furniture from the eighteenth to the twentieth centuries. For kids ages seven and older, the Darnall Young People's Gallery explores Maryland history.

The Maryland Zoo in Baltimore (all ages)

Druid Hill Park, Baltimore 21217; (410) 396-7102, www.baltimorezoo.org. Open daily 10 a.m. to 4 p.m., closed Thanksgiving and December 15 through March 13. $$$. From downtown Baltimore, take Pratt Street to President Street and turn left. Continue straight on I-83 North. Take exit 7 (west) to Druid Park Lake Drive and follow signs to the zoo.

Polar bears, snow leopards, giraffes, chimpanzees, elephants, and prairie dogs are among the hundreds of animals at the third oldest zoo in the nation. Though the entire 180-acre zoo is great for kids, the children's section is specially tailored to youngsters, with pygmy goats that can be brushed, a boardwalk through wetlands, and a slide that goes right through a tree.

There's also a display of cows, pigs, and other farm animals, as well as sculptures that are just right for young climbers.

When the kids get tired of seeing animals, they might want to ride the carousel, climb the rock wall, or ride a tram through the park. And of course, there are snack bars and picnic pavilions for refueling them when they run out of energy.

National Great Blacks in Wax Museum (ages 4 and up)

1601-03 East North Ave., Baltimore 21213; (410) 563-3404, www.greatblacksinwax.org. From March 1 through June 30, open Tuesday through Saturday 9 a.m. to 5 p.m., Sunday noon to 6 p.m.; from July 1 to August 31, open Monday through Saturday, 9 a.m. to 6 p.m.; in September, open Tuesday through Saturday 9 a.m. to 5 p.m. and Sunday noon to 6 p.m.; from October 15 to January 14, open Tuesday through Saturday, 9 a.m. to 5 p.m., Sunday noon to 5 p.m. $$$, children 3 and under are free.

Hampden

This wonderful neighborhood in northern Baltimore is a mix of working-class residences and colorful, locally owned shops and restaurants. The mood here is urban chic, but in a soft-edged, Baltimore kind of way. Think *Hairspray*. Make sure to stroll "The Avenue" (Thirty-sixth Street), with its mix of quirky family-friendly restaurants and stores, including **Hometown Girl,** with Baltimore souvenirs and an old-fashioned ice-cream counter (1001 West Thirty-sixth St.; 410-662-4438). Also check out **Eieio,** a very hip, very cute children's consignment shop selling chic clothes, toys, diaper bags, and more (3616 Falls Rd.; 410-889-2200, www.cluckcluckhere.com).

In the weeks before Christmas, take your kids for a walk past the lavish light displays known as the **Miracle on 34th Street.** On a single residential block (700 West Thirty-fourth St.), you (and thousands of other tourists) will see laughing Santas, flying reindeer, and enough blinking lights to rival Las Vegas.

This unique museum is exactly what its name indicates: It features more than one hundred wax sculptures of African Americans throughout history, including a likeness of President Barack Obama, installed the day of his inauguration. There are sculptures of famous people, such as Martin Luther King Jr. and Harriet Tubman, as well as wax depictions of historic events, such as children chained in the hold of a slave ship or black soldiers fighting in the Civil War. Started in 1983 by Baltimoreans Elmer and Joanne Martin, the museum moved to its larger location in 1988. Look for statues depicting African Americans working on the western frontier, traveling the Underground Railroad, and fighting for Civil Rights. Note: Some children may be upset by images of slavery and lynching.

Walters Art Gallery (ages 3 and up)

600 North Charles St., Baltimore 21201; (410) 547-9000, www.thewalters.org. Open Tuesday through Sunday 10 a.m. to 5 p.m. $, children 17 and under free.

My kids never get tired of seeing the Egyptian exhibit with the real mummy here, and there are lots of other child-friendly exhibits as well. The museum added a Family Art Center in 2001 to encourage children to explore art. The center hosts special art activities on the weekends. Free family festivals are held periodically, usually geared to an event, such as African-American Community Day, or a specific exhibit. Expect hands-on activities, musicians, and films. A museum store has many items that appeal to youngsters, and a cafe on the first floor offers light fare.

The Washington Monument (ages 4 and up)

699 North Charles St., Baltimore 21201; (410) 396-0929. Open Tuesday through Sunday 10 a.m. to 4 p.m. $.

This Washington Monument is not as tall or as famous as the one in Washington, D.C., but it was built fifty-five years earlier, in 1815. Financed by the state lottery, the nation's first tribute to George Washington now anchors the Mount Vernon district. Older children with parents can climb the monument's 228 steps for a great view of Baltimore. Everyone can check out the exhibit at the base about the history of the monument.

Where to Eat

Café Hon. 1002 West Thirty-sixth St., Hampden; (410) 243-1230, www.cafehon.com. No trip to Baltimore is complete without a meal at Café Hon. This very family-friendly restaurant serves home-style food in a fun atmosphere. It's open daily for breakfast, lunch, and dinner, brunch on weekends. $

Golden West Café. 1105 West Thirty-sixth St., Hampden; (410) 889-8891. A casual, fun eatery with unique spins on basic fare. $

Where to Stay

Mount Vernon Hotel. 24 West Franklin St., Baltimore (410) 727-2000 or (800) 245-5256, www.bichotels.com. This hotel is one of three in the city run by Baltimore International College and staffed partly by students who are learning about the hospitality industry. Rooms include bilevel loft suites that are suitable for families. The Bay Atlantic Seafood Company, on the premises, is also run by BIC students. Other hotels in the group are the Hopkins Inn (3403 St. Paul St., Baltimore; 410-

Little Culture Vultures

Baltimore is home to many theaters that often host children's productions.

We've seen *Blue's Clues* at the Lyric Opera House and *Disney on Ice* at the First Mariner Arena. Here are some possibilities:

- **Center Stage.** 700 North Calvert St., Baltimore 21202; (410) 332-0033, www.centerstage.org. A Child's Play babysitting series allows adults to see a Saturday matinee while kids between the ages of four and ten are entertained with theaterrelated crafts and activities in the same building.

- **The Children's Theater Association** (410-366-6403) puts on performances at the Baltimore Museum of Art and travels to schools and theaters throughout the Mid-Atlantic region. It also offers summer drama workshops for children ages seven through seventeen.

- **First Mariner Arena.** 201 West Baltimore St., Baltimore 21201; (410) 347-2020, www.baltimorearena.com. Disney on Ice, Barney, and Sesame Street are just a few of the acts to appear in this downtown sports and entertainment facility.

- **Joseph Meyerhoff Symphony Hall.** 1212 Cathedral St., Baltimore 21201; (410) 783-8100, www.baltimoresymphony.com. The Meyerhoff is devoted to helping young ears learn to appreciate music. Family events include Saturday-morning concerts designed for children as young as three. Tip: Go to www.bsokids.com to read music reviews written by third-grade critics and to read answers to music-related questions posed by real kids.

- **Lyric Opera House.** 140 West Mount Royal Ave., Baltimore 21201; (410) 685-5086, www.lyricoperahouse.com. *Blue's Clues*, *Bear in the Big Blue House*, and other shows for young audiences are always on the schedule here.

235-7051) and the Bay Atlantic Club (206 East Redwood St., Baltimore; 410-752-1448). $$$

For More Information

Hampden Village Merchants Association. 735 West Thirty-sixth St., Baltimore 21211; (410) 235-5800, www.hampden merchants.com.

Mount Vernon Cultural District. 217 North Charles St., Suite 100, Baltimore 21201; (410) 605-0462, www.mcvd.org.

Annual Events

Lunch with the Elephants. Lexington Market. In March, elephants from the Ringling Brothers and Barnum and Bailey Circus parade from the Baltimore Arena to Lexington Market, where they feast on 1,100 oranges, 1,000 apples, and 700 bananas. Clowns, live music, and thousands of fans contribute to the circus atmosphere.

Waterfront Festival. Sailing races, maritime exhibits, and crafts for children are

Other Things to See and Do in Baltimore

- **Evergreen House.** 4545 North Charles St.; (410) 516-0341

- **Homewood House Museum.** Johns Hopkins University, 3400 North Charles St.; (410) 516-5589

- **Mother Seton House.** 600 North Paca St.; (410) 523-3443

- **Mount Clare Museum House.** 1500 Washington Blvd., Carroll Park; (410) 837-3262

- **Poe House and Museum.** 203 Amity St.; (410) 396-7932; www.eapoe.org/balt/poehse.htm

among the highlights of this festival, held at the Inner Harbor in April.

Flower Mart. Founded in 1911, Flower Mart in May is a lot more than vendors selling flowers. Live music fills the air, and contests are held for best hat, best hair, and best ugly tie. Children dance around a maypole. Food for sale includes lemon halves paired with peppermints, a local delicacy known as lemon sticks.

Honfest. Café Hon, 1002 West Thirty-sixth St.; (410) 243-1133, www.cafehon@charm net. This June event is a tongue-in-cheek homage to the women of Baltimore. Big

hair (usually a very obvious wig), skintight leopard-print clothing, and high-heel sandals are required. Polyester is definitely the fabric of choice.

Fourth of July Celebration. Entertainment throughout the day and fireworks at night in the Inner Harbor.

Book Fair. Books and book-related activities for children make this September Mount Vernon event a fun tradition for the whole family.

New Year's Eve. The Inner Harbor puts on a big show with live music, an ice-skating party, and of course fireworks.

Annapolis and Anne Arundel County

I f you and your kids like boats and water sports, you will love Annapolis and Anne Arundel County. Anne Arundel County is to the south and east of Baltimore, with Annapolis perched on a craggy tip of land where the Chesapeake Bay and the Severn River meet. The county, with its astounding 534 miles of coastline, nestles along the Chesapeake Bay. It began developing in the 1600s and remains an important seaport to this day.

Children of all ages will find a lot to do in Annapolis, the state's capital. As you roam the cobblestone streets, you may be delighted that your youngsters suddenly develop a keen interest in American history. Signs of America's past are everywhere in Annapolis.

Four signers of the Declaration of Independence lived here, and Annapolis even served as the United States capital, though only in 1783 and 1784.

Elsewhere in Anne Arundel County, there are beaches, parks, and playgrounds, as well as London Town Public Gardens, an ongoing excavation and reconstruction of a seventeenth-century community, and the Horizon Organic Dairy Farm, where kids can eat ice cream while visiting the cows that helped produce it.

We'll start the chapter by exploring Annapolis, then we'll circle the surrounding county, beginning in the northern part of the county and gradually working southward.

Annapolis

Annapolis, the state capital, is probably best known for the Naval Academy, where the best and brightest young Americans are trained for a career in the United States Navy.

Men and women dressed in spiffy white uniforms can be seen everywhere in the city, alongside wealthy boat owners who have made Annapolis their most recent port of call, and costumed interpreters explaining the city's rich history to attentive visitors.

To get to Annapolis from Baltimore, take the Baltimore Beltway (I-695) to I-97 South, then head east on Route 50. Take Rowe Boulevard (Route 70) to Calvert Street, which will

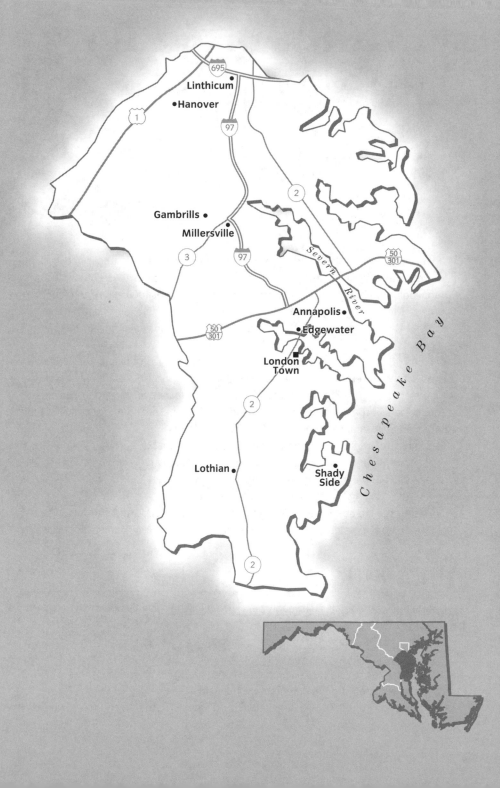

take you to the visitor center at 26 West St., a fine starting place, and one with several nearby parking lots. (If the lots are full, you can go to the Navy–Marine Corps Memorial off Rowe Boulevard and take a trolley shuttle into town.) Once you've parked the car, you and your family can walk to nearly every attraction (unless, of course, you have very young ones who wilt easily).

Annapolis Maritime Museum (all ages)

Second Street at Bayshore Drive, Annapolis 21403; (410) 268-1802, www.annapolismaritime museum.org. Open Saturday 11 a.m. to 4 p.m. and Sunday 1 to 4 p.m. Free. From Route 50, take Rowe Boulevard into Annapolis and bear right to Church Circle. Turn onto Duke of Gloucester Street, then turn right at the end onto Compromise Street. Cross the Spa Creek Bridge. Make the first left onto Severn Avenue. Turn right at Second Street and follow to the end.

A barge house, a former oyster-packing house, and a city park on the water all work together to showcase three hundred years of maritime history. The barge house, built in 1916, is being converted to an interactive children's museum. Kids can walk on the docks and feed the ducks or follow the heritage trail that wanders through Eastport (a quaint village just over the Spa Bridge to the east of Annapolis) noting buildings of historic or maritime significance. A small museum cafe serving crab cakes and sandwiches is on the premises.

Karen's TopPicks for fun in Annapolis and Anne Arundel County

1. State House

2. City Dock and Alex Haley Sculpture

3. Watermark Cruises

4. United States Naval Academy

5. William Paca House and Gardens

6. Chesapeake Children's Museum

7. Sandy Point State Park

8. Banneker-Douglass Museum

9. Pirate Adventures on the Chesapeake

10. Historic London Town and Gardens, Edgewater

Amazing
Maryland Facts

Benjamin Banneker invented a clock, taught himself astronomy and mathematics, and published an almanac that became a local best-seller for the next five years. But he's best known for his role in the construction of Washington, D.C. In 1791, he became the first African-American employee of the federal government when he was asked to help Pierre L'Enfant, the architect who was planning construction of the nation's new capital. When L'Enfant quit the project in a fit of temper, taking the plans with him, Banneker was able to re-create those plans from memory. The Maryland native saved the U.S. government the considerable effort and expense of hiring someone new.

Ballet Theatre of Maryland (ages 5 and up)
801 Chase St., Annapolis 21401; (410) 263-8289, www.btmballet.org. $$$$.

Annual productions of the *Nutcracker* are among the offerings at the only fulltime professional classical ballet company in Maryland. Dance classes are offered for children as young as age three.

Banneker-Douglass Museum (ages 2 and up)

84 Franklin St., Annapolis 21401; (410) 216-6180. Open Tuesday through Friday 10 a.m. to 3 p.m., Saturday noon to 4 p.m. **Free.**

Even young children can enjoy the artifacts from Africa, the colorful local artwork, and the tributes to famous Maryland African Americans at this small museum housed in a former Mount Moriah African Methodist Episcopal Church, built in 1875. The stained-glass window alone makes the trip worthwhile. Older children may want to learn more about Frederick Douglass, the famed abolitionist and author, and Benajmin Banneker, the son of former slaves who became a renowned scientist and astronomer.

Read More about It

One good biography of Benjamin Banneker, who spent most of his life in what is now Howard County, is *The Life of Benjamin Banneker*, by Silvio A. Bedini, published by Charles Scribner's Sons in 1999. For more about Frederick Douglass, consider reading the fascinating *Autobiography of Frederick Douglass*, first published in 1883, which details his life in Maryland.

Chesapeake Children's Museum (up to age 8)

25 Silopanna Rd., Annapolis 21403; (410) 990-1993, www.theccm.org. Open daily except Wednesday 10 a.m. to 4 p.m.; summer hours are 10 a.m. to 5 p.m. $, children under 1 free. From the Naval Academy Stadium, turn right at Taylor Avenue. Go halfway around Westgate Circle and turn right onto Spa Road. Turn left on Silopanna Road and look for the CCM sign to the left. Park in the lot.

This museum, a short drive from downtown, is chock-full of things for kids to see and do, both indoors and out. Your kids won't want to miss Body Works, a 7-foot stuffed person that can be unzipped to see the internal organs; Hard Hats, where young children can build and play with blocks; a dinosaur exhibit with real fossils; a tank with fish and turtles; and plenty of places for kids to create their own artwork. Outside, there's a Harriet Tubman Walk, where kids can follow an imaginary escape route like the famed Maryland native, plus a nature trail, an herb garden, and more. There are also programs and summer camps.

City Dock (all ages)

Between Compromise and Prince George Streets.

The heart of Annapolis was and still is the City Dock, a bustling harbor on the eastern edge of the city, between Compromise and Prince George Streets. Since colonial times, it has been the point of entry from the Severn River, which leads into the Chesapeake. At the dock, you and your family can take a ride on a charter boat, gawk at the enormous yachts, or window-shop.

The upscale setting, with its many restaurants and shops, seems bucolic now, but years ago it was a point of entry for slave ships arriving from Africa. One slave who arrived in Annapolis in 1767 was Kunta Kinte, an ancestor of the author Alex Haley. While you're on the dock, show your children the Alex Haley Memorial, a sculpture of the author reading to three children. The sculpture, installed by the Kunta-Kinte Alex Haley Foundation in 1997, is part of an ongoing project to honor the author for his groundbreaking 1976 book, *Roots,* which detailed the history of Haley's family.

Amazing
Maryland Facts

The lightning rod at the top of the State House has been there for more than two hundred years. It was constructed and grounded to specifications set out by Benjamin Franklin.

Amazing
Maryland Facts

Graduates of the U.S. Naval Academy include one president (Jimmy Carter), eighteen members of Congress, four state governors, four secretaries of the navy, and fifty-one astronauts.

Helen Avalynne Tawes Garden (all ages)

Tawes State Office Building, Taylor Avenue, Annapolis 21401; (410) 260-8189, www.dnr .state.md.us/publiclands/tawesgarden.html. Open daily dawn to dusk; gift shop open weekdays 9 a.m. to 3 p.m. Free.

This five-acre garden, named for the wife of J. Millard Tawes, governor from 1959 to 1967, is a short drive from the historic part of Annapolis. Kids will enjoy the scenery, and they might learn a thing or two as well: The garden showcases environments from Maryland's natural communities, including an Eastern Shore peninsula and a forest in the western part of the state. Free guided tours are available with advance registration.

Pirate Adventures on the Chesapeake (ages 3 to 10)

Sails from the end of Third Street, Eastport; (443) 398-6270, www.chesapeakepirates.com. Goes out at 9:30 and 11 a.m., 12:30, 2, 3:30 and 5 p.m. April through October. Call for reservations. $$$.

Gather your little buccaneers and set sail on a pirate-theme boat tour designed for children and their families. The tour is about an hour and forty-five minutes long, with about a half hour spent on land while kids have their faces painted and get decked out in pirate garb. Then the 41-foot boat sets sail on the Severn River, on a quest for treasure. Along the way, kids will find a message in a bottle; get in a battle with another, smaller, pirate ship; and find a secret stash of "pirate grog" in the water, which is root beer. The boat, which has life jackets on board, can hold as many as thirty-eight people and requires sixteen to set sail.

My Annapolis Adventure

Kids can pick up a free copy of this activity book suitable for second through fifth graders at the Chesapeake Children's Museum, the Naval Academy, the visitor center at 26 West St., or the library on West Street. The book, published by the Chesapeake Children's Museum, highlights places that are appealing to kids and helps them understand local history. Each site has three questions and an activity.

Quiet Waters Park (all ages)

600 Quiet Waters Park Rd., Annapolis 21403; (410) 222-1777, www.aacounty.org. Open Wednesday through Monday 7 a.m. to dusk. $ per vehicle.

This beautiful park located to the west of Annapolis has it all—an enormous playground, an ice rink (open seasonally), biking trails, and boat rentals. The visitor center has formal gardens, an art gallery, and a cafe. And if that isn't enough, the park has a dog park and dog beach. Quiet Waters is a great place for a walk or a picnic.

Sandy Point State Park (all ages)

1100 East College Parkway, Annapolis 21401; (410) 974-2149. Open daily year-round. $. The park is at the western end of the Bay Bridge, exit 32 off Route 50/301.

A large sandy beach makes this an ideal summertime destination for families who want to enjoy a day splashing around in the Chesapeake, and this beach is considered one of the finest in the state. Attractions include a playground, launch areas for kayaks and other small boats, a place to rent rowboats and small motorboats during the warmer months, picnic areas, a snack stand that's open in the warmer months, and two hiking trails. Lifeguards are on duty in the summer.

If your kids like wildlife, they will get an eyeful here, as the park's location makes it ideal for spotting all kinds of waterfowl. Looking out over the water, they'll see plenty of boats, too, from nimble sailboats to enormous freighters.

State House (ages 6 and up)

91 State House Circle, Annapolis 21401; (410) 974-3400. Open Monday through Friday 9 a.m. to 5 p.m., Saturday and Sunday 10 a.m. to 4 p.m. Closed December 25. Half-hour tours at 11 a.m. and 3 p.m. daily, except on Thanksgiving and New Year's Day. Free.

Kids who are old enough to appreciate history and government will enjoy the free half-hour tours of the State House, which has been the headquarters of Maryland's government since 1779, making it the nation's oldest state capital in continuous legislative use.

If the tour itself will test the patience of young kids, they can skip it and focus on some of the other sights open to the public. My kids especially liked the 15-foot wooden ship that dominates the lobby. The small Maryland flag that now graces the wall of the Rotunda went with astronauts Neil Armstrong, Edwin Aldrin, and Michael Collins on the first manned trip to the moon in 1969.

Amazing
Maryland Facts

The homes of all four of Maryland's Declaration of Independence signers have been preserved and can be visited in Annapolis.

Other Historic Houses in Annapolis

Many of the historic houses and buildings in Annapolis provide fascinating glimpses of life during colonial times, particularly life for the upper classes.

Children with an interest in history, and ones that can resist touching fragile objects, may enjoy the following sites:

- **The Barracks.** 43 Pinkney St.; (410) 267-7619. Free. This small eighteenth-century building, open only by appointment, was a center for collecting supplies and troops during the Revolutionary War. It has a kitchen and several rooms.

- **Charles Carroll House.** 107 Duke of Gloucester St.; (410) 269-1737, www .carrollhouse.com. $, children under 10 free. The partially restored home of Charles Carroll, the only Catholic to sign the Declaration of Independence. Living-history tours, eighteenth-century teas, and other programs hold kid-appeal at this beautiful mansion overlooking the Spa Creek.

- **The Chase-Lloyd House.** 22 Maryland Ave.; (410) 263-2723. $ donation. This Georgian home, built in 1769 by Declaration signer Samuel Chase, is ideal for kids who like to gawk at nice houses.

- **Hammond-Harwood House.** 19 Maryland Ave., (410) 269-1714, www .hammondharwoodhouse.org. $$. This National Historic Landmark was built in 1774 and still has furnishing and artwork from that period. Activities focusing on life in colonial times are held throughout the year.

- **Old Treasury Building.** 18 Pinkney St.; (410) 267-7619, www.annapolis.org. Free. The oldest surviving public building in Maryland, built between 1735 and 1737, was once used to house the colony's most important currency, coins, and tobacco. Today, it houses the Research Center for the Historic Annapolis Foundation and contains many photographs that children will find interesting.

- **Shiplap House.** 18 Pinkney St.; (410) 267-7619; www.annapolis.org. Free. Originally built in 1715 as the home and inn of sawyer Edward Smith, the Shiplap House is one of the oldest buildings in Annapolis. The fully restored building now serves as administrative offices for Historic Annapolis Foundation. Kids may want to visit the re-created tavern room on the first floor.

- **Victualling Warehouse.** 77 Main St.; (410) 268-5576. Free. During the Revolutionary War, the warehouse at this site was seized by the state and used to store supplies for the military. Today, the site is home to the museum store and welcome center of the Historic Annapolis Foundation.

- **Waterfront Warehouse.** 4 Pinkney St.; (410) 267-7619. **Free.** This nine-teenth-century building now houses a model of the Annapolis waterfront as it would have looked in the mid-1700s, a neat way to bring history into focus for kids.

On a more somber note, a plaque outside the visitor center commemorates the 1986 *Challenger* disaster. The commander, Michael Smith, was a 1967 graduate of the U.S. Naval Academy.

U.S. Naval Academy (ages 5 and up)

121 Blake Rd., Annapolis 21402; (410) 263-6933, www.usna.edu. Campus open daily 9 a.m. to 5 p.m.; visitor center open 9 a.m. to 5 p.m. March through December, and 9 a.m. to 4 p.m. January and February; museum open 9 a.m. to 5 p.m. Monday through Saturday and 11 a.m. to 5 p.m. on Sunday. **Free.** Tours of the campus ($–$$) are available year-round, 9:30 a.m. to 3 p.m. Monday through Saturday and 12:30 to 3 p.m. Sunday.

Annapolis is probably best known for the Naval Academy, the undergraduate college of the United States Navy. And there's plenty here to entertain kids, from uniforms to model ships and even a real airplane tethered to the lawn.

When it was founded in 1845 as the Naval School, the college had fifty students and a ten-acre campus. Today, a 338-acre campus houses about 4,000 students.

The academy's museum, at 118 Maryland Ave. on the academy campus, includes uniforms and artifacts highlighting the navy's role in armed conflicts, the Cold War, and even the space race. Kids can check out a real space capsule. The Gallery of Ship Models on the ground floor—considered one of the world's finest collections of ship models—is sure to catch the kids' interest.

Also be sure to visit the U.S. Naval Academy Chapel, built in 1904, which has a beautiful copper dome and is adorned with stained-glass windows designed by Tiffany Studios. It's awe-inspiring, even to young ones.

Older kids might like to see the crypt of John Paul Jones, who famously said "I have not yet begun to fight" when his ship was sinking and ablaze during a fierce Revolutionary War battle. Jones managed to prevail, and he is considered the nation's first hero of the navy.

Watermark Cruises (all ages)

City Dock, Annapolis; (410) 768-7600, www.watermarkcruises.com. Open Saturday, Sunday, and holidays April through November as weather permits; also open Thursday and Friday from the end of May through early September. $ for 40-minute tour, $$ for 90-minute tour.

For a cooling view of the city on a hot summer day, your kids may enjoy a cruise with Watermark, a company that offers tours that depart frequently from the City Dock. My kids had a great time on the forty-minute tour. They looked at the huge houses along Spa Creek and the fancy boats in the water, while the breeze provided a break from the summertime heat. Our guide pointed out such sights as the U.S. Naval Academy and other

Walking **Tours**

Many walking tours are available in Annapolis, so it is easy to choose one that fits your fancy and your child's attention span. Here are a few options:

- **Discover Annapolis Tours.** 26 West St., Annapolis 21401 (mailing address: 31 Decatur Ave., Annapolis 21403); (410) 626-6000, www.discover-annapolis .com. Departs from Annapolis and Anne Arundel County Visitor Center. Departure times vary depending on season and special events in Annapolis. $–$$, children 5 and under **free.** Short attention spans cry out for short tours, and this company promises to deliver "350 years in one hour." The minicoach departs from the visitor center and wastes no time introducing riders to the city's history, architeture,and even folklore.

- **Three Centuries Tours.** 48 Maryland Ave., Annapolis 21401; (410) 263-5401, www.annapolis-tours.com. From April through October, tours are daily. Meet the guides at 10:30 a.m. at 48 Maryland Ave. or at 1:30 p.m. at the information booth on the City Dock. From November through March, tours are 1:30 p.m. on Saturday, leaving from the City Dock. No reservation necessary. $$, children under 6 **free.** Guides in colonial attire take visitors on a two-hour tour that includes the U.S. Naval Academy, the State House, St. John's College, exteriors of colonial homes, and interiors when available.

landmarks. A longer "day on the bay" tour goes to St. Michaels on the Eastern Shore and includes a visit to the Chesapeake Bay Maritime Museum.

William Paca House and Gardens (ages 2 and up)

186 Prince George St., Annapolis 21401; (410) 263-5553. March through December, open Monday through Saturday 10 a.m. to 5 p.m., Sunday noon to 5 p.m.; January and February, open Thursday through Saturday 10 a.m. to 5 p.m., Sunday noon to 4 p.m. $$, children under 6 free.

As a hotbed of activity during the Revolutionary War and its aftermath, Annapolis is loaded with historic houses—many of which are not suitable for very young children because they are filled with breakable antiques that can't be touched. One of our favorite Annapolis activities, though, is touring the gardens at the William Paca house. We don't bother going into the building, which is more appropriate for kids at least seven years old.

My daughter loves the tape-recorded audio tour that tells the historic significance of the various buildings and gardens. Once she's done listening, we stroll around, taking the little wooden footbridge across the pond and looking for frogs that lurk on the lily pads.

Where to Eat

Aromi D'Italia. 8 Dock St., Annapolis; (410) 263-1300. Don't miss the excellent gelato at this casual restaurant, which also sells sandwiches, pizza, and other Italian fare. $

Buddy's Crabs and Ribs.100 Main St., Annapolis; (410) 626-1100, www.buddysanap .com. Open daily for lunch and dinner. Kids 5 and under eat **free,** and kids 5 to 10 get half-priced entrees with adult orders. The menu has ribs, seafood, steaks, and of course lots of crabs. No matter what you eat, you'll enjoy the view of City Dock. $$$

Chick and Ruth's Delly. 165 Main St., Annapolis; (410) 269-6737, www.chickand ruths.com. After every election, Annapolis insiders check out the new sandwich names at this popular local deli. Order a Martin O'Malley, named for the state's governor, and get a roast beef and provolone with horseradish and lettuce on rye. At 8:30 every weekday morning and 9:30 on weekends, all patrons stand to recite the Pledge of Allegience. $

Jimmy Cantler's Riverside Inn. 458 Forest Beach Rd., Annapolis; (410) 757-1467, www.cantlers.com. The quintessential Maryland crab house, with a big, sunny deck on the water and mallets for pounding the crabs. Seafood-averse youngsters can enjoy a kid menu with chicken, pizza, grilled cheese, and the like. $–$$$

Where to Stay

Annapolis Marriott Waterfront. 80 Compromise St., Annapolis ; (888) 773-0786, www .annapolismarriott.com. Situated overlooking the water, this hotel is in easy walking distance to downtown shops, restaurants, and attractions. Perks include free bicycles for touring the town, a fitness center, and two 74-foot sailboats. Rooms are no smoking, and get wireless Internet for a small fee. $$$$

Country Inn and Suites by Carlson. 2600 Housley Rd., Annapolis; (410) 571-6700, www .countryinns.com. Located just minutes from downtown, this hotel offers an indoor pool and whirlpool, complimentary continental breakfast, and free shuttle service. $$$

Loews Annapolis Hotel. 126 West St., Annapolis; (800) 526-2593 or (410) 263-7777; www.loewsannapolis.com. As part of the Loews Loves Kids program, this hotel in the heart of historic Annapolis gives kids staying there a bag of toys and kid-geared information about the area. The hotel restaurant, Breeze, has a kids' menu, and kids under five eat **free.** $$–$$$$

Super 8 Motel. 74 Old Mill Bottom Road North, Annapolis; (410) 757-2222. Four miles from the historic district, this inexpensive hotel offers complimentary morning coffee. $$.

Westin Annapolis. 100 Westgate Circle, Annapolis; (410) 972-4300, www.westin.com/ annapolis. Built in 2008, this 225-room hotel has an indoor heated pool and fitness and

Take a **Hike**

Take the kids for a walk or bike ride along the **Baltimore and Annapolis Trail,** a 13.3-mile flat, paved trail that follows the route of the old Baltimore & Annapolis Railroad from Glen Burnie to Annapolis. It is open year-round, from dawn to dusk. The trail passes through suburban communities, wetlands, forests, and meadows. Your kids are likely to spot rabbits or deer.

spa facilities. Look for special family-friendly deals offering **free** meals for youngsters and movies in the room. $$$$

For More Information

Annapolis Accommodations, Inc. (800) 715-1000, (410) 280-0900. More information on places to stay.

Annapolis and Anne Arundel County Conference and Visitors Bureau. 26 West St., Annapolis 21401, (410) 268-7676, www.annapolischamber.com.

Historic Annapolis Foundation. 18 Pinkney St., Annapolis 21401; (800) 603-4020, (410) 267-7619, www.annapolis.org.

Hanover

For families, Hanover's main attraction is Arundel Mills, with its mix of outlet stores, movie theaters, and restaurants. The sprawling mall is one of the state's major shopping and entertainment destinations. It's easy to reach from either Baltimore or Annapolis. From Baltimore, take I-95 South to Route 100 east, then take exit 10A, Arundel Mills Boulevard. You'll see the mall on the right. From Annapolis, take I-97 North to Route 100 west, then take exit 10, Arundel Mills Boulevard. Go left at the light. The mall is open Monday through Saturday 10 a.m. to 9:30 p.m. and Sunday 11 a.m. to 7 p.m.

Medieval Times (ages 6 and up)

7000 Arundel Mills Circle, Hanover 21076; (800) WE-JOUST (ext. 8), www.medievaltimes .com. Open daily, with dinner and performances Wednesday through Sunday. Times vary. $$$$.

Yes, real horses charge at each other, right inside the mall. Stallions prance, falcons fly through the air, and knights on horses save the day. All the while, "serving wenches" dish up bowls of soup, platters of spareribs, and other "medieval" fare. Special packages for birthdays and other special events are available. The dinner theater seats about seven hundred, and tickets must be reserved in advance. On Monday and Tuesday, only the museum and gift shop are open.

Fishing for Fun

Naturally, the Arundel Mills mall has plenty of places to eat and to shop.

When you're tired of spending money, consider stopping by the **Bass Pro Shop,** where kids love to look at the fish in the tanks.

Amazing
Maryland Facts

Maryland is the only state with its own official sport. And believe it or not, it's jousting, a sport that has been important here for nearly four hundred years.

Where to Eat

Kid-friendly restaurants and food courts abound at the Arundel Mills mall. Here are a couple worth trying:

Dave and Buster's Grand Sports Café combines entertainment like video games, billiards, and shuffleboard with a kid-friendly menu of chicken, pasta, burgers, and more. (410) 755-0113, www.daveandbusters.com. $$$

Remomo serves pizza, pasta, and other Italian fare. $$

Where to Stay

Holiday Inn Express. 7481 Ridge Rd., Hanover; (410) 684-3388. A breakfast bar, an outdoor swimming pool, guest laundry facilities, and a fitness cener are among the amenities at this hotel less than 1 mile from the mall and within 3 miles of Baltimore-Washington International Airport. $$

For More Information

Arundel Mills. (410) 540-5110, www .arundelmills.com. The mall has its own tourist department that can help you find a hotel. Call (866) MD-MILLS (866-636-4557).

Linthicum

This town of 7,500 residents is just north of the Baltimore-Washington International Airport. The best route there from Annapolis is I-97, heading north.

Historical Electronics Museum (ages 10 and up)
1745 West Nursery Rd., Linthicum 21090; (410) 765-2345, www.hem-usa.org. Open Monday to Friday 9 a.m. to 3 p.m., Saturday 10 a.m. to 2 p.m. Closed major holidays. Free.

Older kids who are interested in electronics might enjoy a visit to this specialized museum, which highlights electronic advances from the radar to satellites. There are exhibits on radar during World War II, electronics pioneers, and more. The Fundamentals Gallery has hands-on exhibits that can help youngsters learn about the optical spectrum, electricity, and magnetism. Free tours are held during museum hours but must be scheduled in advance.

Thomas A. Dixon Jr. Aircraft Observation Area (all ages)

Dorsey Road, Linthicum; (410) 222-6244, www.dnr.state.md.us/greenways/bwi_trail.html. Open dawn to dusk year-round. Free. From Route 100 east, take exit 10B, which is Route 713. Turn right at the light on Dorsey Road, also called Route 176 east. The playground will be on your right in about 3 miles, right after you cross BW and A Boulevard. There is a large parking lot, but it often fills up on weekends.

What could be better than having fun on a playground while watching planes fly in for a landing? The Thomas A. Dixon playground, near the Baltimore-Washington International Airport, is popular with both children and adults because it provides a perfect view of airplanes touching down on the nearby runway.

The playground has slides, steering wheels, a bouncy bridge, and more. Note, however, that the slides can get uncomfortably hot in the summer. A portable restroom is on the site, but it's wise to bring your own water.

The playground is along the BWI Trail, a 14.5-mile paved path around the airport that's popular with bicyclists and runners. It's also a fine place to take the kids for a stroll.

In the airport itself is the Observation Gallery, a museum and activity center featuring the cockpit of a real Boeing 747, among other things. Kids can enjoy the children's play area while they watch planes take off and land.

Millersville

Millersville is to the north and west of Annapolis, along I-97. The biggest nearby town is Odenton, which is where you'll find places to stay and eat.

Kinder Farm Park (all ages)

1001 Kinder Farm Park Rd., Millersville 21108; (410) 222-6115, www.kinderfarmpark.org. Open daily except Tuesdays 7 a.m. to dusk. $.

This 288-acre park, not far from the Baltimore and Annapolis Trail and just north of Annapolis is the second-most visited Anne Arundel County park, with more than a quarter-million visitors annually. It has an interpretive farm complex with real animals, a disc golf course, a nice playground and tot lot, plus picnic areas and a 2.8-mile paved path for walking, running, and biking. Kid-friendly events include family campfire nights, hikes, and birding for kids. Many programs require advance registration.

Fort Meade

From Millersville, head west on Route 32 to reach Fort Meade, site of the Fort George C. Meade army installation.

National Cryptologic Museum (ages 7 and up)
Colony 7 Road and Route 32, Fort Meade 20755; (301) 688-5849, www.nsa.gov/about/
cryptologic_heritage/museum/index.shtml. Open Monday through Friday 9 a.m. to 4 p.m.
Closed on major holidays. **Free.** From Annapolis, take Route 32 west toward Columbia.
Go past the National Security Agency and take the first right after Canine Road onto Col-
ony 7 Road. Go past the Shell station to reach the museum.

Here's the perfect spot for kids who love playing spy or secret agent. Not long ago, the
National Security Agency, one of the largest employers in Anne Arundel County, was so
secretive that its initials were said to stand for "no such agency." Since 1993, however,
the agency's spy museum provides a behind-the-scenes look at our country's surveillance
methods, especially how enemy codes are cracked. Youngsters will learn about the Code
Talkers, Navajo Indians who encoded their language to fool Allied enemies during World
War II, and they can examine and try out old machines used to decipher some codes. The
National Vigilance Park, adjacent to the museum, is the site of two reconnaissance aircraft
used for secret missions.

Shady Side

This fairly undeveloped town, which still has no traffic lights, is on a peninsula surrounded
by the West River and the Chesapeake Bay. Until the 1920s, it was inhabited mainly by
people who made their living from the water.

Shady Side Rural Heritage Society
and Capt. Salem Avery House (ages 4 and up)
1418 East West Shady Side Rd., Shady Side 20746; (410) 867-4486; www.averyhouse.org.
Open Sunday 1 to 4 p.m., March through December or by appointment. Outdoor exhibits
open daily dawn to dusk. **Free.** From I-97 South take Route 50 east. Get in the right
lane and merge onto exit 22, Aris T. Allen Boulevard. Take the exit for Route 2, Solomons
Island Road, toward Parole/Edgewater. Take Route 2 about 3 miles, then turn left on Route
214, Central Avenue. Go 1.4 miles, then turn right on Muddy Creek Road. Stay on this road
about 11 miles. It will become Shady Side Road. Turn right onto East West Shady Side
Road at the Shady Side ball fields. Follow the road as it forks left. The museum and parking lot will be on your left.

Kids can imagine what life was like for eighteenth-century watermen when they visit this
restored 1860 home of Capt. Salem Avery, a Chesapeake Bay fisherman. The building is
now a museum documenting more than 350 years of local history. Exhibits have included
displays and information about African-African watermen and displays of women's hats
dating from a century ago.

Edgewater

As its name implies, Edgewater is close to the water. It can be reached from Annapolis by traveling south along Route 2, across the South River. Since it's so close to Annapolis, you'll probably want to eat or stay there.

Historic London Town and Gardens (ages 4 and up)

839 Londontown Rd., Edgewater 21037; (410) 222-1919, www.historiclondontown.com. Open Monday through Friday 9 a.m. to 4 p.m., Saturday 10 a.m. to 4 p.m., Sunday noon to 4 p.m. Closed Sunday from January 1 through mid-March. $$. Take Route 50/301 to Route 665 (exit 22, Aris T. Allen Boulevard), exit onto Route 2 south (Solomons Island Road), go over South River Bridge. Continue about 0.6 mile (three traffic lights); turn left at the third traffic light onto Mayo Road. Go about 0.8 mile (two traffic lights) and turn left at the second traffic light onto Londontown Road. Go about 1 mile to end of road. Stay to the left side and enter site through gates.

This gorgeous twenty-three-acre property overlooking the South River was once home to a thriving port community that grew tobacco and shipped it to England. But the town faded in the 1700s and eventually disappeared, except for the majestic brick home of the ferry master, William Brown.

Today, pieces of the old port community are coming back to life. You and your family can wander through the archaeological sites and check the progress of homes that

A Nitkin Family **Adventure**

On a beautiful spring day, David and I took the kids to Historic London Town and Gardens. We thought Ronnie and Sammy would have fun running around outside, while we would enjoy learning about the historic site and the work being done to renovate it. As it turned out, the kids were very interested in the history of the location.

For the price of admission, we were all given audio machines that took us on a leisurely self-paced walking tour of the property. We learned that London Town had started out as a British colony in the 1600s, mainly to grow tobacco and ship it back to England. But in the 1720s, other port cities became more important, and London Town lost population and eventually disappeared. The property is now being restored, using only materials found on the site and only methods that would have been used during colonial times.

The gardens were just starting to bloom when we visited, and they were lovely. We walked along the paths, learning about different plants and why they were grown. What an enjoyable way to deepen our knowledge of Maryland's past!

Other Things to See and Do in Annapolis and Anne Arundel County

- **Amphibious Horizons Kayaking.** 600 Quiet Waters Park Rd., Annapolis; (410) 267-8742, www.amphibioushorizons.com

- **Annapolis Sailing School.** 601 Sixth St., Annapolis; (410) 267-7205, www.annapolissailing.com

- **South River Boat Rentals.** 48 South River Rd., Edgewater; (410) 956-9729, www.southriverboatrentals.com

- **Suntime Boat Rentals.** 2820 Solomons Island Rd., Route 2, Edgewater, 21037; (410) 266-6020

- **Wheels Skating Center.** 1200 Odenton Rd., Odenton; (410) 674-9661, www.wheelsrsc.com

are being reconstructed. A beautiful garden with walking paths is an ideal place for kids to stretch their legs. Pick up audiotapes in the visitor center so you and your family can explore at your own pace.

Smithsonian Environmental Research Center (all ages)

647 Contees Wharf Rd., Edgewater 21037; (443) 482-2218, www.serc.si.edu. Open 9 a.m. to 5 p.m. weekdays and during special events. Free.

This 2,800-acre research center, situated on the Chesapeake, has two nature trails that appeal to kids and that can be navigated by wheelchairs or strollers. The 1.3-mile Java History Trail has interpretive panels and exhibits that examine a Piscataway Indian village, a tobacco plantation exhibit, an early twentieth-century dairy farm, and a marsh walkway.

The 1.5-mile Discovery Trail winds through various ecosystems and has panels discussing topics such as tree diversity and tidal wetlands. Both trails are open to the public, but be sure you visit the Reed Education Center before setting out to check on the condition of the trails. The center is reached by taking the first left upon entering the property.

Special events include an open house held every year the Saturday before Mother's Day, and family canoe trips, which are $5 per person.

Annual Events

Volvo Ocean Race and Annapolis Maritime Heritage Festival. Annapolis; (410) 268-7676, www.aaaccc.org. In April, more than 5,000 boats crowd the bay to watch the contestants in the Volvo Ocean Race head toward France. Events and activities highlight the city's maritime history.

May Day. Annapolis. On May 1, residents and stores throughout Annapolis put May

Baskets filled with flowers in their windows and on their front stoops to commemorate the arrival of spring.

Wednesday Night Sailboat Races.
Annapolis. The largest and oldest sailboat races in the country are held June through September.

Fourth of July Celebration. Annapolis. Old-fashioned parade, waterfront fireworks display, and concert by the United States Naval Academy Band.

Kunta Kinte Celebration. Annapolis; (410) 349-0338, www.kuntakinte.org. Two-day festival in August with food, crafts, performances, and a children's tent.

Eastport Yacht Club's Lights Parade.
Annapolis; (410) 267-9549, www.eastportyc .org. Children love to see boats in their elaborate holiday lights as they cruise the harbor in December.

First Night, December 31. Annapolis; (410) 268-8553, www.firstnightannapolis.org. Ring in the New year with this family event that includes hundreds of performers staged throughout the downtown. Early programs are offered for children, and waterfront fireworks end the evening at midnight.

Central
Maryland

Central Maryland is made up of the bustling communities that surround the city of Baltimore. The counties of Baltimore, Carroll, Howard, and Harford host towns and cities that range from very urban to very rural, but much of this region is suburban, with lots of kid-friendly playgrounds, petting zoos, museums, and historic sites.

Take your kids on a day trip to Havre de Grace, where they can explore the unique Decoy Museum or roam the historic grounds at the Steppingstone Museum. Spend an afternoon on the charming Main Street in Ellicott City, browsing the toy stores and picnicking in one of the pocket parks. If the weather is nasty, consider spending an afternoon indoors at PlayWiseKids in Columbia. Or if it's nice, take the kids swimming and paddleboating at Cascade Lake in Hampstead. Whatever the season, you'll find plenty of family activities in Central Maryland.

In this chapter, we'll start west of Baltimore, in the Howard County towns of Columbia and Ellicott City, then move north in a big arc around Baltimore through Westminster and Towson before heading east to Aberdeen and Havre de Grace. Every attraction in this chapter is within an hour's drive from Baltimore.

Howard County

Family-friendly Howard County is a mix of old and new, from Ellicott City, founded in the 1700s, to the planned community of Columbia, founded in the 1960s. This county is rich with playgrounds, parks, and other places to take the kids.

Columbia

If Columbia were a city or town, it would be among the largest in Maryland, with nearly 100,000 residents. Instead, it's a planned community, designed by developer James Rouse in the 1960s with the goal of creating an inclusive place with a variety of housing types

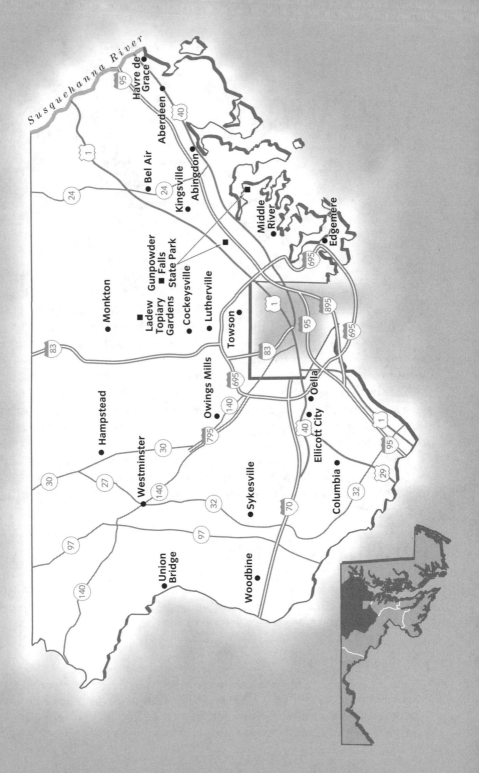

CENTRAL MARYLAND

and with shopping areas close to where people live. Columbia is about thirty minutes to the south and west of Baltimore. From Baltimore, take I-95 South to Route 100 west. From there, you'll connect to Route 29, which is the main north–south road through the community.

EarthTreks (ages 6 and up)

7125-C Columbia Gateway Dr., Columbia 21046, and 1930 Greenspring Dr., Timonium 21093; (410) 872-0060, (800) CLIMB-UP, www.earthtreksclimbing.com. Open Monday through Wednesday 3 to 10 p.m., Thursday and Friday noon to 10 p.m., Saturday from November to April, 9 a.m. to 8 p.m., Saturday from May to October, 9 a.m. to 6 p.m., Sunday 9 a.m. to 6 p.m. $$.

These climbing centers, the largest on the East Coast, are operated by Chris Warner, who has climbed Mount Everest and other notable peaks. The Kids Klimb program for kids ages six to twelve and a Youth Rox Climbing Series for kids ages ten to fourteen teach youngsters the basics of rock climbing in a safe environment. A day camp is offered for aspiring climbers between the ages of nine and thirteen.

Day passes are available, but any child under eighteen must have a waiver signed by a parent or guardian.

PlayWiseKids (up to age 7)

6570 Dobbin Rd., Columbia 21045; (410) 772-1540, www.playwisekids.com. Open Monday through Friday 9:30 a.m. to 5 p.m., Saturday 9:30 a.m. to 7 p.m., Sunday 11:30 a.m. to 6

Karen's
TopPicks for fun in Central Maryland

1. Ellicott City B&O Railroad Station Museum

2. Carroll County Farm Museum, Westminster

3. Cascade Lake, Hampstead

4. Ladew Topiary Gardens, Monkton

5. Hampton National Historic Site, Towson

6. Fire Museum of Maryland, Lutherville

7. Gunpowder Falls State Park, Kingsville

8. Rockfield Park, Bel Air

9. Havre de Grace Decoy Museum, Havre de Grace

10. Susquehanna Museum, Havre de Grace

Holiday **Glow**

For a holiday-season treat, take the kids to Symphony of Lights held in Symphony Woods in Columbia. You'll drive past more than seventy lighted, animated creations, including flying Santas and gingerbread houses. Symphony of Lights runs from the end of November through early January and costs $$$ per car. Proceeds benefit the Howard County General Hospital. For more information, call (410) 740-7666.

p.m. $$, children under 12 months **free.** From Route 29, take Route 175 east for about 3 miles, then turn right on Dobbin Road. It will be on the right in about a half mile.

Climb on a real fire truck, buy pretend groceries, play dress-up, or create your own artwork in this giant indoor play area for children. On a rainy day, it's a great place for kids to blow off steam. My two munchkins can spend hours here, and it's popular for birthday parties too. A cafe serves kid-friendly snacks.

Shadowland Laser Adventures (ages 6 and up)

9179 Red Branch Rd., Columbia 21045; (410) 740-9100, www.shadowlandadventures.com; also in Gaithersburg at 624 Quince Orchard Rd., Quince Orchard Shopping Center 20878; (301) 330-5546. Open Monday 11 a.m. to 6 p.m., Tuesday through Thursday 11 a.m. to 10 p.m., Friday 11 a.m. to midnight, Saturday 10 a.m. to midnight, Sunday 10 a.m. to 10 p.m. $$.

In these adventures, kids (and their parents) strap on high-tech suits, grab handsets, and act out interactive games in an arena filled with mazes, alleys, and turrets. During the adventure, special effects such as lighting and smoke enhance the fantasy. While Shadowland is often rented out by corporations, it is also popular for drop-in play, birthday parties, or family outings.

Toby's Dinner Theatre (ages 3 and up)

P.O. Box 1123, 5900 Symphony Woods Rd., Columbia 21044; (410) 730-8311, www.tobys dinnertheatre.com. Call for specific performance dates. $$.

Amazing
Maryland Facts

Lake Kittamaqundi is named for the first known Native-American settlement in Howard County. The paved path around the man-made lake, off Route 175 in Columbia, is a fine place for a walk. In the summer, canoes and paddleboats can be rented, and live music is often playing.

Round and Round

The merry-go-round at the Mall in Columbia is fairground-quality and a great way to break up an afternoon of shopping.

Winnie the Pooh, the Velveteen Rabbit, and other beloved characters take the stage for shows offered by Toby's Youth Theatre, a part of this popular dinner theater. Kids' shows are about one hour long and are followed by a discussion. Curtain for the children's offerings goes up at 10 a.m. or noon, and food is not included.

Where to Eat

Clyde's. 10221 Wincopin Circle, Columbia; (410) 730-2828. Burgers for the kids and a slightly more sophisticated menu for grownups. After eating, you can take a walk around Lake Kittamaqundi. $$

PastaBlitz. 5805 Clarksville Sq., Clarksville; (443) 535-9777. Pizza, pasta, and salads in a setting that's nicer than the average take-out joint. $

Where to Stay

Hampton Inn Columbia. 8880 Columbia 100 Parkway, Columbia; (800) HAMPTON, (410) 997-8555, www.hamptoninn.com. A nice hotel with an indoor pool, fitness center, complimentary continental breakfast, and cable television. Connecting rooms, cribs, rollaway beds, microwaves, and refrigerators are available options. $$$

Sheraton Columbia Town Centre Hotel. 10207 Wincopin Circle, Columbia, 21044; (410) 730-3900, www.sheratoncolumbia.com. Located close to the mall and Lake Kittamaqundi, this hotel has a fitness facility, outdoor pool, and in-room games and movies. Rooms are smoke-free and have high-speed Internet for a fee. Complimentary breakfast included. $$$$

For More Information

The Columbia Association. 10221 Wincopin Circle, Columbia 21044-3410; (410) 713-3000, www.columbiaassociation.com.

Ellicott City

A day trip to downtown Ellicott City provides plenty of activities for everyone in the family.

The city's historic district, consisting of the hilly Main Street and a few side streets, has buildings dating from the 1700s, when the Ellicott brothers—Joseph, Andrew, and John—set up a gristmill along the Patapsco River, the first step toward creating the town that would later be named for them.

The downtown area is loaded with kid-friendly stores, restaurants, and attractions.

They're arranged here as if you were starting at the bottom of the hill on Main Street and walking up. From Columbia, take Route 29 north to exit 40 east. Turn right on Rogers Avenue and follow the signs.

Stores Kids **Love**

Mixed in with Ellicott City's antiques shops and nice restaurants are several stores with special appeal for youngsters. Best of all, in the opinion of my kids, is **Mumbles and Squeaks** (8133 Main St., 410-750-2803), a locally owned toy store with a Thomas train table set up on the top floor. At the bottom of Main Street is **Forget-Me-Not Factory** (8044 Main St., 410-465-7355), filled with small ornaments, figurines, and other fanciful treats. On the weekends, a large bubble vat and wands are set up outside for kids.

Centennial Park (all ages)

Between Route 108 and Centennial Lane in Ellicott City; (410) 313-4700. Open daily dawn to 7 p.m. Free.

This 325-acre park surrounds a large lake that has a wonderful paved 2.4-mile path for walking or bike riding. The path follows the water's edge, so that kids will likely see geese and, if they peer closely, perhaps frogs. In the summer, you can rent paddleboats for a modest price or purchase burgers, ice cream, and other snacks from an inexpensive concession stand. The playground, sports fields, and tennis courts are open year-round. My kids love to play on the slides and climbing structures and, from their vantage point on the playground, watch the teenagers play basketball.

Clark's Elioak Farm (all ages)

10500 Rte. 108, Ellicott City 21041; (410) 730-4049, www.clarklandfarm.com. Open April 1 through November 1, Tuesday through Saturday, 10 a.m. to 4 p.m. $.

Cows, goats, pigs, bunnies, and sheep are among the animals at this fun petting zoo. Hayrides and pony rides are offered for a small fee, and in the fall kids can try to find their way through a maze made of hay bales. In summer, a produce stand on the property sells some of the best corn in the county, picked right in the adjacent field. Weekend events include an egg hunt in April and demonstrations of blacksmithing and sheepshearing.

More Train Treats

After Thanksgiving each year, Ellicott City's **Fire Station 2,** at 4150 Montgomery Rd., puts together a fantastic train garden that stays in place until early January. Admission is free, but before December 25, donations of unwrapped toys are appreciated and will be distributed to needy children throughout the county. Kids love to see the tiny trains chugging over the tracks.

Amazing
Maryland Facts

Construction of the holiday train garden at the B&O Railroad Station Museum begins in September and takes more than two months to complete.

Ellicott City B&O Railroad Station Museum (ages 2 and up)
2711 Maryland Ave., Ellicott City 21043; (410) 461-1945, www.ecbo.org. Open Friday and Saturday 11 a.m. to 4 p.m., Sunday noon to 5 p.m. $, children under 2 free.

Imagine climbing through a red caboose or watching model trains chug along an elaborate layout. These are just a few of the treats at this museum, housed in the 1830 stone building that is billed as the oldest railroad station in America. It is now a museum with railroad layouts, exhibits, and a 1927 red caboose for children to explore. In December, families flock to the museum to marvel at the fabulous train garden with dozens of toy trains chugging along a complicated, multilayered winter wonderland. And all-year-round, a display with moving trains shows the nation's first train route, between Baltimore and Ellicott City. My son never gets tired of the large Thomas trains that can be activated with the push of a button. For a little holiday or birthday shopping, a museum shop sells Thomas toys and other train-related items.

The Ellicott City Firehouse Museum (ages 5 and up)
3829 Church Rd., Ellicott City 21041; (410) 313-1413 www.howardcountymd.gov/RAP/RAP_HistoricalSites.htm; Open by appointment, Saturday, Sunday, Monday 1 p.m. to 6 p.m. Free.

If your child is like my son and wants to be a firefighter when he grows up, take him (or her) to this museum, where he can explore old-fashioned firefighting equipment, including a hand-drawn hose reel from 1891 and uniforms from the 1930s and 1940s. Kids especially love the display of firefighting-related toys that date from the 1950s.

Patapsco Female Institute Historic Park (all ages)
3691 Sarah's Lane, Ellicott City 21043; (410) 465-8500, www.patapscofemaleinstitute.org. Open April through October, Saturday and Sunday 1 to 4 p.m. $.

Do your kids like ruins? The remains of a nineteenth-century all-girl school dominate this park, which is at the highest elevation of historic Ellicott City and provides a wonderful view of the Patapsco River Valley. You and your gang can explore the elevated walkways through the 8,000-square-foot building. The park hosts many kid-focused activities throughout the year, including egg hunts in the spring, Victorian-style tea parties and a haunted house in the fall.

Patapsco Valley State Park   (all ages)

8020 Baltimore National Pike, Ellicott City 21043; (410) 461-5005. Open daily 9 a.m. to dusk. $ for day use.

This park, established in 1907, meanders along 32 miles of the Patapsco River. It has five areas with amenities: Hollofield, Pickall, Hilton, McKeldin, and Avalon-Glen Artney–Orange Grove.

Check out the Avalon visitor center with exhibits highlighting more than three hundred years of history along the river. Kids love peeking into the nineteenth-century stone house, which even has a re-created forest warden's office showing how it would have looked in the 1930s. At the Avalon visitor center, you can pick up maps of the park, with directions to specific areas. Your fleet-footed youngsters may want to walk the 300-foot swinging suspension bridge that crosses the river in the Orange Grove area. Other popular park activities are canoeing, tubing, hiking, and biking.

Thomas Isaacs Log Cabin   (ages 7 and up)

8398 Main St., Ellicott City 21043; (410) 313-1413, http://thomasisaaclog cabin.ellicottcity.net. Open Saturday, Sunday, and Monday, 1 p.m. to 6 p.m. Free.

In this log cabin, built around 1780, kids can see what life was like in eighteenth-century Ellicott City. The cabin serves as an exhibit center for the Historic Ellicott City Consortium and hosts various kid-friendly programs such as craft demonstrations throughout the year. Forty-five-minute walking tours of Main Street with costumed interpreters discussing such themes as "Women of Ellicott Mills" and "Civil War on Main Street" leave from this site and cost $7 per person with a four-person minimum. Reserve in advance.

A Nitkin Family **Adventure**

We moved to Maryland from Florida when my daughter was two and my son was six months away from being born. On one of the first days in our new home, taking a break from unpacking, I took Veronica to the Hollofield section of the Patapsco Valley State Park. It was late September, and the air had a slight nip, a nice change from the muggy Florida weather. We were the only ones on the small playground. As Veronica clambered on the climbing equipment and swings, I looked around at my new surroundings. Just then, a deer wandered over to us. Veronica and I sat quietly and looked at it, while it stood quietly and looked at us. That was the first time she saw a deer, but it was certainly not the last.

Where to Eat

Great Eggspectations. 6010 University Blvd., Ellicott City; (410) 750-3115. Large, fun dining room and an enormous menu featuring all kinds of eggs, pancakes, and waffles, plus salads and sandwiches. Kids can sit by the window to the kitchen and watch the cooks as they work. $

Johnny's Bistro on Main Street. 8167 Main St., Ellicott City; (410) 461-8210, www .johnnysbistro.net . Great for both parents and kids, this friendly little restaurant has pizzas and gourmet-style sandwiches, as well as inventive salads and delicious desserts. $

Sarah and Desmond's. 3715 Old Columbia Pike, Ellicott City; (410) 465-9700. This vegetarian sandwich shop and bakery has delicious muffins and smoothies. $

Where to Stay

Forest Motel. 10021 Baltimore National Pike, Ellicott City; (410) 465-2090. This old-fashioned twenty-five-room motel has an outdoor pool and a great location next to the Forest Diner and the Soft Stuff ice-cream stand. $

For More Information

Howard County Tourism Council. 8267 Main St., P.O. Box 9, Ellicott City 21041; (800) 288-TRIP (8747), (410) 313-1900, www.visit howardcounty.com.

Carroll County

Carroll County is north of Howard County and extends to the Pennsylvania border. Although it is growing fast, Carroll still has large rural pockets.

Westminster

A glance at a map shows that all Carroll County roads lead to Westminster, the bustling county seat. From the south, Routes 27 and 32 or I-97 will get you there. From the east or west, take Route 140.

Baugher's Orchard and Farm (all ages)

1236 Baugher Rd., Westminster 21158; (410) 857-0111, www.baughers.com. Open daily June through November 8 a.m. to 6 p.m.; open daily December 1–24 10 a.m. to 4 p.m. Free.

Strawberries and cherries in June, pumpkins and gourds in November—Baugher's has been a pick-your-own destination for more than fifty years. The Baughers make every effort to create a fun outdoor experience for the family. Wagons take you to the field, and a petting zoo is open from June through October. Pack a picnic lunch to eat at the outdoor picnic tables, and finish the meal with Baugher's homemade ice cream and famous pies.

Amazing
Maryland Facts

Carroll County is named for Charles Carroll, the only Roman Catholic to sign the Declaration of Independence.

Bear Branch Nature Center (all ages)

300 John Owings Rd., Westminster 21158; (410) 848-2517, http://ccgov.carr.org/hashawha/ bearbrnc.htm. Open Wednesday through Saturday 10 a.m. to 5 p.m., Sunday noon to 5 p.m. Free.

This nature center has lots of fun stuff for kids, including a fish tank, interactive displays about ecology, and an exhibit hall with animals both living and stuffed. There are many programs for children, including ones that use the center's forty-seat planetarium. Walking trails outside the center have educational markers and provide a beautiful view of the rolling countryside.

Carroll County Farm Museum (all ages)

500 South Center St., Westminster 21157; (410) 386-3880, www.carrollcountyfarmmuseum .org. Open weekends May through October, noon to 5 p.m. And in July and August, Tuesday through Friday 10 a.m. to 4 p.m. $, children 6 and under free.

Take your family on a tour of a farmhouse built in 1852 and see skilled artisans at work.

Kids can learn about Maryland's rural past while enjoying the outdoors and the many farm animals on the property.

The museum's centerpiece, the farmhouse, has six antiques-filled rooms open to the public (and is better suited to older kids). Guided tours are available for this building. Elsewhere on the property, a self-guided walking tour takes you through various buildings, explaining their history and importance. These buildings include a smokehouse, one-room schoolhouse, and a wagon shed. In the Living History Center, kids can watch artisans spin cotton, make quilts, carve wood, and shoe horses, among other things.

The General Store sells quilts and other products made by the artisans, plus nickel candies and novelties and gifts.

When the kids get tired of exploring, they can eat at the picnic tables on the property, then play croquet or horseshoes. A recently installed fish pond also provides diversion.

The museum schedules special events, such as a Civil War Living History Encampment in May and fireworks on July 4. Steam Show Days in September show off some cool antique farm machinery.

Union Mills Homestead (ages 5 and up)
3311 Littletown Pike, Route 97, Westminster 21158; (410) 848-2288, www.unionmills.org. Open May through September, Tuesday through Friday 10 a.m. to 4 p.m., weekends noon to 4 p.m. $, children 6 and under free.

While you're exploring history in Westminster, you may want to take the kids to this historic home and real working mill. The home was built in 1797 and is today open for tours. The gristmill, built the same year, still works, and it sells the flour and meal that it grinds from whole grains. Take some home as a souvenir! Events include pancake breakfasts, ice-cream socials, and more.

Where to Eat

Baugher's Family Restaurant. 289 West Main St., Westminster; (410) 848-7413. Baugher's features its famous desserts, plus sandwiches, country-style platters, and Pennsylvania Dutch favorites like scrapple and chipped beef.

Bullock's Family Restaurant. 2020 Sykesville Rd., Westminster; (410) 857-3563. Hamburgers, hot dogs, fish, sandwiches, and more in a casual environment. $

Pour House. 233 Main St., Westminster, 21157; (410) 751-9171. This college-y hangout in downtown Westminster has yummy baked goods and sandwiches. $

Where to Stay

Best Western Westminster. 451 WMC Dr., Route 140 West, Westminster; (410) 857-1900, www.bestwesternwestminster.com.

This hotel next to McDaniel College has tennis courts, an outdoor pool, and a golf course. A complimentary breakfast is served. $$, kids twelve and under stay free.

Days Inn–Westminster. 25 South Cranberry Rd., Westminster; (410) 857-0500, (800) DAYS-INN; www.daysinn.com. A pool and cable television are offered at this ninety-six-room hotel, five minutes from the Carroll County Farm Museum. $$ for rooms with two double beds.

For More Information

Tourism Council of Carroll County. (800) 272-1933, (410) 848-1388, www.carr.org/tourism.

Union Bridge

This small town of about 1,000 residents is to the west of Westminster in Carroll County. From Westminster, you can get there on Uniontown Road.

Western Maryland Railway Historical Society (ages 3 and up)
41 North Main St., Union Bridge 21791; (410) 775-0150; www.moosevalley.org/wmrhsl. Open Sunday 1 to 4 p.m. and by appointment. Free.

The N-scale train layout is the attraction here, as well as the photographs, artifacts, and memorabilia relating to the Western Maryland Railway, which was an independent railway for more than 125 years. The museum is housed in a historic 1902 building that once served as the company's corporate offices.

Hampstead

This rural slice of Carroll County is to the north and east of Westminster. From Westminster, take Route 482 east and then go right on Snydersburg Road. From Baltimore, take exit 19 off I-695 to I-795 to Route 30 north to Hampstead. Turn left on Route 482 and right on Snydersburg Road.

Cascade Lake (all ages)

3000 Snydersburg Rd., Hampstead 21074; (410) 374-9111, www.cascadelake.com. Open 7 a.m. to dusk June through August, with swimming from 10 a.m. to 7 p.m. $–$$, children 2 and under free.

This spring-fed lake has a sandy bottom that makes it a wonderful destination for the whole family. Toddlers can splash in the shallow water and slide down a waterslide shaped like a tongue in a frog's mouth, while older kids can swim out to the rafts, enjoy the high dive, and zoom down the 150-foot twisting waterslide.

There are plenty of picnic tables and grills, as well as a bathhouse, playground, horseshoe pits, arcade, volleyball nets, snack bar, and gift shop. Catch-and-release fishing is included in the admission price. Paddleboats can be rented for $6 on weekends and $5 on weekdays, and a dollar gets you a bag of feed and admission to the petting zoo.

Sykesville

Sykesville got its start as a town after the Baltimore & Ohio extended its main line here in 1831, and the railroad is still the focus of this historic community. Sykesville is easy to reach from Westminster. Just take Route 32 south.

Lilliput Lane Petting Farm (up to age 7)

14160 Forsythe Rd., Sykesville 21784; (410) 489-7291. Open to the public Wednesday 10 a.m. to 2 p.m. from April 1 to end of October; open other days to groups. $, adults free.

Pet the bunnies and cows, climb on the playground, and go for a hayride at this charming farm. There are also tricycles to ride and basketballs to throw.

Little Sykes Railway Park (ages 2 to 7)

Sandosky Road, Sykesville 21784; (410) 795-8959, www.sykesville.net/littlesykes.html. Open May to October, Saturday 9 a.m. to 3 p.m. Free.

Youngsters will love taking a ride on the 1949 12-gauge miniature train at this railway park right near downtown.

Piney Run Nature Center (all ages)

30 Martz Rd., Sykesville 21784; (410) 795-6043. Open April 1 to October 31, Tuesday through Friday 10 a.m. to 5 p.m., and Saturday and Sunday 1 to 5 p.m.; November 1 to March 31, Tuesday through Friday 10 a.m. to 4 p.m. $–$$ per vehicle.

The nature center at this 800-acre park has a children's room with live reptiles and fish, plus a bird-feeding station outside. Boat rentals are available in the summer months, and trails are open for hiking year-round. The 300-acre lake is a good place to let your youngster try his or her hand with a fishing rod. Many of the three hundred or so programs offered each year are designed for kids ages three to six.

Sykesville and Patapsco Railway (ages 2 and up)

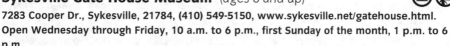

Oklahoma and Baldwin Avenues, Sykesville 21784; (410) 795-3157. Open first Sunday of every month 1 to 5 p.m. Free.

If your youngsters love model trains, take them to the S&P Railway, an organization run by model-train fans who love to show off their skills at putting together fantastic layouts. For added fun, the organization makes its home in a 1910 Pullman car housed in the historic downtown. Special exhibits are held throughout the year.

Sykesville Gate House Museum (ages 6 and up)

7283 Cooper Dr., Sykesville, 21784, (410) 549-5150, www.sykesville.net/gatehouse.html. Open Wednesday through Friday, 10 a.m. to 6 p.m., first Sunday of the month, 1 p.m. to 6 p.m.

Through clothing, toys, photographs, and exhibits such as an antique telephone, this museum traces the history of Sykesville as it grows from a small mill town and survives the Civil War and two World Wars.

Where to Eat

Baldwin's Station. 7618 Main St., Sykesville; (410) 795-1041, www.baldwinsstation.com. American food in a renovated 1883 train station overlooking the Patapsco River. Extensive kids' menu, plus children's plays such as Puss in Boots or Peter Pan held once a month, on Tuesday at 10 a.m. in the spring and summer, and on Sunday at 3 p.m. in the fall and winter. Tickets to the plays should be reserved in advance ($, children two and under free). $$$

E.W. Beck's Pub. 7565 Main St., Sykesville; (410) 795-1001. Popular family dining destination. $

For More Information

Town of Sykesville. 7547 Main St., Sykesville 21784; (410) 795-8959, www.sykesville.net.

Some Berry Good Books

Before we go berry picking, my children and I like to get in the mood by reading two of our favorite books: *Blueberries for Sal*, by Robert McCloskey (Puffin) and *Jamberry*, by Bruce Degen (HarperTrophy).

Woodbine

To conclude your exploration of Carroll County, consider stopping in Woodbine for an afternoon of fruit picking at Larriland. Woodbine is south of Westminster and west of Sykesville.

Larriland Farm (ages 3 and up)
2415 Woodbine Rd., Woodbine 21797; (410) 442-2605, www.pickyourown.com. Late May to August 31, open Tuesday through Friday 9 a.m. to 8 p.m., Saturday and Sunday 9 a.m. to 5 p.m.; in September open Tuesday through Friday 9 a.m. to 6 p.m., Saturday and Sunday 9 a.m. to 5 p.m.; in October open Monday through Friday 9 a.m. to 6 p.m., Saturday and Sunday 9 a.m. to 5 p.m.; in November open the first weekend only, Friday through Sunday 10 a.m. to 5 p.m. Free.

Every summer, we pick blueberries at Larriland, and every fall we go back to pick apples and pumpkins and go for hayrides and make our way through the hay-bale maze. There are plenty of places to eat a picnic lunch. The kids never seem to get tired of our trips to this bucolic farm. Other pick-your-own fruits and vegetables in season include peaches, blueberries, and spinach.

Baltimore County

Baltimore County surrounds the city of Baltimore, forming a doughnut shape. The main road connecting this large patch of geography is the Baltimore Beltway, or I-695, which encircles the city. Most of the county is suburban, but patches, especially to the north, remain quite rural.

Oella

This small historic town is adjacent to downtown Ellicott City, but it's located in Baltimore County.

Benjamin Banneker Historical Park
and Museum (ages 5 and up)

300 Oella Ave., Oella, 21228; (410) 887-1081, www.baltimorecountymd.gov/Agencies/
recreation/countyparks. Open Tuesday through Saturday 10 a.m. to 4 p.m. $ donation sug-
gested. From Baltimore, take Route 40 west and turn left at Rolling Road. At the second
traffic light, go right at Old Frederick Road. After 1.3 miles, turn right onto Oella Avenue.
The park entrance is on the left.

This small but growing museum is situated at the family farm of Benjamin Banneker, the
famed African-American mathematician and astronomer. The Banneker family purchased
more than 1,000 acres in 1737, when Benjamin was six years old. Photographs, exhibits,
and memorabilia tell of Banneker's life and works. The visitor center showcases some
of Banneker's works, plus has a gift shop and patio garden. The park also has many nice
walking trials, including a paved-over trolley line that extends from Main Street in Ellicott
City to the park.

Where to Eat

Dimitri's. 2205 Frederick Rd., Catonsville;
(410) 747-1927. Casual restaurant with Italian
and Greek favorites. In the summer, you can
eat on the deck. $

Owings Mills

Owings Mills is a suburb of Baltimore and mostly residential, with shops and restaurants.
    Yet amid all this development is a great park worth visiting. To get to Owings Mills
from Baltimore, take the Baltimore Beltway (I-695) to Route 140, heading north.

Soldier's Delight Natural Environmental Area (all ages)

5100 Deer Park Rd., near the Liberty Reservoir, Owings Mills 21117; (410) 922-3044, www
.dnr.state.md.us. visitor center open Wednesday through Sunday 9 a.m. to 4 p.m. Free.
Take I-695 to I-795 north, then take exit 7B to Franklin Boulevard West. Turn left on Berry-
mans Lane and left again on Deer Park Road.

This 1,900-acre site is a serpentine barren, meaning the nutrient-poor soil has produced
mostly grassland and very few trees. It doesn't have playgrounds or many amenities, but
it's a neat place to take your kids for a walk. Youngsters get a chance to look for some
special plants in the park, including thirty-nine species that are considered rare, threat-
ened, or endangered. A sturdy stroller can go on most of the 7 miles of marked trails;
bicycles or horses are not allowed. A visitor center has exhibits, such as photographs of
plants, and a few environmental educational games for kids.

Amazing
Maryland Facts

In the nineteenth century, a mine at Soldier's Delight produced almost all the chromium used worldwide.

Where to Eat

Red Robin. 4 Restaurant Park Dr.; (443) 394-0999, www.redrobin.com. Enormous hamburgers, salads, sandwiches, in a fun atmosphere with televisions and distractions. $$

Where to Stay

Hyatt Place Baltimore/Owings Mills. 4730 Painters Mill Rd., Owings Mills; (410) 998-3630, http://baltimoreowingsmills.place .hyatt.com/hyatt/hotels/place/index.jsp. Spacious rooms with large televisions and Internet service.

For More Information

Baltimore County Conference and Visitors Bureau. P.O. Box 5426, Lutherville 21094-5426; (410) 296-4886, www.visitbaco md.com.

Stevenson

Stevenson, a suburb to the north of Baltimore, is best known as the home of the private Villa Julie College.

Irvine Nature Center (all ages)

8400 Greenspring Ave., Stevenson 21253; (410) 484-2413, www.explorenature.org. Open Monday through Saturday 9 a.m. to 4 p.m., Sunday noon to 4 p.m. Free.

Take exit 22 off I-695 and go north for about a mile on Greenspring Avenue. The center is on the left, at the second entrance for St. Timothy's School.

Sometimes with little kids, less is more. This small, charming nature center with its interactive educational displays, live animals, and walking trails was just the thing for me and my three-year-old son on a spring day when his older sister was in school. We spent about a half hour in the nature center, visiting the box turtle, frogs, snakes, and assorted other creatures, and playing with the exhibits that allowed him to match animal tracks with the creatures that made them. Then we went for a short walk, taking a wooden bridge across a tiny creek. Perfect.

The center offers organized programs such as nature crafts and insect hunts, and summer camps for children ages two to fourteen. A small shop has lots of nature-related gifts.

Monkton

Monkton and its top attraction—the Ladew Topiary Gardens—are almost directly east of Gunpowder Falls State Park. From the Baltimore Beltway, take exit 27B and go north on Route 146, Dulaney Valley Road. After the Loch Raven Reservoir Bridge, bear left onto Jarrettsville Pike (Route 146). Ladew Gardens is located on your right, 5 miles north of the stoplight in Jacksonville on Route 146.

Ladew Topiary Gardens (ages 3 and up for gardens, ages 7 and up for house)

3535 Jarrettsville Pike, Monkton 21111; (410) 557-9466, www.ladewgardens.com. Open mid-March through October, Monday through Friday 10 a.m. to 4 p.m., weekends 10:30 a.m. to 5 p.m. $$.

The gardens that Harvey S. Ladew lovingly created from 1929 to 1971 are now open to the public and are a wonderful place for both kids and adults to roam. My children, then three and five, were especially enamored of the water lily garden, where they spent about a half hour inspecting frogs, fish, and water snakes. But they also loved the topiaries fashioned in such whimsical shapes as a Buddha, a unicorn, and a fox hunt, complete with a rider and horse jumping a hedge. There are fifteen gardens in all, including one with roses, one with only pink flowers, and an herb garden. The iris garden, which runs along a small stream, is especially attractive. Secret statues and hidden picnic spots provide constant surprises.

A wooden boardwalk about a third of a mile long is part of a 1.5-mile nature trail that takes you through marshes and wetland forest.

The manor house is open for guided tours, but there are many breakable things inside, so the tours are not recommended for young children. Many events are held at the gardens, including concerts, lectures, and an antique car show in August, but one of the most popular is a children's day in September, featuring music, face-painting, and other activities. In season, a cafe on the premises serves sandwiches, salads, and desserts that can be eaten indoors or taken out for a picnic lunch.

Cockeysville

This suburb almost directly north of Baltimore is easy to reach from I-83.

Oregon Ridge Park and Nature Center (all ages)

3555 Beaver Dam Rd., Cockeysville 21030; (410) 887-1815, www.oregonridge.org. Open 9 a.m. to 5 p.m. Tuesday through Sunday. Free. To get there, take I-695 to I-83 North to exit 20B (Shawan Road West). Follow Shawan Road to the first light, Beaver Dam Road, and turn left. Immediately after making the left onto Beaver Dam Road, there will be a fork in the road. Take the right fork. Follow the driveway to the parking lot. The nature center is located a short walk up the rest of the driveway, at the top of the hill.

Kids can check out an indoor beehive and live reptiles at this wonderful nature center full of displays and live wildlife. Nature trails of varying lengths—but all less than 2 miles—will take you and your kids past a lake and up to a scenic overlook.

Annual events include a pancake breakfast each March when the maple syrup starts to run, and a honey harvest festival every October. Weekend hikes and other nature programs are also offered and are generally **free** of charge. Half-day canoe trips for children eight and older must be reserved in advance and cost $10 per person. Children sixteen and under must be accompanied by an adult.

Where to Eat

Andy Nelson's Southern Pit Barbecue.
11007 York Rd., Cockeysville; (410) 527-1226, www.andynelsonsbbq.com/. This family restaurant is considered by many to have the best barbecue in the state. $

Where to Stay

The Ramada Limited Cockeysville.
10100 York Rd., Cockeysville; (410) 667-4900, www.ramada.com. Rooms with two double beds are available at this hotel, which also offers an outdoor swimming pool, free continental breakfast, and Internet access in the rooms. $$, kids under eighteen stay **free.**

Towson

Towson is both a suburb of Baltimore and a college town, the home of the public Towson University. Although it is only twenty minutes from Baltimore, it is also a destination worth visiting on its own. The unincorporated municipality serves as Baltimore County's seat of government. As a bonus, it's home to the Towson Town Center, one of the region's nicer malls. From Baltimore, simply take the Baltimore Beltway (I-695) to the York Road exit.

Hampton National Historic Site (ages 3 and up)
535 Hampton Lane, Towson 21286; (410) 962-0688, www.nps.gov/hamp. Open daily 9 a.m. to 4 p.m.; tours on the hour. Gift shop open March 1 through early January. $ for mansion; gardens and outbuildings free.

Let your younger kids run around the stately grounds of this historic estate while older ones (and parents) get a dose of history. While outside, everyone can explore the family cemetery, slave quarters and antique carriages. Tours of the mansion are available on the hour and help youngsters understand what life was like for members of the Ridgely family, who lived there for more than 160 years.

The house was the largest in America when it was completed in 1790, and the estate was its own self-contained community, with skilled laborers, slaves, artisans, and more. The site now hosts many activities suitable for children, such as a program that lets them play with reproductions of toys from the eighteenth and nineteenth centuries.

Where to Eat

Bel-Loc Diner. Loch Raven Boulevard and Joppa Road, Towson; (410) 668-2525. This diner has been a local favorite since it opened in 1964. $

Where to Stay

Burkshire Marriott Conference Hotel. 10 West Burke Ave., Towson, 21204; (410) 324-8100, www.marriott.com. Recently renovated suites have kitchens, cable TV, high-speed Internet, and other amenities. $$$$

Lutherville

Lutherville is directly north of Towson. One of its finest kid features is the Fire Museum.

Fire Museum of Maryland (ages 4 and up)

1301 York Rd., Lutherville 21093; (410) 321-7500, www.firemuseummd.org. Open 10 a.m. to 4 p.m. Saturdays in May and September through December, 10 a.m. to 4 p.m. Wednesday through Saturday June, July, and August. $-$$, children 2 and under free. To get to the Fire Museum, take the Baltimore Beltway to exit 26B, York Road/Lutherville. Turn right at the first light onto Greenridge Road. The second driveway on the left leads to the museum parking lot.

You'll find fascinating equipment in every direction at this fun museum, which explores more than four hundred years of firefighting. There are forty antique fire engines, leather buckets, badges, a working fire alarm, a telegraph system, and more, and nearly everything can be touched, operated, or climbed upon. Kids can sit behind the wheel of a 1938 pumper or watch a short video that tells of the 1904 fire that leveled most of downtown Baltimore. In the summer, story times are held on Friday mornings, with readings of *Clifford, Curious George,* and other books that have a firefighting theme.

Kingsville and Gunpowder Falls State Park

Drive north on I-83 past Cockeysville, and you'll see the suburbs give way to more a more rural landscape. Kingsville, a hamlet of around 4,000 residents, is about 15 miles north of Baltimore and is best known as the home of the wonderful Gunpowder Falls State Park.

This enormous park follows the Gunpowder River from Kingsville to the Chesapeake Bay near Joppatowne, sprawling over more than 18,000 acres in Baltimore and Harford Counties. It's one of the state's nicest outdoor destinations, with an incredible mix of nature activities and historic attractions. Like fishing? There are excellent freshwater and tidal fishing areas where you and your kids can sink a hook. How about bike riding? The 21-mile North Central Railroad Trail is ideal for bicycles, strollers, roller skates, and plain ol' feet. Hiking, tubing, canoeing, crabbing, cross-country skiing, and picnicking are just a few of the activities available here.

Hammerman Area (all ages)

2813 Jerusalem Rd., Kingsville 21087; (410) 592-2897, www.dnr.state.md.us/publiclands/central/gunpowder.html. Open daily 8 a.m. to sunset except on Thanksgiving and Christmas. **Free.** Take I-95 to exit 67A for Route 43 east (White Marsh Boulevard). Follow 43 to Route 40 east. Turn right at the first light onto Ebenezer Road and follow it for 4.5 miles. The park entrance will be on your left.

This park has 1,500 feet of beach. Lifeguards are on duty from Memorial Day to Labor Day; at other times swimming is permitted at your own risk. In the summer, you and your family can also rent kayaks and sailboards and enjoy snacks at the concession stand.

Jerusalem Mill and Village (all ages)

2813 Jerusalem Rd., Kingsville 21087; (410) 592-2897, www.jerusalemmill.org. Open Saturday and Sunday 1 to 4 p.m. **Free,** donations appreciated. Take I-95 to exit 74 for Route 152 west (Mountain Road). Follow Mountain Road toward Fallston and turn left onto Jerusalem Road. Jerusalem Mill will be on your left after 1.1 miles. Parking is in the lot on the right, just before the mill.

A 230-year old mill is now a museum and the visitor center for the Gunpowder Falls State Park. Around the mill are several historic buildings that your kids might enjoy exploring—including a blacksmith shop and general store—all listed on the National Register of Historic Places. The museum tells the history of the village and displays the original 1860 plat drawing of the property that shows all the buildings present at that time, most of which are still standing. Regular events include blacksmithing and other living-history demonstrations.

Mill Pond Cottage

2813 Jerusalem Rd., Kingsville, 21087; (410) 592-2897, www.dnr.state.md.us/publiclands/millpond.html. Open year-round. $$$$. The cottage is in the park's northernmost section, the Hereford Area. From the Baltimore Beltway (I-695), take I-83 North 12.4 miles to exit 27, Mt. Carmel Road. Turn right on Mt. Carmel Road. At the traffic light, turn left on York Road. Pass the Hereford High School and turn left on Bunker Hill Road. Continue on Bunker Hill Road to parking lot, located above the river.

Though camping is limited at Gunpowder, the eight-person Mill Pond Cottage is available for rental. Amenities include a full kitchen, cable television, a washer and dryer, central air-conditioning, and a wood-burning fireplace. From Mill Pond, you can go fly-fishing, rent bicycles or tubes, or take part in naturalist-led programs. The park staff can help you design your stay with activities particularly suited to your family.

North Central Railroad Trail (all ages)

Hunt Valley, Maryland, to the Pennsylvania state line; (410) 592-2897, www.dnr.state.md.us/greenways/ncrt_trail.html. Open daily dawn to dusk. **Free.** To get to the Ashland terminus, take York Road (Route 45) to Cockeysville (exit 18 off I-83). Turn right (east) on Ashland Road and bear left onto Paper Mill Road. Go less than a half mile, then look for places to park along the road shoulder near the trail. You can also pick up the trail in Phoenix, Sparks, Monkton, White Hall, Parkton, Bentley Springs, and Freeland.

This flat, paved trail, which starts at Ashland Road in Hunt Valley and continues into Pennsylvania, is ideal for walking, biking, or pushing a stroller. What's more, you don't have to turn around once you get into Pennsylvania: The route continues for another 20 miles after you leave Maryland.

Attractions along the way include the Sparks Band Nature Center, open on summer weekends from 10 a.m. to 4 p.m., and the Monkton Train Station, which is also a museum, gift shop, and ranger station. The station is open Wednesday through Sunday, Memorial Day to Labor Day, and weekends in the spring and fall. There are restrooms, water, telephones, and picnic tables here, but parking is limited.

Middle River

Heading around Baltimore and toward the south, the next stop is Middle River, an unincorporated town of about 25,000 residents. From Route 40, take Martin Boulevard (Route 700) toward Middle River.

Glenn L. Martin Maryland Aviation Museum (ages 5 and up)
Martin State Airport, 701 Wilson Point Rd., Hangar 5, Middle River 21220; (410) 682-6122, www.marylandaviationmuseum.org/index.html. Open Wednesday through Saturday 11 a.m. to 3 p.m. Free.

Your kids will be fascinated by all the real aircraft at this wonderful museum. Dating from the 1920s and continuing to the present day, the aircraft are mostly from the Glenn L. Martin Company. Other cool exhibits include aircraft and rockets, wind-tunnel models, and photographs outlining the growth of the Martin Company and the history of aviation in Maryland.

Edgemere

Edgemere is south of Baltimore and close to Middle River, on an outcropping surrounded by the Patapsco River, the Chesapeake Bay, and the Back River.

North Point State Park
North Point Road, Edgemere 21052; (410) 477-0757, http://dnr.maryland.gov/publiclands/central/northpoint.html; Open Wednesday through Sunday, May 1 to September 30, 10 a.m. to 6 p.m.; and Wednesday through Sunday, October 1 to April 30, 8 a.m. to 4 p.m. Free. From Baltimore, take the Baltimore Beltway to Route 151 (Sparrows Point/North Point Boulevard). Exit and bear right onto Route 151 south to first light. Make a left onto North Point Road (Route 20). Follow through Edgemere for 1.9 miles to North Point State Park on left.

Kids will love seeing the ruins of the Bay Shore Amusement Park that operated here from 1904 to 1947, including a restored trolley shelter and fountain. This park on the water's edge also has a fishing pier and wading beach, and the hiking trails include the Defenders' Trail, which was used during the War of 1812 and runs through the park. A beautiful new visitor center was completed in 2002.

Harford County

Known as the Gateway to the Chesapeake because it is nestled between the Susquehanna River and the Chesapeake Bay, Harford County offers many family destinations, including the charming waterfront town of Havre de Grace, as well as such attractions as the Steppingstone Museum and the U.S. Army Ordnance Museum. I-95 and Route 1 are the county's major roadways.

Bel Air

A short drive east from Monkton in Baltimore County takes you to Bel Air, a residential community that is the seat of government for Harford County.

Hays House Museum (ages 7 and up)

324 South Kenmore Ave., Bel Air 21014; (410) 838-7691, www.harfordhistory.net/HINDEX .htm. Open Sunday 1 to 4 p.m. $, children 4 and under and members of the Historical Society of Harford County Free. From I-95, take Route 24 north for 6 miles, then go right on Business Route 1. At the third light, turn right on Kenmore Avenue. The Hays House is on the right.

In the days before television and video games, children would spend hours working on needlework samplers, painstakingly stitching letters and designs onto a piece of fabric. Blanch Hall Lee began working on just such a sampler when she was eight years old, back in 1830. The sampler is now on display at the Hays House Museum, the oldest home in Bel Air, built starting in 1788.

While touring the house, kids can learn how food was prepared in an eighteenth-century kitchen and see how a home of the time might have been furnished. Local attorney Thomas A. Hays moved into the house in 1811, and he and his descendants lived there for 140 years. It is currently used to teach children and adults about family life in the eighteenth and nineteenth centuries.

To make history come alive for youngsters, you won't want to miss the annual "encampment of living history" held every April. Artisans arrive from far and wide to camp on the property and demonstrate such skills as blacksmithing, weaving, candle making, and period cooking.

Rockfield Park (all ages)

Churchville Road, Bel Air 21014; (410) 638-4561, www.belairmd.org/rockfield.asp. Open Monday through Friday 8 a.m. to noon and 12:30 to 4:30 p.m. Free.

If your child adores playgrounds, then you won't want to miss this Harford County park, considered by many to have the best playground in central Maryland. The massive all-wooden structure has a sandbox, swings, and plenty of nooks and crannies for young ones. The park also has a Grove for the Senses, with trees that have strongly scented flowers or barks that are interesting to touch. This grove was designed by the Bel Air Lions Club specifically for sight-impaired people, but all children can enjoy its tactile features.

And your children won't want to miss the butterfly and hummingbird garden, sponsored by the County Garden Club, which planted flowers that are known to attract the beautiful winged creatures.

Where to Eat

Cracker Barrel Old Country Street. 1440 Handlir Dr., Bel Air; (410) 272-4778. Serving American-style fare for breakfast, lunch, and dinner. $

Where to Stay

Country Inn & Suites by Carlson. 1435 Handlir Dr., Bel Air; (866) 608-9330. This hotel has suites, so kids can sleep in one room and grown-ups in the other. The suites have microwaves and refrigerators. The hotel also serves a complimentary breakfast and has an exercise room and outdoor pool. $$

Abingdon

Abingdon is close to Bel Air. From I-95, take exit 77A, Route 24, toward Edgewood. Keep right at the fork in the ramp, and drive 0.4 mile to merge onto Emmorton Road. In 0.6 mile, go left on Philadelphia Road. In about a mile and a half, you'll be in Abingdon.

Anita C. Leight Estuary Center (all ages)

700 Otter Point Rd., Abingdon 21009; (410) 612-1688, www.otterpointcreek.org. Open Thursday through Saturday 10 a.m. to 5 p.m. and Sunday noon to 5 p.m. Free.

Take your kids on a pontoon or canoe ride at this center, which is part of the Chesapeake Bay National Estuarine Research Reserve. They're likely to see osprey, eagles, great blue herons, snapping turtles, and many other animals.

The pontoon rides are available for children seven and older. Other programs and activities at the center include canoe trips, hikes, and nature lessons. Some of these have a small fee.

Aberdeen

Best known as the home of the Aberdeen Proving Ground, an important military installation, Aberdeen also holds a special place in the hearts of baseball fans as the home town of "Iron Man" Cal Ripken, the great Orioles player.

U.S. Army Ordnance Museum (ages 7 and up)

Aberdeen Proving Ground, Aberdeen 21005; (410) 278-3602, (410) 278-2396, www.ordmus found.org. Open daily 10 a.m. to 4:45 p.m. Closed national holidays except Memorial Day, Armed Forces Day, July 4, and Veterans Day. Free, but must get a visitor's pass at the Maryland Avenue gate of the Aberdeen Proving Ground. Take exit 85 off I-95 and go 3.5 miles east on Route 22 to the museum.

Older kids who are interested in military history will probably love this museum, which traces the history of weapons development from the Revolutionary War to the present day through the world's most extensive collection of combat vehicles, artillery, small arms, and ammunition. The museum, on the grounds of the Aberdeen Proving Ground, features a "tank park" that shows armored vehicles from the time of World War I to the present.

Where to Eat

New Ideal Diner. 104 South Philadelphia Blvd., Aberdeen; (410) 272-1880. A nice one-hundred-seat diner known for its crab cakes. $

Where to Stay

Clarion Hotel. 980 Hospitality Way, Aberdeen; (410) 273-6300, www.clarion aberdeen.com. Nintendo games in the rooms, free breakfast and an outdoor pool are among the amenities at this centrally located hotel. $$$

Holiday Inn Aberdeen-Chesapeake House. 1007 Beards Hill Rd., Aberdeen; (410) 272-8100, www.ichotelsgroup.com/h/d/hi/1/ en/hotel/abdch. Rooms with kitchenettes are available at this hotel, which has an indoor pool and spa as well as in-room movies, cable television, Internet, and a restaurant on the premises. Kids under eighteen stay **Free.** $$–$$$

SpringHill Suites Edgewood Aberdeen. 1420 Handlir Dr., Bel Air; (410) 297-4970, www.marriott.com/hotels/travel/bwiab-spring hill-suites-edgewood-aberdeen. The suites at this hotel have separate areas for eating, sleeping, and hanging out, plus small kitchens with refrigerators, microwaves, and pantries. The hotel also has an indoor swimming pool, exercise room, free Internet access, and complimentary breakfast buffet. $$$

Havre de Grace

Havre de Grace is an ideal place for a day trip with kids. The town, which sits where the Susquehanna River meets the Chesapeake Bay, was founded in 1782 and incorporated as a city in 1785. During the War of 1812, the British burned most of the buildings, despite the efforts of one Lt. John O'Neill, who defended Havre de Grace while its citizens fled in panic.

A good place to begin a tour of Havre de Grace is with the half-mile boardwalk along the bay, which connects the Millard E. Tydings Memorial Park to the Decoy Museum, Maritime Museum, and Concord Point Lighthouse. The park has a nice playground with swings and slides where kids can stretch their legs after the car ride while adults sit at the benches or picnic tables and look out over the water. After lunch, take your family for a stroll through the historic district, with its many antiques shops and other stores.

Concord Point Lighthouse (ages 3 and up)

Concord and Lafayette Streets, Havre de Grace 21078; (410) 939-9040, www.nps.gov/history/maritime/light/concord.htm. Open on weekends April through October 1 p.m. to 5 p.m. Free.

Next on the boardwalk is this beautiful white lighthouse, built in 1827. It is the oldest continuously operating lighthouse in Maryland. Children can climb the stairs to the top (or be carried by their parents) for a sweeping view of the bay.

Havre de Grace Decoy Museum (ages 3 and up)

25 Giles St., Havre de Grace, 21078; (410) 939-3739, www.decoymuseum.com. Open Monday through Saturday 10:30 a.m. to 4:30 p.m., Sunday noon to 4 p.m. $–$$, children 8 and under free.

You have to love a museum with a big sign urging people to "please touch," and that's exactly what you'll find on a display of wooden duck heads at this unique museum dedicated to the art and history of duck decoys. My kids and their cousin, who is seven, had a great time at this museum, which also boasts realistic-looking figurines by renowned carvers. An indoor wooden boardwalk takes visitors on a tour through duck-decoy history, showing how decoys evolved from a hunting tool to a folk art in their own right.

Havre de Grace Maritime Museum (ages 3 and up)

100 Lafayette St., Havre de Grace 21078; (410) 939-4800, www.hdgmaritimemuseum.org. Open Monday, Wednesday, Friday, Saturday, and Sunday noon to 5 p.m. September through May, daily from 10 a.m. to 5 p.m. June through August. $, children 8 and under free.

As you continue along the Havre de Grace boardwalk, you'll come to this waterside museum, which houses the Chesapeake Wooden Boat Builders School and the Susquehanna Flats Environmental Festival. Kids will enjoy the photographs and artifacts that explore the city's maritime history, and they'll like seeing the boats that are under construction.

Martha Lewis Skipjack Discovery Classroom (ages 5 and up)

Chesapeake Heritage Conservancy, 121 North Union Ave., Suite C, Havre de Grace 21078; (410) 939-4078, www.skipjackmarthalewis.org. 90-minute public cruises from June to mid-October offered Thursday, Saturday, and Sunday at 1:30 and 3 p.m. Call ahead to verify. $–$$.

Take your kids for a cruise on this 1955 two-sail bateau, which still dredges oysters on the Chesapeake, making it the last boat to fish commercially, under sail, in the United States.

Children will feel the salty wind on their faces as they learn about a traditional Chesapeake way of life. The *Martha Lewis* hosts educational cruises for children, story-time cruises for children three to eight years old, and camp for children ages eleven to fifteen.

Steppingstone Museum (ages 3 and up)

461 Quaker Bottom Rd., Havre de Grace 21078; (410) 939-2299, www.steppingstone museum.org. Open weekends May through October 1 to 5 p.m. $, children 12 and under **free.**

Once a working farm, this museum just outside the city limits now features artisans who demonstrate the rural arts and crafts of the time period between 1880 and 1920. Children can roam the property, visiting reconstructed buildings that will be of interest to most youngsters, including a blacksmith shop, a carriage barn, the farmhouse, a general store, and a display barn.

Susquehanna Museum of Havre de Grace (ages 3 and up)

Erie and Conesto Streets, Havre de Grace 21078; (410) 939-5780, www.lockhousemuseum .org. Open weekends 1 to 5 p.m. **Free,** though donations accepted.

There are lots of neat things for kids to see in this restored lockhouse, which once guided boats through the southern terminal of the Susquehanna River and the Tidewater Canal.

The building served as home for the lockkeeper, and it is furnished as it would have been in the mid-1800s. The museum also has a reconstructed pivot bridge and a video about the operation of the canal, as well as displays about local history. Activities include tea parties for children, nature walks, and pirate-themed parties.

Amazing
Maryland Facts

The first keeper of the Concord Point Lighthouse was John O'Neill, who remained in charge from 1827 until his death in 1836. The last was his grandson, Harry O'Neill, who remained in service until the lighthouse was electrified in 1920.

Amazing
Maryland Facts

Reefs of oysters, known as oyster bars, were once so large in the Chesapeake Bay they were considered navigational hazards. Today, the oyster population has been significantly depleted.

Susquehanna State Park (all ages)

Rock Run Road, 3 miles northwest of Havre de Grace (mailing address: c/o Rocks State Park, 3318 Rocks Chrome Hill Rd., Jarrettsville 21084); (410) 557-7994, www.dnr.state.md .us/publiclands/central/susquehanna.html. Open daily. Free. From I-95, take exit 89 (Route 155) west to Route 161. Turn right on Route 161 and then right on Rock Run Road. Follow Rock Run Road to the park entrance.

Your kids probably won't want to leave Steppingstone Museum without spending some time in the wonderful 2,500-acre park on which it sits. There's so much to do here, from fishing, canoeing, or kayaking (bring your own gear) in the Susquehanna River to hiking along the 15 miles of marked trails. Kids can eat their PB&J and bananas (or whatever you pack) at the Deer Creek picnic area, which has shaded picnic tables, grills, and restrooms.

Historic sites on the premises include the Carter Mansion, the Rock Run Mill, and the Jersey Toll House. The tollhouse is now a private residence, but the Carter Mansion, with some rooms furnished with period antiques, is open for tours from May to September. Kids may like seeing the antique farm equipment in the barn. The recently restored Rock Run Mill is especially appealing for youngsters because they can see corn ground into meal on weekends. The meal is then bagged and given free to the public.

You might have so much fun that you want to stay overnight, and that's not a problem since there are camping facilities on-site, too.

Where to Eat

Coakley's Pub. 457 Franklin St., Havre de Grace; (410) 939-8888). This casual restaurant and bar offers sandwiches, steaks, crab cakes, and wings. A nonsmoking room is situated away from the bar, and a children's menu is available. Open daily for lunch and dinner. $

MacGregor's Restaurant and Tavern. 331 St. John St., Havre de Grace; (410) 939-3003, www.macgregorsrestaurant.com.

Every table has a view of the water at this large and attractive restaurant that serves lots of crab dishes and seafood. Open daily for lunch and dinner, Sunday for brunch. $$

Where to Stay

Super 8 Motel–Havre de Grace. 929 Pulaski Hwy, Havre de Grace; (410) 939-1880 or (800) 800-8000, www.super8.com. Cribs, king beds, and cable television with HBO,

CNN, and ESPN highlight the amenities at this low-frills motel. $$, children twelve and under stay free

For More Information

Harford County Tourism Council. 3 West Bel Air Ave., Aberdeen 21001; (800) 597-2649, (410) 272-2325, www.harfordmd.com.

Havre de Grace Tourism Commission. 450 Pennington Ave., Havre de Grace 21078; (800) 851-7756, (410) 939-2100, www.hdg tourism.com.

Kids. Pick up a free copy of this monthly magazine that lists things to do, or visit its Web site at www.harfordcountykids.com.

Jarrettsville

Jarrettsville is northwest of Havre de Grace and also along the Susquehanna River. From Havre de Grace, take Lapidum Road heading north.

Rocks State Park (all ages)

3318 Rocks Chrome Hill Rd., Jarrettsville 21084; (410) 557-7994, www.dnr.state.md.us/public lands/central/rocks.html. Open daily 9 a.m. to sunset, closed major holidays. **Free.**

Activities at this park include hiking, tubing, canoeing, fishing, and picnicking. The Falling Branch area of the park has Kilgore Falls, the second-largest vertical drop waterfall in the state. Also, check out the rock formation known as the King and Queen Seats, once a ceremonial place for the Susquehannock Nation of Native Americans.

Annual Events

Chocolate Festival. Downtown Bel Air. Raffles, auctions, and lots of candy in January.

Spring Bear and Doll Show. Historic Savage Mill; (410) 498-6871. Lots of collectible bears, dolls, and accessories for sale in March.

Decoy and Wildlife Festival. Havre de Grace; (410) 939-3739, www.decoymuseum .com. In May, an extravaganza of carving competitions, art for sale, and carving demonstrations.

Outdoor Movies. Bel Air; (410) 638-1023. From May through September family movies are sponsored by the Downtown Bel Air Revitalization Alliance. **Free.**

Ladew Summer Concert Series. Every other Sunday in June, July, and August, bring your own picnics, blankets, chairs, and listen to live music.

4H and FFA Fair. Westminster; (410) 386-2760, www.carrollcountyfair.com. This July fair is advertised as Maryland's largest free fair.

Harford County Farm Fair. The Equestrian Center, Tollgate Road, Bel Air; (410) 838-8663, www.farmfair.org. $ A nonmechanical "kidway" hosts games, craft stands, and other activities, while elsewhere at the fair visitors can enjoy pig races, pie-eating contests, a rodeo, and more. Held in July.

Other Things to See and Do in Central Maryland

- **Aberdeen Room Archives and Museum.** 18 Howard St., Aberdeen; (410) 273-6325, www.aberdeenroom.com/aberdeenroom/index.html

- **BaySail School and Yacht Charters.** 100 Bourbon St., Tidewater Marina, Havre de Grace; (410) 939-2869, www.baysail.net

- **Carroll Arts Center.** 91 West Main St., Westminster; (410) 848-7272

- **Chuck E. Cheese's.** Several locations, including 5 Bel Air Parkway, Bel Air; (410) 515-0207; 5912 Baltimore National Pike, Catonsville; (410) 719-8850; and 8354 Eastern Ave., Dundalk; (410) 288-9393

- **Columbia Ice Rink.** 5876 Thunder Hill Rd., Columbia; (410) 730-0322

- **Liriodendron Mansion.** 502 West Gordon St., Bel Air; (410) 879-4424, www.liriodendron.com

- **Lorenzo's Timonium Young Adult Theatre.** 9603 Deereco Rd., Timonium; (410) 560-1113, www.timoniumdinnertheatre.com

- **Maple Lawn Farm.** 11788 Rte. 216, Fulton; (301) 725-2074, www.maplelawn.com

- **Morris Meadows Recreation Farm.** 1523 Freeland Rd., Freeland; (410) 329-6636

- **Patuxent Research Refuge and National Wildlife Visitor Center.** 10901 Scarlet Tanager Loop, Laurel; (301) 497-5580, www.fws.gov/northeast/patuxent

- **Ripken Stadium.** 873 Long Dr.; (410) 297-9292; www.ironbirdsbaseball.com/stadium

- **Sharp's at Waterford Farm.** 4003 Jennings Chapel Rd., Brookeville; (410) 489-2572, www.sharpfarm.com

Howard County Fair. Howard County Fairgrounds, Friendship; (410) 442-1022, www.howardcountyfair.com. In August, entertainment, livestock shows, tractor pulls, petting farm, and more.

Maryland State Fair. 2200 York Rd., Timonium; (410) 252-0200, www.marylandstatefair.com. Rides, food, animals, contests, you name it. This is the real thing. August.

Capital Region

Maryland's Capital Region surrounds Washington, D.C., and includes Frederick, Montgomery, and Prince George's Counties, areas rich with historic, cultural, and natural attractions. What child can resist a roomful of butterflies? Visit Brookside Gardens in the summer months, and the beautiful winged creatures will probably flutter in for a rest on your child's shoulders. Or how about a lake that's great for swimming, building sand castles, and paddleboating? My family spends many happy summer days at Cunningham Falls. We might grab a meal in nearby Frederick, the state's second largest city, or perhaps we'll take in a Frederick Keys minor-league ball game on the way home. For working farms that take children back to the nineteenth century, it's hard to beat Oxon Hill and the National Colonial Farm, both in Prince George's County.

From the kid-friendly College Park Aviation Museum in College Park to Rose Hill, a museum specifically for children in Frederick, there are many things for youngsters to explore in the Capital Region.

Since the Capital Region basically forms a semicircle around the nation's capitol, that's what we'll do, too. We'll start to the west of the District of Columbia with Montgomery County, then move north to Frederick County, and then head south and to the east of Washington, D.C., to Prince George's County.

Montgomery County

This tony suburb of Washington, D.C., includes the communities of Silver Spring, Bethesda, and Rockville, among others. Residents here often seem to eat, drink, and sleep politics, but this area is actually very family-friendly, with lots of parks, playgrounds, and historic attractions.

CAPITAL REGION

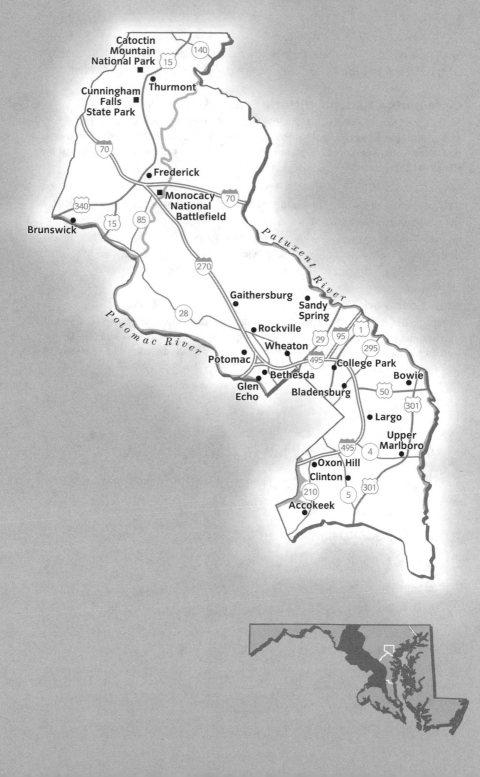

Glen Echo

Just to the north of Washington and perched on the banks of the Potomac River, Glen Echo is the smallest town in Maryland, with a population of about 250 residents.

Clara Barton National Historic Site (ages 8 and up)

5801 Oxford Rd., Glen Echo 20812; (301) 492-6245, www.nps.gov/clba. Open daily 10 a.m. to 5 p.m. House shown by guided tour only, with first tour at 10 a.m. and last tour at 4 p.m. Reservations required for groups of 10 or more. Closed Thanksgiving, Christmas, and New Year's Day. Free.

Boys and girls can learn a lot about American history and the role of women by visiting the home of Clara Barton, the founder of the American Red Cross. Though Barton was born in Massachusetts, this house in Maryland served as her home, as Red Cross headquarters, and as a warehouse for disaster relief supplies from 1897 until her death in 1912 at the age of ninety. Tours of her home illuminate the way she combined her work and private life within the same building.

Glen Echo Park (all ages)

7300 MacArthur Blvd., Glen Echo 20812; (301) 492-6282, www.nps.gov/glec. Open daily dawn to dusk. Carousel operates May through September, Saturday and Sunday noon to 6 p.m. In June through August, the carousel is also open Wednesday and Thursday 10 a.m. to 2 p.m.; in August, it's also open Friday 10 a.m. to 2 p.m. Free.

Karen's TopPicks for fun in the Capital Region

1. Chesapeake & Ohio Canal National Historical Park, Potomac
2. Brookside Gardens, Wheaton
3. Monocacy National Battlefield, Frederick
4. Rose Hill Manor Park, Frederick
5. Cunningham Falls State Park, Thurmont
6. Catoctin Mountain National Park and Catoctin Wildlife Preserve and Zoo, Thurmont
7. College Park Aviation Museum, College Park
8. Six Flags America, Largo
9. Watkins Regional Park, Upper Marlboro
10. Accokeek Foundation/National Colonial Farm, Accokeek

For More Glen Echo **Information**

The Echo is a monthly newspaper published by and for the people of Glen Echo. It is distributed **free** around town, and copies are on file at the local libraries. Or read it online at www.glenecho.org.

The site of a popular amusement park from 1911 until 1968, Glen Echo Park now hosts art education programs, including a children's theater and classes in art and dance. For youngsters, the main attraction is the still-operating wooden carousel, which dates from 1921. There's a small charge for the carousel and some events.

Potomac

The surburb to the north of Washington is easily reached by taking the Washington Beltway to Route 190.

Chesapeake & Ohio Canal National Historical Park and Great Falls Tavern Visitor Center (ages 4 and up)

11710 MacArthur Blvd., Potomac 20854; (202) 653-5190, (301) 767-3714, www.nps.gov/choh. Park open daily sunrise to sunset; visitor center open daily 9 a.m. to 4:30 p.m. with extended summer hours. $ per car.

The Chesapeake & Ohio Canal, better known as the C&O, follows the Potomac River for 184.5 miles, from Washington, D.C., to Cumberland, Maryland. Between 1828 and 1924, it was used mainly to haul coal from western Maryland to the port in Georgetown.

These days, the flat, paved former towpaths are ideal for hiking and biking. Along the way are hundreds of original locks, lock houses, and aquaducts. There are six visitor centers, located at Georgetown, Great Falls, Brunswick, Williamsport, Hancock, and the Western Maryland Station in Cumberland. But Great Falls Tavern Visitor Center has the only lock house still open to the public, Riley's Lockhouse, and thus this center is a favorite with families and kids. The spectacular Great Falls are also visible from this visitor center. Your kids might enjoy taking a mule-drawn boat ride with costumed guides who explain

Amazing
Maryland Facts

When Clara Barton's house was established as a National Historic Site in 1975, it marked the first time a National Historic Site had been dedicated to the accomplishments of a woman.

Amazing
Maryland Facts

Families who lived on boats on the canal would often chain their children to the boat to keep them from falling into the water.

the history of the canal. The rides leave from Great Falls or from the Georgetown visitor center ($–$$).

You and your kids can also rent boats or bicycles to travel along the canal. Rental concessions that are operated near the park include Thompson's Boat Center (near milepost 0), Fletcher's Boathouse (milepost 3.14), and Swain's Lock (milepost 16.1). They all sell snacks as well.

Where to Eat

Potomac Pizza. Potomac Promenade, 9812 Falls Rd., Potomac; (301) 299-7700, www .potomacpizza.com. Plus other regional locations. Pizzas, subs, salads, and Italian specialties. $

Rockville

The county seat of Montgomery County, Rockville is north of Potomac, off I-270. The city has about 50,000 residents, boasts fifty-two parks and playgrounds, two libraries, and one public golf course.

Stonestreet Museum of Nineteenth-Century Medicine and Beall-Dawson Historical Park (ages 8 and up)

111 West Montgomery Ave., Rockville 20850; (301) 762-1492, (301) 340-6534, www .montgomeryhistory.org. Open Tuesday through Sunday noon to 4 p.m. $.

Antique medical instruments, a real skeleton, and a hand-cranked telephone are among the items sure to appeal to children at this museum. Dr. Edward Stonestreet began practicing medicine when he was twenty-one and didn't stop until he died in 1903 at the age of seventy-three. More than one hundred years later, his one-room clinic has been restored as a museum run by the Montgomery County Historical Society. The clinic was moved a short distance in 1972 from its original location near Stonestreet's home to the grounds of the historical society. The clinic displays medical instruments from the time and photographs of Stonestreet and his family.

For Young Theater Buffs

The following Montgomery County theaters have child-appropriate productions.

- **BAPA's Imagination Stage.** Main office: 4908 Auburn Ave., Bethesda 20814; (301) 961-6060; box office (301) 280-1660; Whittier Woods Center: 7300 Whittier Blvd., Bethesda 20817; (301) 320-2550, www.imaginationstage .org. This full-service performing arts center for young people offers acting classes, professional-level performances, and performance opportunities. Founded in 1979 as the Bethesda Academy of the Performing Arts, the organization recently moved into a new home at Auburn Avenue, complete with a cafe, gift shop, and of course stage and classroom areas.

- **Strathmore Hall Arts Center.** 10701 Rockville Pike, North Bethesda; (301) 530-0540, www.strathmore.org. A Georgian-style mansion built around 1900 is now home to more than fifty concerts and programs a year, including many performances, such as jugglers and puppet shows, that are specifically for children. Some performances are free, others cost around $$.

Admission includes a tour of the Beall-Dawson House, a brick, Federal-style home at the same location built in 1815 and now run as a museum. The tour features discussions about what life was like for the upper-class Bealls and their African-American slaves.

Where to Eat

Backstreets Café. 12352 Wilkins Ave., Rockville; (301) 984-0394. Open for breakfast, lunch, and dinner, serving breakfast items, hearty sandwiches, and entrees. $

Silver Diner. 11806 Rockville Pike, Rockville and other regional locations; (301) 770-0333, www.silverdiner.com. Kids' menu plus classic American dishes with flair at a retro-style diner. $

Where to Stay

Best Western Washington Gateway Hotel. 1251 West Montgomery Ave., Rockville; (301) 424-4940. Outdoor pool with sundeck, free breakfast buffet, free Internet access, exercise room, and game room are among the amenities here. $$, children under seventeen stay free.

Courtyard by Marriott Rockville. 2500 Research Blvd., Rockville; (301) 670-6700. A laundry valet, coffee shop, indoor pool, whirlpool, and exercise room are among the features that make this hotel pleasant for families. $$

For More Information

Rockville City Hall. 111 Maryland Ave., Rockville 20850; (240) 314-5000, www.rock villemd.gov.

Gaithersburg

Continuing north along I-270, the next major city is Gaithersburg, with some 50,000 residents in about 10 square miles.

Seneca Creek State Park (all ages)

11950 Clopper Rd., Gaithersburg 20878; (301) 924-2127. Open daily dawn to dusk. Closed Thanksgiving, December 24–25. **Free.**

Kids can walk, run, or bicycle on the 14.75-mile greenway trail that follows Seneca Creek to the Potomac. The park also boasts a 27-hole disc golf course that's fun for both amateurs and professionals, a 90-acre lake for flat-water kayaking and canoeing, and space for cross-country skiing. There are also playgrounds, shelters, a visitor center, picnic areas, and campfire programs.

The Seneca Schoolhouse, located on Route 190 west of Seneca, is a restored one-room schoolhouse that lets kids see what school was like in the nineteenth century.

Shadowland Laser Adventures (ages 6 and up)

Quince Orchard Shopping Center, 624 Quince Orchard Rd., Gaithersburg 20878; (301) 330-5546, www.shadowlandadventures.com. Open Monday 11 a.m. to 6 p.m., Tuesday through Thursday 11 a.m. to 10 p.m., Friday 11 a.m. to midnight, Saturday 10 a.m. to midnight, Sunday 10 a.m. to 10 p.m. $$.

In these adventures, kids (and their parents) strap on high-tech suits, grab handsets, and act out interactive games in an arena filled with mazes, alleys, and turrets. During the adventure, special effects such as lighting and smoke enhance the fantasy. While Shadowland is often rented out by corporations, it is also popular for birthday parties and family outings.

Where to Eat

Hamlet at the Rio. 9811 Washingtonian Blvd., Gaithersburg; (301) 417-0773, www.hamletrestaurants.com. One of the newer additions to the famed Hamburger Hamlet chain that started in Hollywood, California, in 1950, this fun restaurant serves burgers, sandwiches, pasta, and more. $$–$$$.

Noodles and Company. 177 Kentland Blvd., Gaithersburg; (301) 926-5901. Casual restaurant serving noodles in a variety of guises, from pad thai to macaroni and cheese. $

Where to Stay

Comfort Inn Shady Grove. 16216 Frederick Rd., Gaithersburg; (301) 330-0023, www.comfortinn.com. Outdoor pool, complimentary full breakfast, Internet access and Nintendo, microwave, refrigerator, and freezer in every room. $$, kids under eighteen stay **free.**

Holiday Inn Gaithersburg. 2 Montgomery Village Ave., Gaithersburg; (301) 948-8900, www.higaithersburg.com. There are fourteen kitchenette suites here that are ideal for traveling families. Other amenities include an indoor pool, Jacuzzi, fitness center, Internet access, and on-site restaurants. $$

For More Information

Gaithersburg City Hall. 31 South Summit Ave., Gaithersburg; (301) 258-6310, www.gaithersburgmd.gov.

Sandy Spring

The small community of Sandy Spring is to the east of Gaithersburg and Rockville. From I-270, take Route 28 east to the intersection with Georgia Avenue, and go for about 3 miles before turning right at the intersection of Route 97 and Route 108.

Sandy Spring Museum (ages 6 and up)

17901 Bentley Rd., Sandy Spring 20860; (301) 774-0022, www.sandyspringmuseum.org. Open Monday, Wednesday, and Thursday 9 a.m. to 4 p.m., weekends noon to 4 p.m. $, children 12 and under free. The museum is about 3 blocks from the village of Sandy Spring. Turn left on Bentley Road where it intersects with Route 108, and then turn right into the museum's driveway.

The town of Sandy Spring, settled by Quaker farmers in the late 1700s, was growing quickly when this museum was established in 1980 as a link to the community's rural past. Activities such as an annual strawberry festival in June and exhibits of farm equipment, clothing, and photographs evoke a simpler time and are appealing to children.

Wheaton

The unincorporated community of Wheaton is to the north of Washington, D.C., and is easy to reach by taking the Washington Beltway (I-495) to Route 182.

Brookside Gardens (ages 2 and up)

1800 Glenallen Ave., Wheaton 20902; (301) 949-1408, www.brooksidegardens.org. Gardens open daily except December 25 from sunrise to sunset, conservatories open 10 a.m. to 5 p.m., visitor center open 9 a.m. to 5 p.m. Free, although there may be charges for special events.

This fifty-acre garden is a great place for kids to run around while adults enjoy the beautiful flowers. In the winter, many of the more colorful displays are confined to the indoor conservatories, but an annual "garden of lights" held from November to early January will have your kids oohing and aahing at displays in the shapes of animals, fountains, and rainbows.

In summer, don't miss the Butterfly Show. My children were absolutely enchanted when the winged creatures fluttered onto their shoulders and fingertips.

The visitor center hosts children's programs that include a Saturday-morning story time held at 10 and repeated at 10:30, plus various educational programs. A preschooler

Amazing
Maryland Facts

Wheaton is named for Gen. Frank Wheaton, one of the few Civil War generals to reach that rank without attending West Point.

room at the visitor center has hands-on activities specifically designed for children ages two to five.

Wheaton Regional Park (all ages)

2000 Shorefield Rd., Wheaton 20902; (301) 495-2503. Open daily sunrise to sunset. Free.

This park is a delight, with an enormous playground, a miniature train, a carousel, and a shaded picnic area. For a small fee the train, which only operates when the weather is good, takes children on a ten-minute ride through the park. The restored 1915 carousel, with thirty-three jumping horses, three zebras, and two chariots, has the same schedule. Expect to pay a small fee to ride.

Also at the park is an indoor ice-skating rink that is open year-round and offers lessons, rentals, and public skating times; and a horse stable, with both indoor and outdoor facilities for lessons or rides through the mile-and-a-half of trails in the park.

Where to Eat

Ledo Pizza. 2638 West University Blvd., Wheaton; (301) 929-6111. Maryland-based chain of sit-down restaurants serving pizza, pastas, and salads. $

For More Information

Conference and Visitors Bureau of Montgomery County. 11820 Parklawn Dr., Suite 380, Rockville 20852; (301) 428-9702, (800) 925-0880, www.cvbmontco.com.

Montgomery County Department of Recreation. 12210 Bushey Dr., Silver Spring 20902; (301) 528-1480, www.co.mo .md.us/rec.

Frederick County

Frederick County is more rural and less suburban than the rest of the Capital Region, even though it is home to the second-largest city in the state, Frederick. Surrounding the city is bucolic countryside of rolling hills and charming small towns. Be prepared to spot plenty of cows, sheep, and horses along the way.

Frederick

This city is great for strolling with the family, and there are plenty of kid-friendly restaurants, as well as Rose Hill Manor Park, a historic site specifically tailored for curious youngsters.

Barbara Fritchie House and Museum (ages 8 and up)

154 West Patrick St., Frederick 21701; (301) 698-8992, www.fredericktourism.org/members/view/84/sect:v. Visit the exterior year-round, call for hours before planning to see the interior. **Free.**

Kids will like the story of Barbara Fritchie, the ninety-five-year-old who supposedly waved her Union Flag at Gen. Stonewall Jackson and his troops as they marched through Frederick in 1862. Apparently, Jackson was so impressed by her bold action that he spared the town. The event inspired a poem by John Greenleaf Whittier called *Barbara Fritchie,* with the following famous lines:

> "Shoot if you must, this old gray head,
> But spare your country's flag," she said.

Now, the reconstructed house and gardens are open to the public for self-guided tours.

Monocacy National Battlefield (ages 6 and up)

4801 Urbana Pike, Frederick 21703; (301) 662-3515, www.nps.gov/mono/home.htm. Visitor center open 8:30 a.m. to 5 p.m. Memorial Day to Labor Day; 8 a.m. to 4:30 p.m. Labor Day to Memorial Day. Closed major holidays. **Free.** From I-70, take exit 54 (Market Street) and go south on Route 355. The Gambrill Mill Visitor Center is 0.1 mile south of the Monocacy River Bridge. The driveway is on the left.

Few events in American history are more fascinating and important than the Civil War, and a visit to a real battlefield can do more to help kids understand what the war was like than all the homework and lesson plans in the world.

The July 9, 1864, battle at Monocacy was known as the Battle That Saved Washington because even though the Confederates triumphed, the battle cost them a day's march

Amazing
Maryland Facts

Roger Brooke Taney of Frederick was the fifth chief justice of the U.S. Supreme Court. But his brother-in-law is even more famous. He's Francis Scott Key, who wrote the words that became the "The Star-Spangled Banner."

and a chance to capture the nation's capital. After this turning point, the Confederates moved south toward Virginia and ended their quest to take the war farther north.

The Gambrill Mill Visitor Center has interpretive exhibits about the battle, which pitted 15,000 Confederates against a paltry 5,800 Union troops, as well as brochures and maps for self-guided tours. Kids will get to see battle artifacts, and they'll probably enjoy the interactive computer program and electric map that provides orientation.

The center is also the starting point for a 4-mile interpretive drive through the battlefield, as well as for a half-mile loop walk with interpretive signs that passes the mill, which served as a field hospital.

Kids may not understand the details of the battle, but the wonderful monuments and sculptures are sure to impress.

National Museum of Civil War Medicine (ages 8 and up)

48 East Patrick St., Frederick 21705; (301) 695-1864, www.civilwarmed.org. Open Monday through Saturday 10 a.m. to 5 p.m., Sunday 11 a.m. to 5 p.m. Closed major holidays. $–$$, children 10 and under free.

This museum has an undeniable "yuk" factor and is a bit cerebral for youngsters, but kids who are interested in the Civil War, history, or medicine will probably be fascinated. Nearly two-thirds of the 620,000 soldiers who died during the war fell to disease, not battle-inflicted wounds. The Civil War occurred during a time of major medical advancements, and mannequin-populated dioramas in the museum illustrate the ongoing struggle against death. One scene, for example, shows wounded soldiers being loaded onto an ambulance and includes real Union and Confederate stretchers. Another shows an amputation in progress. These scenes may not be appropriate for squeamish kids.

Rose Hill Manor Park (ages 3 and up)

1611 North Market St., Frederick 21701; (301) 600-1646, www.rosehillmuseum.com. Open April through October, Monday through Friday 8 a.m. to 6 p.m., Saturday 10 a.m. to 4 p.m., and Sunday 1 to 4 p.m.; in November open Saturday 10 a.m. to 4 p.m., Sunday 1 to 4 p.m., and the Friday after Thanksgiving. $, children 2 and under free.

Thomas Johnson, Maryland's first elected governor, lived and died in this stately home, which in 1972 became the first hands-on history museum in the United States specifically designed for elementary-age children. A two-hour tour of the house and property gives children plenty of things to touch, including period toys and furniture. The house tours are led by costumed interpreters who are trained in providing age-appropriate information and who might take children to a playroom, a child's bedroom, and the kitchen. The property includes a carriage museum with great old-fashioned sleds and carriages, a blacksmith hall where kids can see horsehoes being made, an icehouse, and more. In a log cabin on the property once used by homesteaders, children can sit on the mattress and ride a wooden rocking horse.

Sleep Tight

"Sleep tight. Don't let the bedbugs bite." I'd said it to my kids a million times without wondering what it meant. But now I know, thanks to Miriam, our kindly guide at Rose Hill Manor Park.

While we were visiting the log cabin on the property, she lifted the thin mattress off one of the wooden beds in the room to show the ropes that had been woven to form a platform underneath. The ropes had to be tight so the mattress wouldn't sink, she explained. And the hay inside the mattress was changed once a year, when the new crop came in. That hay would be alive with insects when it was stuffed between the pieces of cloth. So, after parents tucked their kids into bed, they said what we still say today: "Sleep tight. Don't let the bedbugs bite."

Where to Eat

Barbara Fritchie Restaurant. 1513 West Patrick St., Frederick; (301) 662-2500. A local landmark serving homemade pies and meals, including chicken potpie and roast turkey, in an old-fashioned establishment. $

Crabapples Delicatessen. 101 West Patrick St., Frederick; (301) 694-0208. Sandwiches and salads in a casual atmosphere. $

Where to Stay

Comfort Inn Red Horse Frederick. 998 W. Patrick St., Frederick; (301) 662-0281, www.comfortinnfrederick.com. This centrally located hotel offers an exercise room, free breakfast, and an adjacent restaurant. $$

Sleep Inn. 5361 Spectrum Dr., Frederick; (301) 668-2003, www.sleepinn.com. Fitness center and complimentary continental breakfast. $$, kids stay **free** in parents' room.

Thurmont

I have a soft spot for Thurmont, a rural community to the north of Frederick. I really like its small-town, relaxing ambience. And I'm not alone. Presidents seem to like it, too. Thurmont is the home of Camp David, a country getaway for the president and his guests. So that helicopter you see whirring overhead just might contain the most powerful person on the planet.

Catoctin Mountain National Park (all ages)

6601 Foxville Rd., Thurmont 21788; (301) 663-9388, www.nps.gov/cato. Open year-round during daylight hours; visitor center open Monday through Thursday 10 a.m. to 4:30 p.m., Friday 10 a.m. to 5 p.m., and weekends 8:30 a.m. to 5 p.m. Closed New Year's Day, Martin Luther King Jr.'s Birthday, President's Day, Veterans Day, Thanksgiving Day and Christmas Day. **Free.**

Camping and hiking are the main activities at this park, but rock climbing, picnicking, fishing, and cross-country skiing are also possibilities. The park has 25 miles of trails. Two three-sided Adirondack shelters are available, and these rough shelters can provide a nice introduction to camping. They are free of charge, with permits issued on a first-come, first-served basis at the visitor center.

Catoctin Wildlife Preserve and Zoo (all ages)

13019-A Catoctin Furnace Rd., Thurmont 21788; (301) 271-3180; www.cwpzoo.com. Open end of March, April weekdays 10 a.m. to 5 p.m. and weekends 9 a.m. to 5 p.m.; May daily 9 a.m. to 5 p.m.; Memorial Day to Labor Day daily 9 a.m. to 6 p.m.; September daily 9 a.m. to 5 p.m.; October limited schedule 10 a.m. to 5 p.m., weather permitting. From Frederick, take Route 15 north 15 minutes. Look for the brown signs 2 miles south of Thurmont. The exit is almost exactly at mile marker 26. $$–$$$, children 2 and under free.

One nice thing about this zoo is that it's small enough to explore in a single afternoon. Opportunities to touch, feed, and learn about animals are offered every day. Under the guidance of a zoo professional, your children might touch a prickly hedgehog, feel the grip of a mighty python, or feed the goats at this thirty-acre, family-owned zoo that houses more than 350 animals. Check the Web site for a schedule of shows and events.

The zoo hosts summer camps for kids ages four to fourteen. Sleepover nights for the whole family include a picnic dinner, a guided tour of the zoo, and special games and activities for children such as campfire stories, marshmallow roasting, and a twilight tour of the zoo. You bring your own tents, flashlights, sleeping bags, and insect repellent.

Cunningham Falls State Park (all ages)

14039 Catoctin Hollow Rd., Thurmont 21788; (301) 271-7574 (888-432-2267 for camping reservations), www.dnr.state.md.us/publiclands/western/html. Open daily dawn to dusk. $ from Memorial Day to Labor Day, honor system the rest of the year, children in car seats free.

One of Maryland's great places to spend a sweltering summer day is Cunningham Falls State Park. The lake in the park has sandy beaches and a nice sandy bottom that stays shallow for a long time, so even kids too young to swim can splash around in the water. Lifeguards are on duty during the day.

Surrounding the beach is plenty of grass dotted with shade trees, so a picnic lunch is a good idea. Tables and grills are available. But if you don't want to bring your own food, a snack bar serves up the usual burgers and other snacks during the summer months.

Away from the water, a half-mile hike rewards children with a view from the base of the 78-foot falls. The walk feels like a real hike because it goes through woods and climbs a bit, but it is easy enough for all but the youngest toddlers. For older kids, there are longer trails, too.

Canoes and rowboats can be rented at a boat ramp off Catoctin Hollow Road, or private boats may be launched for a small charge. If you wish to bring your own boat, be aware that gasoline motors are prohibited, but small electric motors are OK. Call for details.

Campsites can be found at the park's Houk Area and Manor Area, both with bath-houses that have hot showers. The park also has a nice playground.

Where to Eat

Cozy Restaurant. 105 Frederick Rd., Thurmont; (301) 271-7373. This unique blend of restaurant, inn, and shops is still run by the same family that established it in 1929. The restaurant has eleven dining rooms, each with a different personality. Buffets and family-style platters are the specialties. $–$$

Where to Stay

Cozy Inn. 103 Frederick Rd., Thurmont; (301) 271-4301. Since this establishment is near Camp David, rooms and cottages are decorated in the style of various presidents. The Kennedy Room, for example, has a replica of the president's famous rocking chair. The Clinton Room has a Murphy bed that's good for kids. Continental breakfast included. $–$$$

Ole Mink Farm. 12806 Mink Farm Rd., Thurmont; (301) 271-7012, www.olemink farm.com. Luxury cabins with kitchens and fireplaces, smaller cabins with kitchenettes, a large cabin suitable for family reunions, or campsites, all in a beautiful Cactoctin Moun-tain park with a swimming pool, playground, hiking, and fishing. $$$, two-night minimum.

Brunswick

This city of 5,300 lies to the west of Frederick County, along the Potomac River. From Frederick, it can be reached by traveling west along I-340. Visitors will most likely eat or stay in Frederick or in nearby Harper's Ferry, West Virginia.

Brunswick Railroad Museum (ages 3 and up)

40 West Potomac St., Brunswick 21716; (301) 834-7100, www.brrm.net. Friday 10 a.m. to 2 p.m., Saturday 10 a.m. to 4 p.m., Sunday 1 p.m. to 4 p.m. $, children 3 and under **free.**

For train fans like my son, Sammy, the highlight of this museum is the fabulous model rail-road on display. Dozens of locomotives and more than five hundred freight cars rumble along an elaborate layout with more than 150 switches. The museum, in a 1904 building, also has period rooms showing typical turn-of-the-twentieth-century homes, plus photo-graphs of men laying track. The first floor has a hands-on activity rooms specifically for

Amazing
Maryland Facts

Brunswick is known as the Home of the Iron Horse because of its long railroad history.

youngsters, and a railroad view park has picnic tables with a good view of passing trains on the "real" railroad tracks.

For More Information

Frederick Magazine. Everedy Square, 6 North East St., Suite 301, Frederick 21701; (301) 662-8171; www.fredmag.com.

Tourism Council of Frederick County. 19 East Church St., Frederick 21701; (301) 228-2888, www.visitfrederick.org.

Prince George's County

It seems impossible to run out of things to do in Prince George's County. Just east of Washington, D.C., this county is practically bursting with museums, from historic working farms like the National Colonial Farm in Accokeek to the exciting Aviation Museum in College Park, which explores the aviation history at the site of the oldest continually operating airport in the nation. And if that's not enough, there's always Six Flags America, in Largo, where the roller coasters and other rides will have your family screaming in delight (or fear) for hours.

As we move through Prince George's County, we'll travel from north to south, starting with College Park, then Largo, then going to Bowie, Upper Marlboro, Oxon Hill, and Accokeek.

College Park

The city College Park is best known as the home of the University of Maryland–College Park, but this college town is also a fun place for families. College Park is at the intersection of Route 1 and I-95.

College Park Aviation Museum (ages 3 and up)

1985 Cpl. Frank Scott Dr., College Park 20901; (301) 864-6029, www.collegeparkaviation museum.com. Open daily 10 a.m. to 5 p.m., groups of ten or more can schedule a guided tour by calling in advance. $. From the Washington Beltway, take exit 23, Kenilworth Avenue, and turn south at the end of the ramp. Turn right at traffic light onto Paint Branch Parkway. Turn right at traffic light onto Cpl. Frank Scott Drive. Continue to the entrance of the airport parking lot. Turn right onto the service road and proceed to the museum parking lot.

When brothers Orville and Wilber Wright first took to the skies in 1903, the world responded with a collective yawn, not realizing the significance of the event. But soon their flying inventions would change the world. The famed aviation pioneers founded the

College Park Airport in 1909 in order to train military aviators. It's now the oldest continually running airport in the world and the home of many aviation milestones.

This museum, built as part of the airport in 1998, explores aviation history in a surprisingly kid-friendly way. Outside, airplane-shaped pedal bikes and rockers set the mood. Inside, kids can climb in the cockpit of a replica airplane, try on aviation jackets and leather helmets and goggles, and experiment with a flight-simulation computer program. Throughout the museum, there are art projects and hands-on activities for kids, and when they leave they get a goody bag filled with knickknacks such as a rubber ball, small foam airplane, plastic whistle, and colorful eraser.

The airport runway can be seen from the museum. On nice days, you might bring a picnic lunch to eat at tables on the museum's outdoor balcony, where your kids can watch planes take off and land. If you visit in summer, ask about summertime activities that include a Peter Pan Club for preschoolers and craft days; both are included with the price of admission.

Where to Eat

94th Aero Squadron Restaurant. 5240 Paint Branch Parkway, College Park; (301) 699-9400. Continue your aviation theme with lunch, dinner, or Sunday brunch at this restaurant and banquet hall, which serves burgers and sandwiches for lunch, and more sophisticated entrees for dinner. $$

A Nitkin Family **Adventure**

On a raw, rainy spring day, a couple of friends and I decided to take our kids to the College Park Aviation Museum. Four out of the six kids were boys, and before we left, my daughter put up a protest. "It sounds boylie," she said. (*Boylie*, for the uninitiated, being the opposite of *girlie*.)

When we got there, she turned up her five-year-old nose at the airplane-shaped pedal bikes that were outside. "Too boylie," she announced, as her brother and friends pedaled away. Once we got inside, though, her mood changed. As we looked at the antique airplanes, we talked about the early days of aviation and how scary it must have been for those first pilots.

At first, she didn't want to try on the kid-size leather jackets and helmets, but she soon relented. She watched, fascinated, as her three-year-old brother moved a joystick on a computer flight simulator to make the airplane on the screen crash again and again.

As we were leaving, we passed the pedal bikes. This time, my daughter decided to give them a try. Of course, she had lots of fun. As we left, I asked if she still thought the museum was too boylie. She thought for a minute, and decided it was good for girls, too.

More Air Museums

Though North Carolina has the First in Flight license plates, Prince George's County's claim to modern, controlled flight is far from shabby. Besides being home to the first aviation school in the country, it also hosts Andrews Air Force Base. Here are two other aviation attractions for kids interested in taking to the skies.

- **Airmen Memorial Museum** (ages 6 and up). 5211 Auth Rd., Suitland; (301) 899-3500, www.hqafsa.org/AM/Template.cfm?Section=Airmen_Memorial_ Museum&Template=/CM/HTMLDisplay.cfm&ContentID=1574. Open Monday through Friday 8 a.m. to 5 p.m. Free. This privately owned museum celebrates enlisted life with artifacts and artwork starting with personal belongings from the first enlisted airman, Eddie Ward (who signed on in 1907), through two world wars and up to the present day.

- **Goddard Visitor Center/Museum** (ages 4 and up). Explorer Road, Greenbelt; (301) 286-3978, www.nasa.gov/centers/goddard/visitor/home/index .html. Open September through May, Tuesday through Friday 10 a.m. to 3 p.m. weekends noon to 4 p.m., June through August, Tuesday through Friday 10 a.m. to 5 p.m., Saturday, noon to 4 p.m. Free. This ultramodern center gives kids and adults a hands-on, gee-whiz exploration of space travel, with lots of artifacts and photos. Exhibits include Hubble telescope images and "Science on a Sphere," which projects animated data onto a 6-foot sphere, so youngsters can picture activity on the curved surface of the earth. Elementary school students and their families are invited to the Goddard Visitor Center on the third Sunday of every month, from September to May, 1 to 3 p.m. for free hands-on activities showcasing Goddard's world-renowned technologies.

Plato's Diner. 7150 Baltimore Ave., College Park; (301) 779-7070. Breakfast, hamburgers, and some Greek food. $

Where to Stay

Best Western College Park Inn and Fundome. 8601 Baltimore Blvd., College Park; (866) 273-9330. Billiards, electronic games, indoor pool, sauna, putting green, shuffleboard, and restaurant make this hotel a fun destination. The hotel also boasts an excellent restaurant, E.J.'s Landing Restaurant and Lounge, with steak, pasta, seafood, and kid-friendly fare like cheese steaks and chicken fingers. $$

Holiday Inn-College Park. 10000 Baltimore Ave., College Park; (301)345-6700, www.ichotelsgroup.com/h/d/hi/1/en/hotel/ wascb. Amenities here include an exercise room, indoor pool, and hot tub.The on-site Moose Creek Steak House has a billiards table and televisions tuned to sports. $$

Amazing
Maryland Facts

College Park is home to the National Archives, a state-of-the-art facility that houses many important documents, tapes, and films, including Richard Nixon's infamous Watergate tapes.

For More Information
CollegePark.com has detailed listings of local restaurants, hotels, and activities.

Bladensburg

Bladensburg is to the south of College Park, along Route 1.

Bladensburg Waterfront Park (all ages)
4601 Annapolis Rd., Bladensburg 20710; (301) 779-0371, www.pgparks.com/places/nature/ bladensburg.html. Open daily sunrise to sunset. Free. To get to the park from the Washington Beltway, take exit 23, Kenilworth Avenue, south toward Bladensburg. Go 5 miles. After the traffic light for the Upshur Street intersection, go right on the exit ramp to Route 450 (Annapolis Road). Go left at the end of the exit ramp onto Route 450 west. Park entrance is 2 short blocks on the left.

Kids will find fun things to do here year-round, but especially in the summer. This beautiful waterfront park features a paved riverside walk, a free boat ramp, and weekend rentals of canoes, kayaks, and rowboats May through October. From April through October, naturalists take visitors on a forty-seat pontoon boat for a free forty-five-minute narrated tour of the Anacostia River.

Canoe and kayak lessons are offered, and events include an annual clean-up around Earth Day, the Paddlesport Regatta, and nature programs. If it's too cold for the water, your kids will still enjoy the playground and the B&O Railroad caboose.

Amazing
Maryland Facts

Prince George's County was a leader in flight even before the College Park Airport. In 1784, the first unmanned hot-air balloon lifted off from Bladensburg.

Largo

The small community of Largo is almost directly east of Washington, D.C. To get there, take Route 214 off the Washington Beltway.

Six Flags America (ages 6 and up)

P.O. Box 4210, Largo 20775; (301) 249-1500, www.sixflags.com. Open April to October, hours vary. $$$$. From Baltimore, take the Beltway (I-695) to exit 4, I-97 South. Follow I-97 to exit 7, Route 3 south, toward Crofton/Bowie. Route 3 will become Route 301 at the Route 50 intersection. Remain on Route 301 south for approximately 5 miles. Exit onto Route 214 west, Central Avenue. Six Flags America is located on Central Avenue, Route 214, approximately 3 miles ahead on your right.

This massive amusement park has more than one hundred rides and attractions for children of all ages. Older kids may want to check out the famously terrifying roller coasters, while younger children will enjoy the musical performances, comedy shows, live entertainment, and the children's section where young ones can meet Looney Tunes characters and choose from a dozen rides, including Sylvester's Pounce and Bounce and Movie Town Airport.

The Hurricane Harbor Water Park, included in the general admission price, has a range of watery thrills, from the relatively tame Castaway Creek to the Tornado, which sends your child hurtling through a 132-foot long funnel.

There are plenty of kid-friendly places to eat in the park, including a new Johnny Rockets restaurant serving burgers and the like, and vendors selling funnel cakes, hot dogs, subs, and Chinese food.

Where to Stay

Doubletree Club, Largo. 9100 Basil Court, Largo; (800) 310-6154. This hotel has an indoor heated pool, exercise room, and on-site restaurant. $$$

Plan Your Visit

Since Six Flags America is so large, it pays to spend a few minutes coming up with a game plan before you arrive. The park recommends starting at the farthest point from the entrance and working your way back. It also suggests trying to hit your favorite rides either when the park first opens or after 5 p.m. To avoid crowds, schedule your visit on a weekday during the summer or during the months of April, May, June, or September.

Bowie

Bowie, the largest municipality in Prince George's County, is 12 miles from Washington and 20 miles from Baltimore at the intersection of Routes 50, 450, and 301. It was incorporated as a town in 1916 and named in honor of resident Oden Bowie, president of the Baltimore & Potomac Railroad.

Radio-Television Museum (ages 8 and up)

2608 Mitchellville Rd., Bowie 20716; (301) 390-1020, www.radiohistory.org, www.cityof bowie.org/comserv/museums.htm. Open Friday 10 a.m. to 5 p.m., Saturday and Sunday 1 p.m. to 5 p.m. Free.

From a radio made out of a Quaker Oats container to an old "spark gap" transmitter similar to the one aboard the *Titanic,* this museum is loaded with cool old gadgets that provide insights into radio and television history. It's especially good for kids with a knack for the mechanical. Events include showings of television shows from the 1950s from the museum's vast archive. If you've been yearning to explain *Howdy Doody* and *Lassie* to your child, you'll want to check it out.

Where to Eat

Luigi's Pizza and Pasta. 3552 Crain Hwy, Bowie; (301) 805-5725. Pizza, pasta, and other Italian specialties. $

Memphis Bar-B-Q. 4449 Mitchellville Rd., Bowie; (301) 809-9441. Pulled pork sandwiches, burgers, catfish platters, and other barbecued favorites. $

Where to Stay

Hampton Inn–Bowie. 15202 Major Lansdale Blvd., Bowie; (301) 809-1800. This 103-room hotel has an indoor fitness center, outdoor pool, and complimentary breakfast. $$$

For More Information

Greater Bowie Chamber of Commerce. 6770 Race Track Rd., Bowie 20715; (301) 262-0920, www.bowiechamber.org.

Amazing Maryland Facts

The first telegraph message sent by Samuel Morse was sent in Prince George's County.

Upper Marlboro

To the south of Bowie along Route 193 is the town of Upper Marlboro, a tiny community with a population of fewer than 1,000 people.

Darnall's Chance House Museum (ages 4 and up)

14800 Governor Oden Bowie Dr., Upper Marlboro 20772; (301) 952-8010; www.pgparks .com. Open Friday and Sunday noon to 4 p.m., and by appointment Tuesday through Thursday 10 a.m. to 4 p.m. $.

Tours of this historic house highlight the differences between the lives of the wealthy and the lives of the enslaved—definitely an important lesson for children. Built in 1742 by wealthy Scottish immigrant James Wardrop, Darnall's Chance was nearly lost to history before it was saved from demolition in 1986 and restored to its 1742 appearance. At one point, the property had thirty-two slaves. Of the special events held on the property, some of the most kid-friendly are a ghost walk in October and a gingerbread-house show and contest held every November.

Duvall Tool Museum and Tobacco Farming Museum
(ages 5 and up)

1600 Croom Airport Rd., Upper Marlboro 20772; (301) 627-6074. Open April to October, Saturday and Sunday 1 to 4 p.m. Free.

These museums, located in the Patuxent River Park, give you insight into nineteenth-century life. The tool museum has more than 1,000 pieces of nineteenth-century farm implements, tools, and household appliances, and the tobacco museum has exhibits about the history of tobacco in Maryland. You can take guided tours by reservation. Demonstrations are given during special events.

Merkle Wildlife Sanctuary (all ages)

11704 Fenno Rd., Upper Marlboro 20772; (800) 784-5380, (301) 888-1410. Sanctuary grounds open daily 7 a.m. to sunset; visitor center open Monday and Friday 10 a.m. to 4 p.m. and Saturday and Sunday 10 a.m. to 5 p.m. Free.

Kids who love animals will get their fill here. Every October, more than 5,000 Canada geese arrive at Merkle for the winter and stay until late February or early March. The sanctuary is also home to red fox, white-tailed deer, hummingbirds, and more. The visitor center, which focuses on the lives of Canada geese, has a Discovery Room with live snakes, frogs, turtles, and other animals. There are also hiking trails and a driving tour through key areas.

Watkins Regional Park (all ages)

301 Watkins Park Dr., Upper Marlboro 20774; (301) 218-6702, www.pgparks.com. Nature center open Monday through Saturday 8:30 a.m. to 5 p.m., Sunday and holidays 11 a.m. to 4 p.m. Free.

As a parent, you have to love a park that offers something for everyone. You could easily entertain the kids all day here. For starters, there's the Old Maryland Farm (301-218-6770) with ponies, goats, chickens, and other animals. Kids who are ages two and up can even go on pony rides.

Then there's the Antique Chesapeake Carousel, a turn-of-the-century carousel with forty-five hand-carved animals that is open Memorial Day through Labor Day, Tuesday through Sunday 10 a.m. to 7 p.m., and weekends in September, weather permitting. A miniature train, built in the 1960s to look like an 1863 locomotive with three coaches, takes children on an enchanting ride through the park. $, call (301) 218-6757 to confirm carousel and train hours and fees.

The park's Watkins Nature Center has an indoor turtle pond, an outdoor frog pond, a songbird feeding area, and more. At the gift shop, you can borrow a trail discovery back-pack and explore 6 miles of trails, learning as you go.

This 850-acre park offers plenty of other activities and amenities, too, including a miniature-golf course, campsites, picnic tables, playgrounds, and a snack bar.

Oxon Hill

Oxon Hill is to the east and south of Washington, D.C., easy to reach by taking I-95 South to Route 5 south.

Oxon Hill Farm (ages 3 and up)
6411 Oxon Hill Rd., Oxon Hill 20745; (301) 839-1176, www.nps.gov/oxhi. Open daily 8 a.m. to 4:30 p.m. except major holidays. Reservations required for activities such as egg gathering or wagon rides. Free.

This working farm gives kids an up-close view of life on a farm in the early twentieth century. They can see cows being milked, check out the antique farm machinery, or hike the steep half-mile Woodlot Trail to learn why this wooded ravine was important to early farmers. Animals include goats, chickens, horses, and pigs. Seasonal activities include sheepshearing in the spring and corn harvesting in the fall. No food is sold, but there are picnic areas to enjoy a meal if you bring your own.

Where to Eat

Henry's Soul Café. 5431 Indian Head Hwy, Oxon Hill; (301) 749-6856. Great macaroni and cheese, fried chicken, and sweet potato pie at this supercasual American-style restaurant. $

Ranch House Restaurant. 6355 Oxon Hill Rd., Oxon Hill; (301) 839-2433. Family restaurant serving American-style food. $

Where to Stay

Clarion Hotel National Harbor. 6400 Oxon Hill Rd., Oxon Hill; (301) 749-9400, www.clarionhotel.com. This eight-floor hotel includes several suites that have sofa beds for children. The hotel has a fitness center and restaurant. Free Internet in rooms. $$–$$$, children under seventeen stay **free,** continental breakfast is offered free on weekday mornings.

Red Roof Inn. 6170 Oxon Hill Rd., Oxon Hill; (866) 244-9330. This hotel advertises that it allows small pets. Cribs are provided at no charge, and rollaway beds are available. $$ kids eighteen and under stay free.

Clinton

After Oxon Hill, the next town to the south is Clinton, a suburb of about 25,000 residents.

Clearwater Nature Center (all ages)

11000 Thrift Rd., Clinton 20735; (301) 297-4575. Open Monday through Saturday 8:30 a.m. to 5 p.m., Sunday and holidays 11 a.m. to 4 p.m. Free.

A butterfly garden and an exploration of gems and rock cutting help make this nature center so popular with children. The exhibit *Natural Treasures of Prince George's County* lets kids explore life underground, and a laboratory on the premises shows them how jewels are made and cut. The park also has a boathouse on a lake, playgrounds, nature trails, and picnic areas.

Poplar Hill on His Lordship's Kindness (ages 5 and up)

7600 Woodyard Rd., Clinton 20735; (301) 856-0358, www.poplarhillonhlk.com. House tours are from 10 a.m. to 4 p.m. Thursday and Friday, noon to 4 p.m. Sunday. $, children 6 and under free.

A beautiful eighteenth-century home, a carriage house, and stunning historic gardens make a trip to Poplar Hill a worthwhile adventure for the whole family. Kids are sure to enjoy the annual Easter egg hunt and a hands-on history day in May that lets them churn butter, learn about weaving, try on costumes, and play games. A mother-daughter tea in May lets little girls indulge their romantic side with an elegant light lunch in an antique setting.

Surratt House Museum (ages 6 and up)

9118 Brandywine Rd., Clinton 20735; (301) 868-1121, www.surratt.org. Open mid-January to mid-December, Thursday and Friday 11 a.m. to 3 p.m., Saturday and Sunday noon to 4 p.m. $, children under 5 free.

The dramatic story of the Surratt family is sure to appeal to kids with an interest in history. Built in 1852, this family plantation was a tavern, post office, and Confederate "safe house" during the Civil War. But its real claim to fame is that the Surratts were involved in a plot to kidnap President Abraham Lincoln. After twenty-six-year-old John Wilkes Booth killed the president on April 14, 1885, he stopped at this home before fleeing into Virginia, where he was killed on April 26, 1885. Through exhibits and programs, the museum helps visitors explore the history and culture of nineteenth-century Maryland through the story of the Surratts. Every spring, an open house is held, featuring free tours and activities for children.

Where to Eat

Fish Market. 7611 Old Branch Ave., Clinton; (301) 599-7900, www.mamastellasrestaurant .com. Known for its pasta and seafood. $$

Mama Stella's Pasta House. 7918 Old Branch Ave., Clinton; (301) 868-3057. Pizza and other Italian favorites. $

Where to Stay

Colony South Hotel & Conference Center. 7401 Surratts Rd., Clinton; (301) 856-4500. In this luxury hotel, guest rooms have two double beds, and amenities include an indoor swimming pool, a sauna, and a tennis and raquetball facility. $$$

Econo Lodge–Clinton. 7851 Malcolm Rd., Clinton; (800) 553-2666, (301) 856-2800, www .econolodge.com Some rooms have kitchens with microwaves and refrigerators. $$–$$$

Accokeek

Accokeek borders the Potomac River in the western part of Prince George's County. It can be reached from I-95 by taking Route 210 south.

Accokeek Foundation/National Colonial Farm

(ages 3 and up)

3400 Bryan Point Rd., Accokeek 20607; (301) 283-2113, www.accokeek.org. Park open dawn to dusk year-round. $.

What was life like on a middle-class tobacco farm in 1775? The National Colonial Farm can take children back to that time with costumed interpreters leading the way through period buildings that include an out-kitchen and a "necessary." The farm is known for its historic plant preservation, growing varieties of herbs, flowers, and vegetables that were cultivated in the eighteenth century.

As a bonus, the farm is located in beautiful Piscataway Park. On clear days, you can see George Washington's home, Mount Vernon, across the river. Bring your own lunches and enjoy them on picnic tables by the river. If your youngsters love history events, you might plan to visit the farm on special events days, which include colonial days, when costumed reenactors re-create an eighteenth-century day, and children's days, when children and their families can participate in the daily workings of the farm.

The Ecosystem Farm, also in Piscataway Park, shows kids ecologically sound ways to produce crops such as garlic, tomatoes, and zucchini.

Fuel Up

If you're heading to the National Colonial Farm for the day, pick up sandwiches and other snacks at **B and J Carryout,** which you'll pass on Route 210 on the way to the farm, and have a picnic at the tables along the river. Or stop at B and J for ice cream after a day of fun.

Other Things to See and Do in the Capital Region

- **American Indian Cultural Center and Piscataway Indian Museum.**
16816 Country Lane, Waldorf; (301) 782-7622, www.piscatawayindians.org/
museum.html.

- **Belair Mansion and Stable Museums.** 12207 Tulip Grove Dr., Bowie; (301)
809-3089, www.cityofbowie.org/comserv/museums.htm

- **Bowie Baysox Baseball Club.** 4101 NE Crain Hwy, Bowie; (301) 805-6000,
www.baysox.com

- **Fairland Regional Park.** 13950 Gunpowder Rd., Laurel; (301) 206-2359;
www.pgparks.com

- **Frederick Keys Baseball.** 21 Stadium Dr., Frederick; (877) GO-KEYS; www
.frederickkeys.com

- **Greenbelt Museum.** 15 Crescent Rd., Greenbelt; (301) 507-6582

- **Monocacy Natural Resource Management Area.** Route 28 and Park Mills
Road, Dickerson; (301) 924-2127

- **National Fallen Firefighters Memorial Park.** 1682 South Seton Ave.,
Emmitsburg; (301) 447-1365, www.firehero.org

- **National Shrine of Elizabeth Ann Seton.** 333 South Seton Ave., Emmitsburg; (301) 447-6606, www.setonshrine.org

- **North Hampton Slave Quarters and Archeological Historical Park.** 100700
Lake Overlook Dr., Mitchellville; (301) 218-9651

- **Seabrook Schoolhouse.** 6116 Seabrook Rd., Lanham; (301) 464-5291

- **Skate Frederick.** 1288 Riverbend Way; Frederick; (301) 662-7362, www
.skatefrederick.com

- **Way Off Broadway Children's Theater.** 5 Willowdale Plaza, Frederick;
(301) 662-6600, www.wayoffbroadway.com

- **Weinberg Center for the Arts.** 20 West Patrick St., Frederick; (301) 228-
2867, www.weinbergcenter.org

- **Wells Ice Rink.** 5211 Paint Branch Parkway, College Park; (301) 277-3186

For More Information

Prince George's County Conference and Visitors Bureau. 9200 Basil Court, Suite 101, Largo, 20774; (301) 925-8300, (888) 925-8300, www.visitprincegeorges .com.

Prince George's County Department of Parks and Recreation. 6600 Kenilworth Ave., Riverdale, 20737; (301) 699-2407, www .pgparks.com.

Annual Events

Maryland Day. University of Maryland, College Park; (800) UMTERPS. The university's flagship campus is open to the public for a free day of family-friendly learning in April.

Bowie Heritage Day. Belair Mansion/Stable Museum, Bowie; (301) 809-3089, www.cityof bowie.org/comserv/museums.htm. A May celebration of Maryland history and horseracing.

Children's Day at National Colonial Farm. Accokeek; (301) 283-2113. In May children and adults can take part in the activities of a typical day on an eighteenth-century colonial farm.

Summer Concert Series. Frederick; (301) 694-CITY, www.cityoffrederick.com. Free performances held at the Baker Park Bandshell on Sunday evenings in June, July, and August.

Fourth of July Celebration. Frederick; (301) 694-CITY, www.cityoffrederick.com. Children's activities, live entertainment, fireworks, boat rides, and more.

The Great Frederick Fair. Frederick Fairgrounds, Frederick; (301) 663-6313, www .thegreatfrederickfair.com. September.

Olde Towne Gaithersburg Day. Gaithersburg; (301) 258-6350, www.ci.gaithersburg .md.us. Family-friendly entertainment on six stages, food, items on sale from local artists. September. Free

Western Maryland

A s Maryland extends west, it becomes longer and narrow, a thin, bumpy finger, with West Virginia to the south and west and Pennsylvania to the north. The wide-open spaces get wider and more open, and the landscape grows more mountainous. The state's only ski resort, Wisp, is in its westernmost county, Garrett County. The three counties of western Maryland are Allegany, Washington, and Garrett. Lakes, mountains, and other natural features are the main attractions here, but don't miss a visit to historic Cumberland. Kids of all ages who like trains, boats, and cars will love this traditional transportation hub. Stop by Canal Place, the western terminus of the Chesapeake & Ohio Canal National Historical Park, and see a full-scale replica of a canal boat, an amazing exhibit center, and the old-fashioned trains of the Western Maryland Scenic Railroad.

Another important stop is Antietam National Battlefield, site of the bloodiest one-day battle in United States history. Wherever you go in western Maryland, you're sure to enjoy the adventure. The main east–west road in Western Maryland is I-68, which often overlaps with Route 40. This chapter is organized from east to west, mostly along that road, starting with Washington County, then going to Allegany and Garrett Counties.

Washington County

Civil War buffs who come to Washington County just to visit Antietam, the national battlefield, will find plenty of reasons to linger in the county's beautiful parks and family-friendly towns.

Boonsboro

Boonsboro, located to the south and east of Hagerstown, can be reached from Baltimore by taking Route 70 west to exit 35 (Boonsboro/Smithsburg, Route 66). Turn left off the exit, and follow Route 66 to Boonsboro.

WESTERN MARYLAND

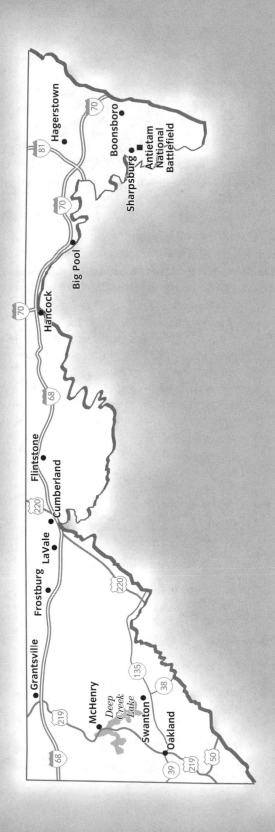

Amazing
Maryland Facts

The very first monument to honor George Washington is a rugged stone tower dedicated by the citizens of Boonsboro in 1827. The monument is now a focal point of Washington Monument State Park, located 4 miles east of Boonsboro.

Crystal Grottoes Cavern (ages 3 and up)

19821 Shepherdstown Pike, Boonsboro 21713; (301) 432-6336, www.crystalgrottoes.com. Open daily April to October, 10 a.m. to 5 p.m.; from November to March open weekends 11 a.m. to 4 p.m. $–$$.

Kids will ooh and ah over the beautiful formations here. Crystal Grottoes claims to have more formations per square foot than any other cave known to man. It is also the only cave in Maryland that is open as a tourist attraction. The interior is beautiful, with stalagmites, stalactites, and other formations in a variety of colors.

A forty-minute tour takes you on dry walkways with guides who explain the history and geology of the formations.

Karen's
TopPicks for fun in Western Maryland

1. Crystal Grottoes Cavern, Boonsboro
2. Hager House and Hagerstown City Park, Hagerstown
3. Antietam National Battlefield, Sharpsburg
4. Rocky Gap State Park, Flintstone
5. Dans Mountain State Park, Flintstone
6. Canal Place Heritage Area, Cumberland
7. Thrasher Carriage Museum, Frostburg
8. Deep Creek Lake State Park, Swanton
9. Wisp Resort, McHenry
10. Swallow Falls State Park, Oakland

Greenbrier State Park (all ages)

21843 National Pike, Boonsboro 21713; (301) 791-4767, www.dnr.state.md.us/publiclands/western/greenbrier.html. Open daily 8 a.m. to 4:30 p.m. $, children in car seats free.

This popular park, 8 miles east of Hagerstown, is in the beautiful Appalachian Mountains and features a forty-two-acre freshwater lake where families can rent or launch small boats, go swimming, or try their luck with a rod and reel. There are nature trails, picnic spots, and playgrounds, as well as 165 campsites offering bathhouses with hot showers.

Rural Heritage Museum (ages 3 and up)

7313 Sharpsburg Pike, Boonsboro 21713; (240) 420-1712, www.ruralheritagemuseum.org. Open weekends April through October 1 to 4 p.m., other times by appointment. Free, but donations appreciated.

This museum, which opened in 2001, shows what life was like in Washington County through such displays as three rooms of Victorian-era home furnishings, a rendition of a country store, and a replica of a 1914 post office. You'll also see many buggies and sleighs.

South Mountain State Park (ages 6 and up)

21843 National Pike, Boonsboro 21713; (301) 791-4767, www.dnr.state.md.us/publiclands/western/southmountain.html. Open daily dawn to dusk. Free.

The main attraction here is a portion of the 2,167-mile Appalachian Trail, which runs from Maine to Georgia. You can choose from several trailheads to pick up the trail. Even though some ascents are steep, they reward hikers rather quickly with scenic overlooks. The park is also interesting because the Civil War battle of South Mountain was waged here in September 1862. Note that there are no facilities in the park, however, aside from a few primitive camping sites.

Where to Eat

Heather B's Pub. 1 North Main St., Boonsboro; (301) 432-5100. Burgers, sandwiches, seafood, and more, plus a nice kids' menu in a two-hundred-year-old building in the heart of downtown Boonsboro. $

Asaro's Pizza & Sub Shop. 4 North Main St., Boonsboro; (301) 432-6166. You can never go wrong with a pizza shop. $

Amazing Maryland Facts

Boonsboro, founded in 1792, was named for brothers George and William Boone, cousins to the famous Daniel Boone.

Hagerstown

The small city of Hagerstown has enough attractions to make a day trip here worthwhile. The city can be reached from Route 40 to the east and west, Route 65 from the south, or I-81 from the north.

Beaver Creek School Museum (ages 3 and up)

9702 Beaver Creek Church Rd., Hagerstown 21740; (301) 797-8782, www.rootsweb.ancestry .com/~mdwchs/beaver.html. Open Sundays April through November, 1 p.m. to 4 p.m.

What was school like in the early 1900s? This refurbished classroom has desks, books, and other items that give your kids a glimpse of an educational world without computers, guidance counselors, or cafeterias. It's definitely worth a stop if you're in the area.

Hager House (ages 7 and up)

City Park, 110 Key St., Hagerstown 21740; (301) 739-8393, www.hagerhouse.org. Open April through December, Tuesday through Sunday 10 a.m. to 4 p.m., Sunday 2 to 5 p.m. $, children under 6 **free.**

The Hager House, right in Hagerstown's City Park, was built in 1740 by Jonathan Hager, the German immigrant who founded the city. Today, the house is furnished as it would have been in the eighteenth century and is the centerpiece for local events, including a German Easter celebrated in late March and Frontier Craft Days held each August. Kids will especially like the herbal gardens that surround the house. And they'll probably be fascinated by the spring that runs through the cellar, which provided a protected water supply during a time of frequent attacks by Native Americans.

Next door is the Hager Museum. It houses hundreds of artifacts that were discovered when the Hager House was restored in 1953. These include coins, pottery, buttons, and other items from the eighteenth and nineteenth centuries.

After touring the house or museum, you might want to spend a couple of hours at the park itself. It's considered one of the nation's most beautiful city parks, with three man-made lakes on fifty acres of open space. The park has playgrounds, a restored steam engine, picnic areas, and hiking trails with views of the lake.

Sounds of Summer

Every Sunday from June through August, live music is played at the bandshell in **Hagerstown City Park.** The show starts at 8 p.m. Bring a blanket if you want, or sit on the park benches—there's enough seating for five hundred people.

Hagerstown Roundhouse (all ages)

300 South Burhans Blvd., Hagerstown 21741; (301) 739-4665, www.roundhouse.org. Open Friday to Sunday 1 to 5 p.m. $, children under 4 **free.**

Train lovers of all ages will get a kick out of this museum, which has four model-train layouts, including a Thomas the Tank Engine that kids can play with, plus railroad memorabilia like lights, lanterns, whistles, and photographs. A holiday-theme train layout runs from November through February.

The actual roundhouse no longer exists, but the museum is located in what was the old engineering building on the Western Maryland Railway parking lot.

The Train Room (ages 2 and up)

360 South Burhans Blvd., Hagerstown 21740; (301) 745-6681, www.the-train-room.com. Open Monday and Friday 9 a.m. to 8 p.m., Tuesday, Thursday, and Saturday 9 a.m. to 6 p.m. Sunday noon to 6 p.m. $, children under 12 **free.**

Any child interested in trains will love the Train Room. It's part store and part model-train museum. The store part sells tons of model trains, including Brio, Lionel, and Thomas the Tank Engine. The museum portion has one of the largest train layouts on the East Coast, plus model airplanes and other items.

Washington County Museum of Fine Arts (ages 4 and up)

P.O. Box 432, City Park, Hagerstown 21741; (301) 739-5727, www.wcmfa.org. Open Tuesday through Friday 9 a.m. to 5 p.m., Saturday 9 a.m. to 4 p.m. and Sunday 1 to 5 p.m. Closed major holidays. **Free.**

This small museum has a big reputation for excellent artwork and cultural events. Situated right in Hagerstown City Park, it features the work of both regional and national artists and has a selection of works from Europe, Africa, and Asia. It's a nice place to take kids, because there is so much to see in a small space. Exhibits in the permanent collection that may hold special appeal for kids include works by Norman Rockwell, a display of paperweights, and beautiful floral paintings. The museum schedules special events for children throughout the year, such as art classes and dance classes.

Where to Eat

Brother's Pizza III. 1573 Potomac Ave., Hagerstown; (301) 790-2667. Some say it has the best pizza in town. $

The Gourmet Goat. 41 N. Potomac St., Hagerstown 21740; (301) 790-2343. A very nice restaurant and deli. $–$$$

Where to Stay

Days Inn. 900 Dual Hwy, Hagerstown; (301) 739-9050. Outdoor pool, some rooms with microfridges, complimentary hot breakfast, plus full-service restaurant. $–$$

Holiday Inn Express. 241 Railway Lane, Hagerstown; (301) 551-0222, www.hagers townexpress.com. Indoor pool and fitness center, complimentary breakfast bar, and cable television. Suites with microwaves, refrigerators, and sofa beds are a good option for families. $$, children under nineteen stay **free** with parents.

Super 8 Motel. 1220 Dual Hwy, Hagerstown; (301) 739-5800, (800) 800-8000, www.super8.com. Complimentary coffee and toast

bar, cable television. $$, children seventeen and under stay **free.**

For More Information

Hagerstown/Washington County Convention and Visitors Bureau. Elizabeth Hager Center, 16 Public Sq., Hagerstown 21740; (800) 228-7829, (301) 791-2601, www.marylandmemories.org.

Sharpsburg

A visit to the national battlefield at Antietam, considered one of the nation's best preserved Civil War sites, will bring American history into focus for your children. Antietam is in Sharpsburg, which is 10 miles south of Hagerstown. To get to the battlefield from I-70, take exit 29A onto Route 65 south. In about 10 miles, you'll see the visitor center on the left. To get there from I-81, take exit 1, Route 68, and go about 6 miles east to Route 65. Turn right at the light on Route 65, and the visitor center will be on the left in about 5 miles.

Antietam National Battlefield (ages 7 and up)
P.O. Box 158, Sharpsburg 21782; (301) 432-7672, www.nps.gov/anti. Open daily 8:30 a.m. to 6 p.m. in June, July, and August; from 8:30 a.m. to 5 p.m. the rest of the year. Closed Thanksgiving, Christmas, and New Year's Day. $, children 17 and under **free.**

Clearly, the story behind the battlefield and related activities will be too shocking or confusing for very young children. But older ones will learn about a day that changed the course of American history. That day was September 17, 1862. Gen. Robert E. Lee tries to push his Confederate Army into the north, but his 41,000 southerners meet fierce resistance from 87,000 northerners fighting under Gen. George B. McClellan.

Fighting rages for twelve hours. When it is over, 23,110 souls are killed, lost, or wounded, making the Battle of Antietam the single bloodiest one-day battle in U.S. history.

And also one of the most important, even though neither side really won. Because Lee failed to carry the war into the North, Great Britain postponed its plans to recognize the Confederate government. Within days, President Abraham Lincoln wrote the first draft of the Emancipation Proclamation, which was issued on January 1, 1863.

The national battlefield was established as an act of Congress in 1890. Today, you can take a self-guided 8.5-mile tour through the fields, past memorials and markers. Most people drive, but walking and biking are allowed. You can rent or purchase audiotapes of the tour at the visitor center, where exhibits and films provide a good introduction to the battle and its ramifications. The twenty-six-minute movie, narrated by James Earl Jones,

Civil War Books for Kids

A basic understanding of the Civil War can greatly enhance your family's experience of Antietam and other Maryland attractions, since the War between the States raged heavily on Maryland soil, a state just south of the Mason-Dixon Line yet close to the nation's capital. There are jillions of books on the Civil War, and it seems like more are being published every day. The ones listed below were written specifically for children and are some of my favorites.

- *Civil War*, John E. Stanchak, Eyewitness Series, DK Publishing, 2000, $15.99. An informative and entertaining look at the war.

- *The Civil War for Kids: A History with 21 Activities*, Janis Herbert, Chicago Review Press, 1999, $14.95. Hands-on activities, some requiring adult supervision, that can help kids understand what life was like during the Civil War.

- *Fathers, Sons and Brothers*, James Gus Filegar, PublishAmerica, 2003, $19.95. The dramatic fictional tale of Nathan Clark, who joins the Twentieth Maine Infantry Regiment in 1862.

- *Story of the Civil War Coloring Book*, Peter Copeland, Dover, 1991, $3.95. Simplistic introduction to the war.

recreates the battle as well as President Abraham Lincoln's visit to the Union commander, General McClellan. Young children may find the film frightening.

In the summer, rangers or costumed interpreters give scheduled talks. Various ranger programs and special events, such as hikes and bikes through the park, are also held throughout the year and might be fun for older children.

Personally, I just like driving through the park, getting out to look at the various monuments. It's a great history lesson for me, and my kids enjoy the beautiful countryside and the chance to get out of the car every few minutes and run around. Some of the monuments seem to hold their attention, too.

Where to Stay

Antietam Hagerstown KOA. 11759 Snug Harbor Lane, Williamsport; (301) 223-7571, (800) KOA-SMOR, www.hagerstownkoa .com. Luxury campground (for those who don't consider that an oxymoron!) with all kinds of activities, including hayrides, miniature golf, a heated pool, and creekfront sites. Cabins have heat, air-conditioning, and cable television. $

Amazing
Maryland Facts

Washington County, created on September 6, 1776, was the first county in the country to be named for George Washington, who was then Commander in Chief of the American army. Today, it is one of thirty-one counties named after the father of our country.

Big Pool

Big Pool, west of Hagerstown along I-70, was named for the "big pool" that formed during construction of the Chesapeake & Ohio Canal.

Fort Frederick State Park (all ages)
11100 Fort Frederick Rd., Big Pool; (301) 842-2155, www.dnr.state.md.us/publiclands/western/ fortfrederick.html. Open daily April to October 8 a.m. to sunset; November to March, open Monday through Friday 8 a.m. to sunset; Saturday, Sunday, and holidays 10 a.m. to sunset. $ to view the fort.

The restored stone fort in this park was the major defense position for Maryland against the French and their Indian allies during the French and Indian War, which took place between 1754 and 1763. The stone wall and two barracks have been restored to their original 1756 appearance, and children can learn about their architecture from guides in period dress. The fort was also used during the Revolutionary and Civil Wars. A ten-minute film on the fort's role is shown by request at the visitor center.

But for kids, the real fun can be found in all the activities within the park: fishing, hiking, cross-country skiing, or camping. There are also playgrounds, a concession area and canoes and rowboats to rent for use in Big Pool, the park's lake. Special programs for children include campfire events, craft making, and historical programs.

Western Maryland **Rail-Trail**

This 20-mile trail, which starts a half mile to the west of Fort Frederick, travels through rolling farmland along the Potomac River. The paved and flat surface is ideal for walking, running, biking, roller-skating or pushing a stroller.

To reach the eastern terminus, take I-70 to exit 12, Route 56. Turn east and go to Big Pool. The trail parking lot is across the street from the post office.

Hancock

Located 33 miles west of Hagerstown, Hancock is your next major stop as you travel west.

Sideling Hill Exhibit Center (ages 3 and up)

300 Sideling Hill, Hancock; (301) 768-5442, www.dnr.state.md.us. Open daily 9 a.m. to 5 p.m. Free.

As you're driving along I-68, stop by this four-story visitor center to pick up information about the region and explore the really neat exhibits showing the archaeology of the exposed rock layers on Sideling Hill. When the highway was built, the rock was cut, exposing nearly 850 feet of layered rock, considered one of the best examples of exposed rock in the northeastern United States.

On nice days, an outdoor walkway gives an up-close view of the exposed rocks, and picnic areas overlooking the valley provide a nice break during a long drive.

Where to Eat

Park-N-Dine Restaurant. 189 East Main St., Hancock; (301) 678-5242. A lengthy menu is big on such home-style favorites as macaroni and cheese, beef stew, hamburgers, and ham potpie. The portions are huge and the prices are rock bottom. $

The Lockhouse Restaurant. 11 East Main St., Hancock; (301) 678-6991. Located next to the rail-trail parking lot in Hancock, this restaurant offers a little bit of everything, from steaks and seafood to burgers and chicken sandwiches. $$

For More Information

Hancock Chamber of Commerce. 126 West High St., Hancock; (301) 678-5900, www.hancockmd.com.

Allegany County

This county is all about trains, boats, and cars, with some gorgeous lakes and mountains thrown in for good measure. One of the main attractions here is Cumberland, a city with a beautiful downtown and a rich heritage. The city became known as the Gateway to the West because it is the home of the first federal road, the Chesapeake & Ohio Canal, and railroads.

Flintstone

There isn't much in the town of Flintstone except forests and Rocky Gap State Park. But that's enough.

Dans Mountain State Park (all ages)

17410 Recreation Area Rd., Flintstone 21539; (301) 463-5487. Open daily sunrise to sunset. Free. Take I-68 to exit 24 and travel south on Route 36 for about 9 miles.

With its waterslide-equipped Olympic-size swimming pool and large recycled-tire playground, Dans Mountain is a great place to spend an afternoon with the kids. A bathhouse and concession stand are open from Memorial Day to Labor Day. There are also some picnic areas and a small fishing pond. If your kids are feeling adventurous, climb to Dans Overlook for a panoramic view of the surrounding countryside from a height of 2,898 feet.

Green Ridge State Forest (ages 6 and up)

28700 Headquarters Dr., NE, Flintstone 21530; (301) 478-3124. Open daily year-round. Free.

The state's second-largest state forest has opportunities for canoeing, kayaking, and angling on the Potomac River, as well as camping and hiking. The park has a hundred designated primitive campsites, which means they have no amenities and so may not be suitable for young children.

Rocky Gap State Park (all ages)

125 Pleasant Valley Rd., Flintstone 21530; (301) 777-2139, www.dnr.state.md.us. Open year-round. Free.

Rocky Gap has been developed as a year-round family vacation destination, highlighted by a magnificent lodge with three restaurants that are fine for the kids, an indoor-outdoor pool, and an eighteen-hole golf course for families that like to hit the links. Lake Habeeb has several sandy beaches with playgrounds and places for renting canoes and kayaks, plus it's good for fishing.

The resort has a kid-friendly nature center with books, small interactive exhibits, and the Scales and Tales Aviary, where live reptiles and birds of prey can be seen. Camping is also popular here, and campers can use all the lodge's facilities, including its indoor-outdoor pool, whirlpool, and exercise room.

Educational programs are held in the summer, usually on weekends, and adventure packages featuring kayaking, rapelling, and other activities can be arranged through the Rocky Gap Lodge and Golf Resort.

Where to Stay

Rocky Gap Lodge and Golf Resort.
16701 Lakeview Rd., NE, Flintstone; (301) 784-8400, (800) 724-0828, www.rockygapresort.com. This resort in the heart of Rocky Gap State Park has it all—indoor-outdoor pool, great golf course, a lake with sandy beaches, playgrounds, a nature center, and an aviary with live animals, plus nature trails for hiking and biking. $$$–$$$$

A Nitkin Family **Adventure**

My husband and I have always loved camping, and when our children were six and three, we decided to introduce them to the fun of campfires, s'mores, and round-the-clock bug spray. We knew camping wouldn't be the same with young children in tow, but we didn't realize how different it would be.

We decided to take them to Rocky Gap, which is about two hours from our house and has a lot of fun things to do. It turned out to be a great decision.

The tent we had from our before-kid days, though, was barely large enough for our two sleeping bags. There was no way our whole family could squeeze in. We went shopping for a larger one and came home with one so enormous that I dubbed it the Tent Majal. It had a screened mud room that was larger than our old tent, plus two rooms inside, one for kids and one for grown-ups.

Back in the prekids days, our camping gear fit easily into the back of our little Acura. This time, we had so much stuff we filled our minivan. We took a propane stove, folding chairs for everyone, a coffee percolator, air mattress for the grown-ups (we're not so comfortable sleeping on the ground anymore), a cooler full of food, and more.

When we got to Rocky Gap, the kids helped set up the tents and unfurl the sleeping bags. We spent the rest of the day at the beach, then came back to the tent to cook dinner and s'mores before taking a nighttime stroll around the park. When it was time to sleep, the kids poked each other and giggled a while before finally dozing off. Amazingly, despite the loud chirping of birds at dawn, we all slept past 8 a.m.

The next day, we rented a canoe, then played on the beach and playground some more before packing up. It was almost a perfect trip, except that my husband and I forgot to bring mugs. Having kids sure changes things.

We drank our morning coffee out of sippy cups!

Cumberland

Cumberland, a quaint city of about 25,000 nestled in the Appalachian Mountains, is a worthwhile destination for a day trip or longer family getaway. In addition to its many historic attractions, Cumberland has a wonderful downtown that's fun just to stroll through. It's easy to reach from I-68.

Canal Place Heritage Area (all ages)

13 Canal St., Cumberland 21502; (301) 724-3655, www.canalplace.org. Free.

Located at the western terminus of the Chesapeake & Ohio Canal, Canal Place has a variety of attractions for youngsters, including a replica of a canal boat and several old-fashioned trains.

The Queen City Transportation Museum here is amazing, with tons of kid appeal. Interactive exhibits explain the importance of the canal system and the system of seventy-four lift locks that made it work. Look for plenty of lights, sound effects, and even jokes as the kids are encouraged to push buttons, listen to audiotapes, and lift the lids of barrels to find the answers to riddles. There is even a box of old-fashioned stuffed animals for children to play with and compare to their own toys. Museum hours are May through October, Monday through Sunday 10 a.m. to 5 p.m. and November through April, Tuesday through Saturday 10 a.m. to 4 p.m. $, children under 6 are Free.

Canal Place also hosts an ice-skating rink, a replica of a canal boat, and a retail area with restaurants and stores. Also here are walking tour starting points and bicycle rentals for the C&O Canal. Of course, you can bring your own bicycle. Go as far as you like—the canal is 184.5 miles long and will take you all the way back to Potomac!

Events include summertime concerts and the annual Canalfest/Railfest, which each September features a three-day weekend's worth of live entertainment, fireworks, and other family-friendly entertainment.

Gordon-Roberts House (ages 6 and up)

218 Washington St., Cumberland 21502; (301) 777-8678, www.gordonrobertshouse.com. Tours are offered year-round Tuesday through Saturday 10 a.m. to 4 p.m. on the hour; last tour at 4 p.m.

Costumed docents give tours of the 1867 Victorian home built for Josiah Gordon, president of the C&O Canal. Kids will especially like the frilly pink child's bedroom decorated with period dolls, and the day nursery (basically a playroom) with its gray rocking horse and child-size table and chairs. A costume room shows intricate gowns from the 1860s. The site includes beautiful gardens and a gift shop with children's books, dolls, teapots, and more.

Children can ask for handouts that identify specific items to search for in the house. (Older children are given clues, younger children get pictures.)

Western Maryland Scenic Railroad (all ages)

13 Canal St., Cumberland 21502; (800) TRAIN-50, www.wmsr.com. Hours and schedule vary. $$–$$$$, children 2 and under not occupying a seat free.

What fun! Ride a 1916 Baldwin steam locomotive from downtown Cumberland to Frostburg and back. The entire 32-mile scenic trip takes three hours. The steam and diesel excursions have many themes, including Polar Express, Musical Express, Train Robberies, and more. For the Polar Express, which is offered seasonally in both the afternoon

The **Canal**

The Chesapeake & Ohio Canal was obsolete before construction was finished, but for a time it was the centerpiece of a magnificent plan to connect the Chesapeake Bay to the east with the Ohio River to the west, so that goods such as lumber, coal, and grain could be shipped.

Construction began in 1828. The project was supposed to cost about $3 million and take ten years, but instead it cost $13 million and took twenty-two years. The canal also stopped at Cumberland, instead of Pittsburgh as originally planned.

By the time construction was complete in 1850, railroads had arrived in Cumberland several years earlier, providing a much simpler mode of transportation than the canals. Still, the canals continued to operate until 1924.

These days, the 184.5-mile length of the C&O Canal, which begins in Georgetown in Washington, D.C., is a popular destination for tourists and locals alike. The paths along the canal, designed for the mules that pulled the boats, are flat and wide, ideal for bike riding, walking, or running. Visitor centers along the way provide fascinating history about the canal.

and evening, children are invited to come in their pajamas to listen to stories of the Polar Express and enjoy hot chocolate, cookies, and a present.

Where to Eat

Curtis' Coney Island Famous Weiners. 35 North Liberty St., Cumberland; (301) 759-9707. An old-fashioned counter-style restaurant serving hot dogs since 1918. $

Queen City Creamery and Deli. 108 Harrison St., Cumberland; (301) 777-0011. After a deli meal, treat the kids to something cool from the old-fashioned soda fountain, which dishes out homemade frozen custards, shakes, sundaes, and more. $

Where to Stay

Holiday Inn. 100 South George St., Cumberland; (301) 724-8800, www.cumberlandmd holidayinn.com. Within walking distance of Canal Place and the downtown mall, this 130-room hotel has a fitness room, outdoor pool, and restaurant. $$, children under nineteen stay **free,** children twelve and under eat free with a paying adult.

For More Information

Allegany County Tourism Department. www.mdmountainside.com.

City of Cumberland. P.O. Box 1702, 57 North Liberty St., Cumberland 21501-1702; (301) 722-2000, www.ci.cumberland.md.us.

LaVale

LaVale is a short distance from Cumberland, heading west. How to get there? Take the National Road, of course!

National Road and Toll House (ages 3 and up)
14302 National Hwy, LaVale 21502; (301) 729-3047, (301) 729-1681. Open weekends May through October 1:30 to 4:30 p.m., or by appointment. Free, donation encouraged.

The nation's first federally funded road, the National Road, was started in 1811 and made Cumberland the Gateway to the West. It's still possible to take your family for a drive along it, starting at mile marker 1 in Cumberland.

The seven-sided Toll Gate House, about 3 or 4 miles west of Cumberland, was constructed after the state took ownership of the section of road in 1835. It's the only tollhouse left in Maryland, though others exist in other states. All the tollhouses along the road were built in the same seven-sided style, as mandated by Thomas Jefferson.

Youngsters enjoy going inside the tollhouse, with its furnishings from around 1836. Be sure to look for the original chalkboard used to keep track of who passed through. You'll see that wagons and coaches with wide wheels paid less than those with skinny wheels, because the wide wheels packed down the dirt roads and the skinny wheels made ruts.

Where to Eat

Gehauf's Restaurant. 1268 National Hwy, LaVale; (301) 729-1746. Like Henny's, this restaurant is part of the Best Western. Unlike Henny's below, it has a more vegetable-focused menu, with an emphasis on home-made soups and baked goods. $

Henny's Grill and Bar. 1268 National Hwy, LaVale; (301) 729-1746. Located within the Best Western, this grill serves burgers, salads, sandwiches, and other American-style food. $

Penny's Diner. 12310 Winchester Rd., SW, LaVale; (301) 729-6700. Adjacent to the Oak Tree Inn, this old-fashioned place with 1950s memorabilia is open twenty-four hours a day, serving burgers, shakes, malts, and other food for breakfast, lunch, and dinner. $

Where to Stay

Best Western. 1268 National Hwy, LaVale; (301) 729-1746, www.bestwesternbraddock

Amazing
Maryland Facts

Initial cost estimates for building the National Road were $6,000 per mile, but as often happens with government projects, the actual price was higher. In hilly places, the cost was as much as $13,000 per mile.

.com. Amenities here include an indoor pool, fitness center, whirlpool, and game room. $$

Comfort Inn and Suites. 1216 National Hwy, LaVale; (301) 729-6400, (800) 4CHOICE,

www.choicehotels.com. Indoor heated pool and whirlpool, continental breakfast, and small refrigerators and coffeemakers in many rooms. Within walking distance of restaurants and shopping in LaVale. $$$$

Frostburg

Home to Frostburg State University, Frostburg has a lovely historic downtown and several family-friendly attractions. To get there from La Vale or Cumberland, stay on I-68 and continue west.

Thrasher Carriage Museum (ages 3 and up)

Depot Center, Frostburg, 21532; (301) 689-3380, www.thrashercarriagemuseum.com. Open March to December, Wednesday to Saturday 10 a.m. to 4 p.m., Sunday 10 a.m. to 3 p.m., and other times by appointment. $.

Any child interested in horse-drawn vehicles will have a blast at the Thrasher Carriage Museum, which has one of the top collections in the country. Everything is here, from funeral wagons to milk carts to carriages that carried United States presidents, and it's all in the historic Depot Center, built in 1891. Also on display are accessories such as lap blankets, bridles, and charcoal foot warmers. Guides and interpretive signs tell kids about the lives of the people who rode in the wagons, and events here include Victorian teas that older children will enjoy.

The depot is one terminus of the Western Maryland Scenic Railroad, which offers rides between Frostburg and Canal Street in Cumberland.

Where to Eat

Princess Restaurant. 12 West Main St., Frostburg; (301) 689-1680. A family restaurant with a soda fountain and gourmet candy case, plus kids' menu. $

Where to Stay

Hampton Inn. 11200 New Georges Creek Rd., Frostburg; (301) 689-1998, (800) HAMP-TON, www.hampton-inn.com/hi/frostburg. Indoor pool, continental breakfast, and rooms with refrigerators, microwaves, and coffeemakers. Connecting rooms, rollaway beds, and cribs are also available. $$

For More Information

Allegany County Convention and Visitors Bureau. Western Maryland Railway Station, 13 Canal St., Suite 406, Cumberland, 21502; (301) 777-5132, www.mdmountainside.com.

Garrett County

Garrett County, founded in 1872, was named for John W. Garrett, then president of the Baltimore & Ohio Railroad. That makes sense, because the county's growth was spurred by construction of the railroad in the 1850s. Today, the state's westernmost county is a popular year-round vacation destination, home to the state's largest freshwater lake, Deep Creek Lake, and its only alpine ski resort, Wisp. A full 20 percent of the county is reserved for parks, lakes, and publicly owned forests.

Grantsville

As you drive into Garrett County heading west on I-68, your first major stop will be Grantsville, a small town surrounded by farmland.

Savage River State Forest and
New Germany State Park (all ages)
349 Headquarters Lane, Grantsville 21536; (301) 895-5759, www.dnr.state.md.us/public lands/western/savageriver.html. Open daily 8 a.m. to dusk. $ on weekends and holidays, **free** the rest of the time.

For the outdoorsy family, Maryland's largest state forest (52,812 acres) has hiking trails, primitive camping, horseback riding trails, and places to fish. Big Run State Park, surrounded by the Savage River State Forest, offers camping and day-use facilities, plus access to a reservoir for fishing and nonmotorized boating. It has a picnic pavilion, large enough for one hundred people, that can be rented.

The smaller New Germany State Park is also within the boundaries of the Savage River State Forest. It has a thirteen-acre lake with sandy beaches, good for swimming, fishing, and summertime boat rentals. There are campgrounds, pavilions, trails for hiking and biking, and cross-country ski trails. Eleven furnished cabins are available, too. Since they have electricity, fireplaces, and kitchens, the cabins are popular year-round.

For a Customized Nature Adventure

Consider taking part in Maryland's "nature tourism" program, which links visitors with private guides and outfitters who can tailor an adventure to the ages and interests of your children. To try a nature tourism adventure, call the nature tourism coordinator at (301) 784-8403.

Spruce Forest Artisan Village (all ages)

177 Casselman Rd., Grantsville 21536; (301) 895-3332, www.spruceforest.org. Open May through October, Monday through Saturday 10 a.m. to 5 p.m.; hours vary November through April. Free.

Kids can watch artisans produce traditional local ware such as hand-stitched quilts and wooden toys in this cluster of studios. The site also include a 1797 gristmill and the Casselman River Bridge, the largest single-span stone bridge when it was constructed in 1813. In 1933, it was replaced by a steel bridge. The old stone structure is no longer in use.

Where to Eat

Penn Alps. 125 Casselman Rd., Grantsville; (301) 895-5985, www.pennalps.com. This casual, Amish-style restaurant is located in the Spruce Forest Artisan Village. A buffet of country fare is offered on weekends, but there are plenty of menu options the rest of the time, including soups, sandwiches, baked ham, and fried chicken. $

Annie's Kitchen Country Restaurant. 414 South Main St., Accident; (301) 746-8578.

The specialty of the house is a Reuben on homemade, grilled rye bread, but patrons also come for the generous weekend buffets. The restaurant has twenty kinds of pie, plus a kids' menu. $

For More Information

Greater Grantsville Business Association. P.O. Box 790, Grantsville, 21536; (301) 895-3144, www.granstvillemd.com.

Swanton and McHenry

As the home of Deep Creek Lake State Park, Swanton and McHenry are family tourist destinations in every season. Despite its increasing popularity, the area retains a rustic feel. From I-68, Swanton, which is on the southern end of the lake, can be reached by taking Route 495 south. McHenry, which is on the northern end of the lake, can be reached by taking I-68 to Route 219 south.

Deep Creek Lake State Park (all ages)

898 State Park Rd., Swanton 21561; (301) 387-5563, www.dnr.state.md.us/publiclands/western/deepcreeklake.html. Open daily dawn to dusk. Free.

A summer day or a week at Deep Creek Lake State Park is the stuff of childhood memories. Your kids can splash in the water along the mile-long shore while you set out a picnic lunch. The whole family might rent a canoe. Or you might get out of the sun to explore the Discovery Center, which opens at 9 a.m. daily and lets kids touch fossils, look into a microscope, and enjoy an aquarium while learning about the natural wonders and history of the area. Another option is to take a hike. Trails range in length from a half mile to 6 miles.

Organized Activities in Deep Creek Lake

Here is a sampling of some of the organized activities that are available for families in the Deep Creek Lake area.

- **Camp Earth** (P.O. Box 35, Friendsville 21531; 800-446-7554, 301-746-4083, www.campearth.org) offers farm tours, hiking trips, family adventure camps, and even programs for toddlers.

- **Circle R Ranch** (4151 Sand Flat Rd., Oakland; 301-387-6890, www.deepcreek lakestable.com) has a dairy farm and trail-riding facilities.

- **Deep Creek Outfitters** (1899 Deep Creek Dr., McHenry; 301-387-6977, www .deepcreekoutfitters.com) has boat rentals and boating excursions in the summer, cross-country ski equipment rental in the winter.

- **The Deep Creek Sailing School** (365 Back Bay Lane, Swanton; 301-387-4497. www.saildeepcreek.com) offers on-water lessons for kids as young as six, provided that they know how to swim. The school, based in Swanton, offers group or private lessons.

- **Elk Ridge Nature Works** (283 Elk Ridge Lane, Grantsville; 301-895-3686, www.elkridgenatureworks.com) provides custom-designed nature programs or classes that might include a search for stream critters, bike rides, and a night watch.

- **Precision Rafting** (715 Morris Ave., Friendsville; 800-477-3723, www.precision rafting.com) offers family float trips and beginner whitewater trips, as well as more adventurous raft and kayak excursions. They say they've taken kids as young as age two.

- **Western Trails Riding Stables** (400 Mayhew Inn Rd., Oakland; 301-387-6155, www.westerntrails.net) offers indoor or outdoor horseback riding lessons for all ages, plus hayrides and trail rides.

One amazing perk of the 12-mile lake is that it has hardly any mosquitoes! Nobody seems to know why the area is free of biting insects, but the result is delightful.

Activity schedules posted throughout the park tell of nature hikes, evening campfire programs, and other events.

And don't forget that Deep Creek is a year-round resort. In winter, snowmobiling on the park's 6 miles of trails is a popular pursuit. The nature center has plenty of winter activities, too, including scavenger hunts, crafts, and encounters with live reptiles and birds of prey. No mosquitoes then, either.

Smiley's Fun Zone Family Entertainment Center (ages 4 and up)

75 Fort Dr., McHenry 21541; (301) 387-5121, www.smileyfunzone.com. Open 10 a.m. to 11 p.m. Memorial Day to Labor Day, schedules vary the rest of the year depending on weather. Admission free, activities $.

Bumper boats, batting cages, arcade games, a laser-tag arena, miniature golf, and other activities make this a popular destination. The restaurant serves reasonably priced pizza, burgers, wings, ice cream, and other kid-friendly fare, plus beer and wine for the grown-ups.

Wisp Resort (ages 3 and up)

Wisp at Deep Creek Mountain Resort, P.O. Box 629, 296 Marsh Hill Rd., McHenry 21541; (301) 387-4911, www.skimaryland.com. The mountain is generally open from early November to mid-March, depending on the weather. $$$–$$$$.

The state's only ski resort is a great place to introduce kids to the sport of downhill skiing. The resort offers lessons and programs just for youngsters and has a year-round youth center, called Willy Wisp, for kids ages three to fourteen.

The ski season starts as soon as it's cold enough to make snow, typically around Thanksgiving, and runs through mid-March. But there are plenty of other things to do at Wisp if you're a person who doesn't think gliding down a mountain with two sticks strapped to your feet seems like much fun.

In addition to skiing down the 610-foot vertical drop, kids can tube down the mountain at the Bear Claw Snow Tubing Tubing at the Bear Claw Snow Tubing Park.

Snowmobile tours, introduced in 2006, offer exhilarating rides through the pristine Western Maryland countryside. Kids younger than 10, meanwhile, can ride special safety-featured mini snowmobiles.

Snowmobiles are rented at the Nordic Center, which is also the base of operations for snowshoeing and cross-country skiing, offering lessons, rentals, guided tours, or simply access to the groomed trails that transform the resort's golf course into a playground for winter, too.

The Wisp Resort Hotel and Conference Center has suites and rooms with fireplaces. Indoor activities include a spa, restaurants, and an arcade. Parents can get a few hours to themselves by enrolling their children in an evening of tubing, snowmobiling, and other activities through the Kids Night Out program.

In the off-season, the resort offers scenic chairlift tours with views of the surrounding countryside; a new skate park for skateboarders, bikers, and in-line skaters; golf, mountain biking, fishing, and much more.

Where to Eat

Black Bear Restaurant. Route 219, Fort McHenry; (301) 387-9400. With the kids in tow, you'll be focusing on the restaurant side of this combination family-style restaurant, tavern, and nightclub. The casual dining area has views of the lake and ski slopes, and there's an outdoor deck for eating when the weather is nice. $–$$

Vacation Rentals

If you're planning to stay more than a few days in Swanton and McHenry, or if you're going with another family, a good option is to rent a house or apartment. For rental information, contact **Coldwell Banker** (301-387-6187, 800-769-5300, www.deepcreekrentals.com) or **Railey Mountain Lake Vacations** (800-846-RENT, www.deepcreek.com), or **Long and Foster Realtors** (800-336-7303, www.deepcreekresort.com).

Canoe on the Run. 2622 Deep Creek Dr., McHenry; (301) 387-5933. A stylish little coffee and sandwich shop with great soups and an outdoor deck and working fireplace. $

Where to Stay

Comfort Inn. 2704 Deep Creek Dr., McHenry; (301) 387-4200. Located a halfmile from the lake, this hotel serves a complimentary continental breakfast and has some rooms that are suites. $$–$$$

Panorama Motel. 921 Mosser Rd., McHenry; (301) 387-5230, www.deepcreek times.com/panorama. A choice of apartments, efficiencies, or deluxe rooms, all reasonably priced and within a mile of Deep Creek Lake and Wisp. All the rooms have cable television, refrigerators, and individually controlled heating and air-conditioning. The site has a picnic area and tot lot. $$, children under twelve free.

Wisp Mountain Resort Hotel and Conference Center. 290 Marsh Hill Rd., McHenry; (800) 462-9477, www.wispresort .com. This resort center, located at the base of Wisp Mountain, has 102 suites and 64 efficiencies or deluxe rooms, all with refrigerators, separate sleeping quarters, and a television. $$–$$$

For More Information

Garrett County Chamber of Commerce. 15 Visitors Center Dr., McHenry 21541; (301) 387-4386, www.garrettchamber.com.

Lake-Front Magazine. Pick up a free copy at various locations.

Oakland

Oakland is nearly as far west as it's possible to go in Maryland before hitting West Virginia. The town, with about 2,000 residents, is surrounded by beautiful countryside. It's about three hours from Baltimore. Get there by taking I-68 West to exit 42. Bear left onto Route 220, then turn right onto Route 135. In about 30 miles, you'll be in Oakland.

Funland (ages 2 and up)

24450 Garrett Hwy, Oakland 21541; (301) 387-6168, www.deepcreekhospitality.com/FU_ Funland.asp. Open daily 10 a.m. to 10 p.m. throughout the summer and as long as weather allows. $–$$.

When the kids crave a little excitement, take them to Funland, where they can try their luck at a rock-climbing wall, ride go-karts, take a spin on a carousel, play miniature golf, indulge in video games, and ride bumper cars. Pizza and soft-serve ice cream are sold. Admission is **free,** but you pay for the rides.

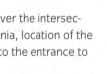

Potomac-Garrett State Forest (ages 3 and up) ⊗
1431 Potomac Camp Rd., Oakland 21550; (301) 334-2038, www .dnr.state.md.us. Open daily dawn to dusk. Free.

A 1-mile hike in this park will reward you with a vista from the top of Backbone Mountain, the state's highest point at 3,360 feet. The mountain, near the West Virginia state line, also forms part of the Eastern Continental Divide, meaning water to the east of the mountain drains into the Atlantic Ocean, and water to the west flows into the Gulf of Mexico. A mile-long hiking trail takes you to the highest point, where you can record your visit on a register.

To get to the trail from Oakland, go south on Route 219, crossing over the intersection of Route 50 at Red House and continuing to Silver Lake, West Virginia, location of the smallest church in forty-eight states. From here, proceed 1 mile south to the entrance to the logging road leading to Maryland's highest point.

Other activities here are mountain biking and fishing. Campsites are available.

Swallow Falls and Herrington Manor State Parks (all ages) ⊛⊗⊛Ⓐ
222 Herrington Manor Lane, Oakland, 21550; (301) 334-9180, www.dnr.state.md.us/public lands/western/herringtonmanor/html. Open daily dawn to dusk. $.

These two parks, connected by a 5.5-mile hiking trail, boast some of the most pristine scenery in the state. Muddy Creek Falls, the highest waterfall in the state, is at Swallow Falls, which also has three other beautiful falls, plus sixty-five campsites with bathhouses, a children's play area, a beach volleyball court, and hiking trails.

Herrington Manor State Park is home to Herrington Lake, which has swimming areas with lifeguards on duty during the summer. Rowboats, canoes, and paddleboats are available for rental from May through September. There are two tennis courts, a volleyball court, picnic shelters, a concession stand open in the summer, and twenty furnished log cabins for rental year-round.

In winter, you can snowshoe or cross-country ski on 10 miles of trails. Rent equipment at the concession stand, which is open daily (except Christmas and New Year's) from 8:30 a.m. to 4 p.m. when conditions are good. The stand has a snack bar, restrooms, and a cozy fireplace.

Kids might enjoy attending one of the park's annual activities, including a demonstration of maple-syrup making held every March, and an apple-butter boil and corn roast held in August.

Other Things to See and Do and See in Western Maryland

- **Boonsborough Museum of History.** 113 North Main St., Boonsboro; (301) 432-6969

- **C and O Bicycle.** 9 South Penn Ave., Hancock; (301) 678-6665, http://cando bicycle.com

- **Cumberland Theatre.** 101 Johnson St., Cumberland; (301) 759-4990, www .cumberlandtheatre.com

- **Family Recreation Park.** 21063 National Pike, Boonsboro; (410) 733-2333, www.familyrecreationpark.com

- **Frostburg State Planetarium.** Frostburg State University, Room 302 of Tawes Hall, Frostburg; (301) 687-4270

- **Garrett 8 Cinemas.** 19736 Garrett Hwy, Oakland; (301) 387-2500

- **George Washington's Headquarters.** Riverside Park, Greene Street, Cumberland; (301) 777-5132

- **Hagerstown Speedway.** 15112 National Pike, Hagerstown; (301) 582-0640, www.hagerstownspeedway.com

- **Hagerstown Suns.** Municipal Stadium, 274 East Memorial Blvd., Hagerstown; (301) 791-6266, www.hagerstownsuns.com

- **Heritage Koaches.** 16 Howard St., Building 1, Cumberland; (301) 777-0293, www.wstmr.com

- **Simon Pearce.** 265 Glass Dr., Mountain Lake Park; (301) 334-5277, www .simonpearce.com

Where to Stay

Swallow Falls Inn. 1691 Swallow Falls Rd., Oakland; (301) 387-9348, www.swallowsfalls cabins.com. Fully equipped cabin rentals, near Swallow Falls and Herrington Manor State Parks. $$

For More Information

Oakland Town Hall. 15 South Third St., Oakland 21550; (301) 334-2691, www.oak landmd.com.

Annual Events

Pancake Breakfast and Syrup-Making Demonstration. Herrington Manor State Park, Oakland; (301) 334-9180. $. Held in March.

Egg Dying and Hunting. Deep Creek Lake State Park Discovery Center, McHenry; (301) 387-7067. Children can color eggs with natural dyes, then hunt for plastic eggs. April.

C&O Canalfest. 13 Canal St., Cumberland; (301) 724-3655 ext. 2. Living history events—including artisans, children's events and live music—celebrate the heritage of Canal Place in May.

Heritage Days Festival. Cumberland; (301) 777-2787, www.HeritageDaysFestival.com. An old-fashioned celebration of history and art on the streets of Cumberland in June includes storytellers, face painting, carnival rides, pony rides, crafts, and food.

McHenry Highland Festival. Garrett County Fairgrounds, McHenry; (301) 387-9300, www.highlandfest.info. In June, celebrate the return of warm weather with Scottish-themed music and activities for the whole family, including crafts, sheepdog demonstrations, athletic competitions, and dancing.

Youth Fishing Rodeo. Herrington Manor State Park; (301) 334-9180. Children sixteen and under fish for **free,** and prizes are awarded in three categories. Usually held the first Saturday in June, 8 a.m. to noon. Free food for contestants.

July Fourth Fireworks over Deep Creek Lake; (301) 387-4386, www.garrettchamber.com. Also, live music and fireworks at Constitution Park, Cumberland; (301) 759-6636.

Garrett County Fair. Garrett County Fairgrounds, McHenry; (301) 245-4564, www.countryfest.org. Fun for the whole family in August. Activities include a tractor pull and aerial candy drop. Lots of food, crafts, and rides. **Free.**

Autumn Glory Festival. Garrett County; (301) 387-4386, www.garrettchamber.com. Five days of fun in October, including railroad excursions, fiddling contests, parades, music, storytelling festival, and other activities for the whole family.

Southern Maryland

Southern Maryland is less than two hours from Washington, D.C., and Baltimore, yet it is a world apart from the hustle and bustle of those major metropolitan areas. There are no big cities here, just small towns and plenty of open spaces. The pace is a little slower, the air a little saltier.

As the name implies, this region is at the southern tip of the state, on the western side of the Chesapeake Bay. Calvert County is to the east, separated from the others by the Patuxent River. Charles and St. Mary's Counties are to the west. This chapter is organized from north to south, first traveling south along Route 2/4 in Calvert County, then south along Route 301 in Charles County, and finally south along Route 5, which turns into Route 235, in St. Mary's County.

In all three counties, you and your family will find pristine beaches, charming historic communities, and museums dedicated to the people who make their living from the bay.

Calvert County

If your youngsters are interested in fossils, they will love Calvert County, where fascinating fossils of teeth and bones seem to turn up just about everywhere, from shark teeth at the Flag Pond Nature Park to the bones of extinct whales at Calvert Cliffs State Park. That's because Southern Maryland was covered by a shallow ocean about ten million to twenty years ago.

Though the county is no longer covered by water, it is surrounded by it. Sandwiched between the Chesapeake Bay and the Patuxent River, Calvert County seems to have a beach or marina around every corner. In this chapter, we'll tackle Calvert County from top to bottom, starting with the town of North Beach and continuing south to the tip of the county at Solomons Island, following the main north–south route, which is Route 2/4.

SOUTHERN MARYLAND

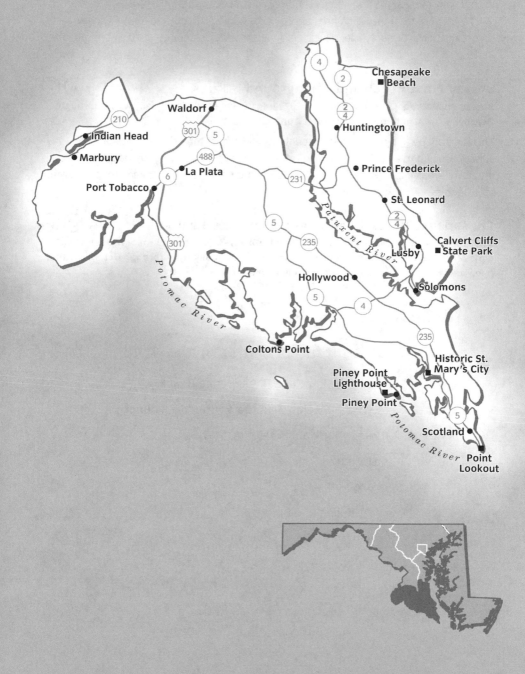

Chesapeake Beach

The charming bayside town of Chesapeake Beach, only 28 miles from Washington, D.C., was developed as a resort community in the late 1800s. These days, it has many year-round residents but retains its quiet waterfront allure. Since many of the homes here are vacation properties, the community is more crowded in the summer.

To get here from the Baltimore Beltway, take Route 301 south to Route 4 south. Just across the Calvert County line, take a left on Route 260. Go about 5 miles to Chesapeake Beach.

Breezy Point Beach and Campground (all ages)
Breezy Point Road, Chesapeake Beach 20732; (410) 535-0259. Open daily May 1 through October 31, 6 a.m. to dusk. $, children 2 and under free.

This bayfront park, operated by the county, can't be beat for a day or more of fun in the sun. In addition to a half-mile-long sandy beach, it has a playground, shaded picnic areas, and a volleyball court. There is also a pier for crabbing or fishing. Camping for as many as four people is $30 a night.

Chesapeake Beach Railway Museum (ages 3 and up)
4155 Mears Ave., Chesapeake Beach 20732; (410) 257-3892, www.cbrm.org. Open weekends March 15 through November 30, 1 p.m. to 4 p.m., daily April through October, 1 to 4 p.m., and weekends 11 a.m. to 5 p.m. June through August. Free.

Karen's
TopPicks for fun in Southern Maryland

1. Chesapeake Beach Water Park, Chesapeake Beach

2. Battle Creek Cypress Swamp Sanctuary, Prince Frederick

3. Jefferson Patterson Park and Museum, St. Leonard

4. Calvert Cliffs State Park, Lusby

5. Flag Pond Nature Park, Lusby

6. Calvert Marine Museum, Solomons

7. Annmarie Garden on St. John, Solomons

8. Sotterley Plantation, Hollywo.od

9. Piney Point Lighthouse Museum and Park, Piney Point

10. Historic St. Mary's City, St. Mary's City

At the turn of the twentieth century, Chesapeake Beach was a major tourist attraction. In the late 1890s, a 1,600-foot boardwalk was constructed, and attractions included a roller coaster, carousel, band shell, and entertainment booths. A rail line was constructed at the same time, cementing the resort's popularity as a summertime destination. But the Great Depression and the growing popularity of the automobile took their toll, and the railway closed in 1935, spelling the end of the amusement park. In 1979, the empty railroad station was turned into a museum celebrating the town's amusement-park past.

The museum's photographs and artifacts here provide a charming glimpse of what Chesapeake Beach was like during its heyday. Kids may like the photos of roller coasters and other attractions on the boardwalk. Events include a summer concert series on Thursdays, a family fun day in spring and fall, and children's programs on Thursday mornings during the summer.

Chesapeake Beach Water Park (all ages)

4079 Gordon Stinnett Ave., Chesapeake Beach 20732; (410) 257-1404, www.chesapeake beachwaterpark.com. Open daily in the summer 11 a.m. to 7 p.m., weather permitting. $$–$$$.

Your kids will beg you to spend the afternoon at this popular water park, owned and operated by the citizens of Chesapeake Beach. It has eight waterslides, a children's activity pool, a lagoon, waterfalls, fountains, and other fun. An adjacent recreation center houses a basketball court, pool table, and more. If you plan to stay all day (and you easily can), you'll be able to fuel up at the snack bar. Children younger than thirteen must go with an adult.

Where to Stay

Chesapeake Beach Resort and Spa.
4165 Mears Ave., Chesapeake Beach; (410) 257-2735, toll-free (877) 763-6733. Rooms at this waterfront hotel include sitting areas, flat-screen TVs with DVD players, and Internet access. $$$–$$$$.

Where to Eat

Rod and Reel. 4160 Mears Ave., Chesapeake Beach; (410) 257-2735, toll-free (877) 763-6733. Visitors come by car and boat to this popular restaurant, founded in 1946. Seafood is the specialty, but there are other dishes, plus a kids' menu. You can eat inside or take in the sea air outside at the Boardwalk Café. $$$. The adjacent Smokey Joe's Grill serves pulled pork sandwiches and other barbecue in a casual setting. $$

For More Information

Chesapeake Beach Town Hall. P.O. Box 400, Chesapeake Beach, 20732; (410) 257-2230, www.cheapeake-beach.md.us.

Huntingtown

From Route 4, you can reach the small town of Huntingtown by taking Route 521.

Kings Landing Natural Resources Management Area (all ages)

End of Kings Landing Road, Huntingtown, 20639; (410) 535-5327, www.calvertparks.org. Open weekends only January, February, March, November, and December 8:30 a.m. to 5 p.m.; open daily Memorial Day weekend through Labor Day weekend 8:30 a.m. to 8 p.m., and open April, May, September, and October, Monday through Friday 8:30 a.m. to 4:30 p.m., weekends 8:30 a.m. to 6 p.m. Free.

A sandy shoreline, 200-foot fishing pier, canoe and kayak access, and plenty of hiking trails are among the natural attractions for families at this 260-acre scenic spot on the Patuxent River.

Where to Stay

Serenity Acres Bed and Breakfast. 4270 Hardesty Rd., Huntingtown; (410) 535-3744. Children are welcome at this bed-and-breakfast, situated on five acres with nature paths. Each of the four rooms has a king-size bed and private bath, and cots and portable cribs are available. Other amenities include an exercise room, outdoor swimming pool, and complimentary continental breakfast. $$

Prince Frederick

Continuing south along Route 2/4, our next stop is Prince Frederick, an inland community of fewer than 2,000 residents.

Battle Creek Cypress Swamp Sanctuary (all ages)

Grays Road, Prince Frederick 20678; (410) 535-5327, www.calvertparks.org. Open year-round Tuesday through Saturday 10 a.m. to 4:30 p.m., Sunday 1 to 4:30 p.m. Closed Thanksgiving, Christmas, and New Year's Day. Free. From Route 2/4 south of Prince Frederick, turn west on Sixes Road, then turn south on Grays Road. The swamp will be on the right.

You'll feel like you're stepping into prehistoric times when you take your children to this one-hundred-acre sanctuary. Walking among trees that are 100 feet tall and listening to the sounds of frogs and songbirds are sure to evoke a sense of mystery and awe.

This sanctuary boasts the nation's northernmost range of bald cypress trees. A quarter-mile boardwalk over swamps and through the trees lets you and your family look for wildflowers and animals while enjoying the beauty of the surroundings. Keep your eyes open for raccoons, owls, and flying squirrels. The nature center here has exhibits and live animals, and it offers programs for children as young as age two.

Amazing
Maryland Facts

Some of the trees at the Battle Creek Swamp Sanctuary are more than 1,000 years old!

Where to Stay

Super 8 Motel. 40 Commerce Lane, Prince Frederick; (800) 800-8000 or (410) 535-8668, www.super8.com. A basic motel with complimentary continental breakfast, plus a fitness room and whirlpool. Internet access and local calls are free, and suites are available. $$, children twelve and under free.

St. Leonard

The next stop on our drive south is St. Leonard, located off Route 2/4 on the Chesapeake Bay.

Jefferson Patterson Park and Museum (ages 3 and up)

10515 Mackall Rd., St. Leonard 20685; (410) 586-8500, www.jefpat.org. Open April 15 to October 15, Wednesday through Sunday 10 a.m. to 5 p.m. Free.

If your kids are at all interested in bones and fossils, you shouldn't miss this fascinating museum of history and archaeology, which includes more than seventy archaeological sites and houses the state's archaeological collections.

Short trails take visitors to active archaeological sites that range from ones with 9,000-year-old fossils to ones that explore remains from colonial times and even from the 1814 Battle of St. Leonard Creek, the largest naval engagement in Maryland's history.

The discovery room in the visitor center has colonial clothes for the kids to try on, as well as archaeology-themed games. Also on display is a permanent exhibit called *12,000 Years in the Chesapeake*. Your kids can visit the farm exhibit building and see the collection of regional farm equipment, including a 20,000-pound steam traction engine. Kid-friendly events include a Children's Day on the Farm, held in June, with music, art, food, a talent show, and more.

Lusby

The town of Lusby, near the southern tip of Calvert County, is home to several attractions. It's a good place to stop on the way to Solomons.

Stay Off the Cliffs

Climbing on the Calvert Cliffs is strictly forbidden. This is to protect the cliffs, which are fragile, and to protect people, in the very real likelihood that the cliffs would crumble if disturbed.

Calvert Cliffs Nuclear Power Plant Visitors Center (ages 4 and up)

Constellation Energy, 1650 Calvert Cliffs Parkway, Lusby 20657; (410) 495-4673. Open daily 10 a.m. to 4 p.m. Closed New Year's Day, Easter Sunday, Thanksgiving, and Christmas. Free.

It might seem strange to see the state's only nuclear-power plant listed as a tourist attraction, but this one is remarkable. First of all, the visitor center is housed in a nineteenth-century tobacco barn. And second, on clear days, it boasts gorgeous views across the bay and all the way to the Eastern Shore. The visitor center has hands-on exhibits about energy and nuclear power and exhibits about local agriculture and archaeology.

Calvert Cliffs State Park (ages 5 and up)

Route 765, Lusby 20657; (301) 872-5688, www.dnr.state.md.us. Open sunrise to sunset daily. $ donation requested. From Route 2/4, drive 14 miles south of Prince Frederick and look for signs for the park. It will be on the left.

The only thing that makes this magnificent site tricky for youngsters is the 2-mile walk to the beach, which may be daunting for little legs. However, if your youngsters are up for it, the end result is worth the effort, bringing you to the Chesapeake Bay and the soaring Calvert Cliffs, formed more than fifteen million years ago. Other hikes range in length from 1.2 to 3.6 miles. Be sure to take plenty of water; the only fountain is in the parking lot. The cliffs and surrounding areas contain more than six hundred species of fossils, which can be collected on the open beach. However, no climbing is allowed on the cliffs. There's also a playground, picnic tables and grills.

Flag Pond Nature Park (all ages)

North Solomons Island Road, Lusby 20657; (410) 586-1477, www.calvertparks.org. Open daily Memorial Day to Labor Day, 9 a.m. to 6 p.m. weekdays; 9 a.m. to 8 p.m. weekends;

Shark Teeth

Why are there so many shark teeth near the Calvert Cliffs? One reason is simply that sharks have a lot of teeth, which are set in layered rows in the gums. If one tooth falls out, another moves forward to take its place.

from April to Memorial Day and Labor Day to the end of October, open weekends only 9 a.m. to 6 p.m.; from last weekend in October to first weekend in April, weekends only 9 a.m. to 5 p.m. $ per vehicle.

Fossil hunting is a popular activity on the beaches of this scenic 463-acre park on the Chesapeake Bay. And yes, you get to keep the fossils you find. Though there is a sandy beach, there are no lifeguards so swimming is at your own risk. Better activities are picnicking and hiking along the trails that include a boardwalk over wetlands. Two ponds on the property boast observation platforms, and a fishing pier juts into the Chesapeake Bay. Take your kids to see the wildlife displays at the visitor center and to visit the shanty that in the first half of the 1900s served as a shelter for local fisherman. Today it houses an exhibit on the fishing industry.

Solomons

Solomons is at the tip of Southern Maryland, surrounded by the Patuxent River and Chesapeake Bay. The former fishing village has grown into a popular destination for water sports and activities.

Annmarie Garden on St. John (all ages)

Dowell Road, Solomons 20629; (410) 326-4640, www.annmariegarden.org. Open daily 10 a.m. to 4 p.m. **Free.** From Baltimore, take I-97 to Route 301 south, then Route 4 south to Solomons. Turn left on Dowell Road at Solomons Firehouse. The garden is in less than a quarter mile, on the left.

Introduce your children to art while enjoying the great outdoors. This public sculpture and botanical garden has sculptures that will appeal to young children, as well as plenty of nature trails to explore. The park sits on thirty acres along St. John Creek, on land donated by Francis and Ann Koenig and dedicated in 1993. The first work of art was *Tribute to an Oyster Tonger,* a sculpture at the entrance to the garden of a man scooping oysters out of the water. Another fascinating sculpture is the *Surveyor's Map,* a floating walkway with images and inscriptions related to Calvert County.

Calvert Marine Museum (ages 3 and up)

14200 Solomons Island Rd., Solomons 20688; (410) 326-2042, www.calvertmarinemuseum .com. Open daily 10 a.m. to 5 p.m. $, children under 5 **free.** From Baltimore, take I-97 South to Route 3. Then take Route 301 south to Route 4. Continue south and east to Route 2/4 to Solomons.

For my animal-loving kids, the highlight of this museum was the outdoor tank with live, and very playful, otters. But they also loved climbing to the top floor of the historic Drum Point Lighthouse and seeing what life was like for the families who lived there from 1883 until it was decommissioned in 1962. In the museum's discovery room, my youngsters played with plastic bones and looked at sea creatures in jars. Meanwhile, I had a hard time pulling my husband away from the exhibits about maritime life from the 1700s to the

Amazing
Maryland Facts

During World War II, Solomons was chosen as the staging area for amphibious invasion training.

present day. And my favorite thing was the giant Miocene-era shark skeleton that's part of the paleontology exhibit.

This museum is actually several buildings, with enough activities to keep a family busy for an entire day. On the weekends in spring through fall, museum interpreters demonstrate oyster tonging—a method of scooping up the tasty shellfish—and fishing techniques, and they lead nature walks through the saltwater and freshwater marshes on the site.

When you visit the Marine Museum you can also take a shuttle to the Cove Point Lighthouse, built in 1828 and the state's oldest in continuous use (open daily 10 a.m. to 5 p.m.). Since the lighthouse is still in use, visitors can only go into the base and look up the spiral staircase.

The museum admission price also includes entry to the Joseph C. Lore and Sons Oyster House, just south of the museum, a restored 1934 seafood-packing house with exhibits showing how watermen harvested and packed seafood.

Where to Eat

Boomerang's Original Ribs. 13820 Solomons Island Rd. South, Solomons; (410) 326-6050, www.loveribs.com. Burgers, ribs, chicken, and other fare in a casual environment. Kids' menu. $$–$$$

Captain's Table. 275 Lore Rd., Solomons; (410) 326-2772, http://massarosrestaurants .com/captainstable/index.htm. This waterfront family restaurant serves breakfast, lunch and dinner and has a popular weekend breakfast bar. Kids' menu. $$$

Where to Stay

Comfort Inn Beacon Marina. 255 Lore Rd., Solomons; (410) 326-6303. Sixty-room renovated waterfront complex with a marina, restaurant, outdoor pool and hot tub, and

Amazing
Maryland Facts

Oysters can live to be twenty years old. They are eligible for harvest when they are 3 inches long, usually at around three years of age.

complimentary continental breakfast. Bicycle renting and boating available. All rooms have Internet access. $$$

For More Information

Calvert County Department of Economic Development. 176 Main St., Suite 101 of the Courthouse Annex, Prince Frederick 20678; (800) 331-9771, www.co.cal.md.us/cced.

Calvert County Historical Society. P.O. Box 358, Prince Frederick 20678; (410) 535-2452, www.somd.lib.md.us/CALV/cchs.

Charles County

Quiet Charles County was once the tumultuous center of national events, thanks to a country doctor named Samuel Mudd who set the leg John Wilkes Booth broke jumping from a balcony of the Ford Theater after killing President Abraham Lincoln. Though Mudd maintained he didn't recognize Booth when he treated him, he was convicted of conspiracy to murder the president, though later pardoned by President Andrew Johnson.

Mudd's house is now a museum, one of many reasons to visit this beautiful county only twenty minutes southwest of Washington, D.C. Port Tobacco, settled in 1634, was once Maryland's second-largest seaport. It now features a historic downtown with a replica of the original courthouse, a one-room schoolhouse built in 1876. Port Tobacco was the county seat until the government was moved to La Plata in1895.

Waldorf

Located off Route 301 in Charles County, Waldorf is something of a shopping mecca. It has a mall, the St. Charles Towne Center, at the intersection of Crain Highway and Smallwood Drive. The food court there provides good lunch options for the kids.

Samuel A. Mudd House (ages 8 and up)
Dr. Samuel Mudd Road, Waldorf 20601; (301) 645-5870. Open end of March to end of November, Wednesdays and Saturdays 11 a.m. to 4 p.m. and Sundays noon to 4 p.m. Also open in December for the annual Victorian Christmas event. $, children 6 and under free.

This unassuming clapboard house, built around 1754, is a popular destination for Civil War buffs and history lovers re-creating the escape route of John Wilkes Booth, who killed Abraham Lincoln on April 14, 1865, and then fled toward Virginia.

The house, furnished with original pieces from the nineteenth century, is now open to the public. Costumed docents give historical tours. Older children with an interest in history will probably enjoy seeing where Mudd lived and learning about Booth's flight from justice.

Where to Eat

Lefty's Bar-B-Que. 2064 Crain Hwy, Waldorf; (301) 374-6554. Ribs, chicken, sandwiches, and other barbecued fare, plus a children's menu. $$

Mama Mia's Pizza. 12526 Mattawoman Dr.,Waldorf; (301) 645-1433. Pizza and other Italian favorites at a family-owned restaurant. $$

Where to Stay

Holiday Inn Waldorf. 45 St. Patrick's Dr., Waldorf; (301) 645-8200, (800) 645-8277. A fitness center, guest laundry facilities, and an outdoor pool are among the amenities in this 191-room hotel, including some suites with kitchenettes. Kids eat free at the in-house restaurant, Damon's Grill, which serves ribs and other American-style fare. $$

Super 8 Motel. 3550 Crain Hwy, Waldorf; (301) 932-8957. Cribs and cots are available, and some rooms have refrigerators and microwaves. All rooms have remote-control cable television. There's a fitness area and complimentary continental breakfast. $$, kids twelve and under stay free.

La Plata

To the south of Waldorf is La Plata, the county seat. Get there by taking Route 301 (Crain Highway) to Route 488 east.

Gilbert Run Park (all ages)

Route 6, 7 miles east of La Plata; (301) 932-1083, www.charlescountyparks.com. Open Wednesday through Sunday, March to the end of October, 8 a.m. to dusk. $ to park.

Paddleboats, rowboats, and canoes can be rented for an afternoon of watery fun on the sixty-acre freshwater lake in this park. There's also a nature center with a 150-gallon aquarium, playgrounds, and nature trails through the wooded parkland. Keep your eyes open for the bald eagles that live here, and pack a lunch to enjoy at the picnic areas, which have grills and tables.

Laurel Springs Regional Park (all ages)

Radio Station Road, La Plata. Open daily 9 a.m. to dusk. Free.

Perfect for an afternoon getaway, this park has a tot lot and playground, as well as picnic tables, athletic fields, and a 1.6-mile trail through the wooded perimeter of the park.

Where to Eat

Johnny Boy Ribs. 7540 Crain Hwy, La Plata; (301) 870-2526, www.johnnyboysribs.com. Located right next to the renowned Twin Kiss, this restaurant serves chicken sandwiches, barbecue, burgers, and fries. Eat in or take your food out to the picnic tables by the parking lot. $

Twin Kiss Drive Inn. 7415 Crain Hwy, La Plata; (301) 934-4025. The place that invented the double-flavor soft-serve swirl in 1959 has been serving ice cream to happy customers ever since. $

Where to Stay

Best Western La Plata. 6900 Crain Hwy, Route 301, La Plata; (301) 934-4900, (877) 356-4900. Single rooms and two-room suites with microwave, refrigerator, and cable

television. Amenities include an outdoor pool, exercise room, guest laundry facilities, and complimentary continental breakfast. $$

Indian Head

Indian Head is along the Potomac River, on the western edge of the county. Get there by taking Route 210 south.

Purse State Park (ages 4 and up)

Route 224 on Riverside Road, Indian Head; www.dnr.state.md.us. Open daily sunrise to sunset. Free.

Fossil hunting along the shoreline is a popular activity for both kids and adults at this ninety-acre preserve on the shore of the Potomac River. Your explorations may be rewarded by discoveries of fossilized shark teeth, bones, and shells, which you and your children can take home. It's best to come during low tide, as there's not much shore area when the tide is high. The park is almost completely undeveloped, but there are a few unmarked trails through the woods and wetlands. The spot is also known as a prime fishing location for carp, largemouth bass, and perch, among other species.

For More Information

Town of Indian Head. 4195 Indian Head Hwy, Indian Head 20640; (301) 743-5511, www.townofindianheadmd.org.

Marbury

Just to the south of Indian Head on Route 224, the village of Marbury is located along the Mattawoman Creek, which feeds into the Potomac River.

Smallwood State Park (all ages)

2750 Sweden Point Rd., Marbury 20658; (301) 743-7613, www.dnr.state.md.us. Open daily April through October 5 a.m. to sunset, and November through March 8 a.m. to sunset. $ on weekends and holidays. Take Route 301 south to La Plata, go west on Route 225 to

Route 224. At the light at Route 224, turn left (south). Park entrance is approximately 3 miles on the right.

For children, a highlight of this park is the great playground made of recycled tires. For adults, it may be Smallwood's Retreat, the plantation home of Gen. William Smallwood, Maryland's fourth governor. The restored home, built in 1760, is open to the public from 1 to 5 p.m. on Sundays from May through the end of September, with tours conducted by costumed docents.

The park also has a marina on the Mattawoman Creek, called the Sweden Point Marina, boat-launching ramps, picnic areas, nature trails that travel through forest, and campsites. The trail system is about 2 miles long, with exit points along the way if the kids get tired. Canoes, rowboats, and paddleboats can be rented at the marina from May through September on a first come, first served basis.

Port Tobacco

Colonized in 1634, Port Tobacco is one of the oldest communities on the entire East Coast. The downtown has many historic buildings and attractions that are interesting to children. Get to Port Tobacco by taking Crain Highway to Route 6, then head east on Route 6.

Chapel Point State Park (ages 3 and up)

Chapel Point Road, Port Tobacco 20677; (800) 784-5380. Open daily sunrise to sunset. Free.

This six-hundred-acre park on the Port Tobacco River has a sandy launch area for canoes, kayaks, and other small boats. Fishing and hunting are permitted (hunting season is late autumn). A paddle-in campsite is available by permit. Next door is another point of interest, the St. Ignatius Catholic Church, founded in 1641, which is the nation's oldest Catholic Parish in continuous service.

Port Tobacco Historic District

Off Route 6 on Chapel Point Road, Port Tobacco. Open April through December, Wednesdays and weekends, 11 a.m. to 4 p.m. Admission is free, but donations are accepted.

For more than 150 years, the site where this small cluster of buildings now stands was a major river port on the East Coast. The Historic Port Tobacco Courthouse (301-934-4313) and the Port Tobacco School House (301-932-6064) are open for self-guided tours. More formal tours of the school house can be arranged.

Thomas Stone National Historic Site (ages 4 and up)

6655 Rose Hill Rd., Port Tobacco 20677; (301) 934-6027, www.nps.gov/thst. Open Wednesday through Sunday 9 a.m. to 5 p.m. September to mid-June, and daily from mid-June to September. Free.

The plantation home of Thomas Stone, a signer of the Declaration of Independence, is the centerpiece of this 322-acre site, which also contains several colonial-era outbuildings and the family cemetery. Twenty-minute tours of the house, which is called Haberdeventure, start every hour on the hour from 10 a.m. to 4 p.m., and the visitor center has a short orientation film, plus exhibits about local history.

There's plenty to do outside, too. Families can roam the grounds, following self-guided hiking and birding trails past eighteenth-century farm buildings and garden terraces.

For More Information

Charles County Office of Tourism. P.O. Box 2150, La Plata 20646; (800) 766-3386, (301) 645-0558, www.explorecharlescomd .com.

St. Mary's County

St. Mary's County is the birthplace of Maryland. In 1634, 140 settlers led by Governor Leonard Calvert arrived from England and established a community, turning St. Mary's into the state's first capital. When the seat of state government was moved to Annapolis in 1695, St. Mary's foundered.

Today, Historic St. Mary's City is a living history museum. Costumed interpreters will show you around buildings that are being reconstructed along the same site plan as the original development. There's something wonderfully untouristy and laid back about the place, which does not get the attention it deserves as an attraction and destination.

Coltons Point

Located on a spit of land overlooking the Potomac River, Coltons Point is a worthwhile family destination. Get there by taking Route 5 south to Route 242 south.

St. Clement's Island State Park and Potomac River Museum (ages 4 and up)

38370 Point Breeze Rd., Coltons Point 20626; (301) 769-2222. Museum open October through March 24, Wednesday through Sunday noon to 4 p.m., and March 25 through September 30, weekdays 9 a.m. to 5 p.m. and weekends noon to 5 p.m. Closed major holidays. $, children 12 and under free. Island accessible only by boat from May to October, weekends only, weather permitting. The first boat leaves at 12:30 p.m. and returns at 2:15, the second leaves at 2:30 p.m. and returns at 3:45. $.

A nineteenth-century country store and a restored 1820 one-room schoolhouse are among the exhibits that fascinate children at this museum, which explores the history of St. Mary's County and includes watermen's tools and other artifacts. On the grounds around the museum are picnic spots.

But for most children, the real fun is taking a short ride aboard a twenty-six-passenger boat to the forty-acre St. Clement's Island, where a marker indicates the spot where Maryland's first colonists landed in 1634. The island has hiking trails, a portable restroom, and places where your family can enjoy a couple of hours of picnicking and fishing before returning on the boat.

Where to Eat

Morris Point Restaurant. 38869 Morris Point Rd., Abell; (301) 769-2500, www.morris-point.com. Casual family-owned restaurant with seafood, steaks, burgers, and more in a setting overlooking St. Clement's Bay. Outdoor seating in nice weather. $$

Hollywood

Hooray for Hollywood. Actually, the Hollywood in Maryland, unlike the one in California, is a small town with no movie stars in sight. But it's still worth a visit with the kids. Hollywood is right off Route 235, near the larger community of Leonardtown, which is the county seat.

Greenwell State Park (all ages)

25450 Rosedale Manor Lane, Hollywood 20636; (301) 872-5389, www.dnr.state.md.us. Open daily 8 a.m. to sunset. Donation box, proceeds benefit the Greenwell Foundation to help operate the park.

This 596-acre park on the Patuxent River has a fishing pier, 10 miles of trails, and a sandy beach area that can be used to launch canoes and kayaks. There are no lifeguards, though, so swimming is at your own risk. The trails are all less than 2 miles long. Some run along the Patuxent, and others wind through fields to take you to tidal ponds or historic barns. Programs include an egg hunt in April and summer day camps.

Sotterley Plantation (ages 3 and up)

P.O. Box 67, Hollywood 20636; (800) 681-0850, www.sotterley.com. Manor house open for guided tours May through October, Tuesday through Saturday 10 a.m. to 4 p.m., and Sunday noon to 4 p.m.; grounds open year-round for self-guided tours. $–$$, children 5 and under free. From Route 4, cross onto Solomons, turn right on Route 235 and head north about 5 miles to Route 245 (Sotterley Road). Turn right at the Shell gas station and proceed approximately 4 miles to Sotterley.

This seventeenth-century tobacco farm is a great place for kids to learn about Maryland history, since they are encouraged to grind corn, write with a quill pen, feed the sheep, and try to tell time with a sundial. The twenty-eight outbuildings include slave quarters, a corncrib, and two "necessaries." (We had a lot of fun watching my daughter try to guess the purpose of the necessary. She finally figured it out when we explained that there had been no indoor plumbing in the 1800s.)

Tours of the manor house, which dates from 1710, are more suitable for kids eight and older, since there are many valuable items that cannot be touched. The tours provide fascinating tidbits about the history and inhabitants of the house, including one who is said to linger on as a ghost.

The property, with its well-manicured grounds and gardens, is absolutely gorgeous. It overlooks the Patuxent River, and bald eagles live in the sycamore trees. The grounds are ideal for a picnic lunch when the weather is nice.

Where to Eat

Bert's 50's Diner. 28760 Three Notch Rd., Mechanicsville; (301) 884-3837, www .berts50sdiner.com. Fried chicken, sandwiches, salads, and great milkshakes in a diner with 1950s memorabilia and furnishings, including real Wurlitzer jukeboxes. $

Do Dah Deli. 22696 Washington St., Leonardtown; (301) 997-1604, www.dodahdeli.com. Sandwiches and pastries to eat in or take out. Sunday breakfast. $

Where to Stay

Hampton Inn. 22211 Three Notch Rd., Lexington Park; (301) 863-3200, (800) HAMPTON. Outdoor pool, complimentary continental breakfast, guest laundry. $$

Sleep Inn & Suites. 23428 Three Notch Rd., California; (301) 737-0000, www .sleepinn.com/hotel-california-maryland-MD097?promo=gglocal. Indoor heating pool and hot tub, an exercise room, free continental breakfast, and an on-site restaurant are among the amenities at this comfortable hotel. $$$.

Piney Point

Piney Point, near St. George Island, is southeast of Coltons Point, closer to where the Potomac River flows into the Chesapeake Bay.

Piney Point Lighthouse Museum and Park (ages 3 and up)

Lighthouse Road, Piney Point (mailing address: c/o St. Clement's Island Museum, 38370 Point Breeze Rd., Coltons Point 20626); (301) 769-2222, www.baygateways.net/general. cfm?id=28. Grounds open daily sunrise to sunset; gift shop open Friday through Monday noon to 5 p.m., May through December. $ donation. To get there follow Route 5 south through Leonardtown to Callaway. Turn right on Route 249. Drive 9 miles to Piney Point, making a right onto Lighthouse Road to the end.

From a kid's perspective, the key attractions here are a short boardwalk along the Potomac River, a pier for fishing, and a historic lighthouse. Alas, an offshore sunken German submarine can only be seen by experienced divers.

Inside the museum are exhibits about the construction and operation of the lighthouse, which was built in 1836, and an exhibit about the U-1105 *Black Panther* German submarine, which was captured in Scotland at the end of World War II and intentionally sunk after it was extensively tested and examined in the United States.

Where to Eat

Evans Seafood. St. George Island, Piney Point; (301) 994-2299. Seafood, seafood, and more seafood, plus hamburgers and a kids' menu at this casual waterside establishment. $$

Where to Stay

Camp Merryelande Vacation Cottages. 15914 Camp Merryelande Rd., St. George Island; (800) 382-1073, www.campmd.com. Fully furnished cottages with full kitchens, cable television, and air-conditioning, on an island with swimming, sailing, fishing, volleyball, and more. The cottages range from one bedroom to six bedrooms, and prices vary accordingly. Guests must bring their own linens. $$–$$$

St. Mary's City

Located on the banks of the St. Mary's River, near the southern tip of St. Mary's County, this community is dominated by Historic St. Mary's City, a fantastic family destination.

Historic St. Mary's City (ages 4 and up)

P.O. Box 39, St. Mary's City, 20686; (800) SMC-1634, (240) 895-4990, www.stmaryscity.org. **Self-guided tours January through early March, Wednesday through Sunday 10 a.m. to 5 p.m. Living history exhibits open mid-March through mid-June, Tuesday through Saturday 10 a.m. to 5 p.m.; mid-June through mid-September, Wednesday through Sunday 10 a.m. to 5 p.m.; mid-September through mid-November, Tuesday through Saturday 10 a.m. to 5 p.m. $–$$, children 6 and under free. From Route 301 south, take Route 4 south toward Prince Frederick. Continue onto Solomons Island, going across a large bridge over the Patuxent River, and stay on Route 4 until it ends at the intersection of Route 5. Turn left onto Route 5, travel south about 14 miles, and pass St. Mary's College. Look for Rosecroft Road on the right. Take Rosecroft Road, then take the first right to visitor center.**

The pace at this living history museum is remarkably relaxed. You and your children can stroll around more than eight hundred acres of reconstructed history. Costumed interpreters go about their business, stopping to talk to you about what they are doing.

The re-created town is really as it must have been in colonial times: The historic buildings have been reconstructed on the original foundations, leaving lots of room for kids to roam the beautiful bayside location.

Most of the exhibits are within walking distance of each other, even with small children, but you may want to drive to the Godiah Spray Plantation, a real farm tended by people in colonial garb. A "servant" will introduce your kids to pigs wallowing in mud and explain how soap is made.

On the reconstructed freight boat, the *Maryland Dove,* children may be asked to help stuff a mattress or to step back when a cannon is fired. In the tavern, they can play a colonial game of checkers. Kids can even pound a gavel at a replica of the State House, constructed in 1934. A video about the history of the area and how it has been preserved is shown in the visitor center.

Amazing
Maryland Facts

Margaret Brent, who lived in St. Mary's City, was the first American woman to be a lawyer, landowner, taxpayer, and suffragist. You can find a plaque about her in Historic St. Mary's City.

Where to Eat

St. Mary's College. 18952 East Fisher Rd., St. Mary's City; (800) 492-7981. Walk (or drive, if you want) across the street to the college and grab a meal in the student union. It has pizza, sandwiches, bagels, fruit, and more. $

Scotland

Way on the southern tip of St. Mary's County, jutting out between the Potomac River and the Chesapeake Bay, is Scotland. Get there by taking Route 5 south to the very end.

Point Lookout State Park Civil War Museum and Nature Center (all ages)

Junction of Chesapeake Bay and Potomac River, Route 5, Scotland 20687; (301) 872-5688, www.dnr.state.md.us/publiclands/southern/pointlookout.html. Open daily 8 a.m. to sunset. $ weekends and holidays May through September, other times **free.**

With the Chesapeake on one side and the Potomac on the other, there's no shortage of waterfront activities at this park. You and your family can rent rowboats or canoes or simply play on the playground. Lifeguards are on duty from Memorial Day to Labor Day, and the beach area has picnic tables, grills, restrooms, and a playground. If it's too cold to swim, you can explore some of the hiking paths, which are generally flat and take you along the waterfront. The entire route is 5 miles long, but there are shortcuts if shorter strolls are better for your family.

During the Civil War, this location served as a prison camp that held nearly 53,000 Confederate soldiers in captivity. Today, you and your family can learn about this history at the Civil War Museum on the property.

As many as six people at a time can camp in cottages for rent on the property. Reserve by calling (888) 432-CAMP May through September, or call (301) 872-5688 in other months.

A Nitkin Family **Adventure**

The woman on the deck of the boat was wearing a long dress with a corset, and she was barefoot. She was stuffing straw into a mattress and looked up as we approached.

"Oh, hello," she said as my children and I walked across a ramp onto a replica of the *Maryland Dove*, the boat that had transported supplies for the 140 passengers who had settled in Maryland. "Want to help?"

"Sure," said both my children instantly, much more eager to help than they are at home. Following the woman's instructions, they pummeled and stepped on the mattresses to evenly distribute the straw.

When they were done, we continued our walk around the living history museum of Historic St. Mary's City. Even though it was a beautiful June day, the grounds were not crowded. In fact, it seemed as though there were more costumed interpreters than visitors. We explored the garden, walked through the reconstructed State House, and visited the Godiah Spray Plantation. At every stop, the kids were encouraged to explore, ask questions, and touch things. They could pet the pigs, feed the chickens, smell the homemade soap, play a game of checkers, or pound a gavel.

St. Mary's City was shaping up to be one of my favorite attractions in the state. It was filled with fascinating history, and there were so many things for the kids to touch and do.

As is often the case, Ronnie and Sammy were most enchanted by something that was not part of the exhibit at all. On our way home, I asked them what they liked best about St. Mary's City. Without hesitation, they both began raving about the tiny fingernail-size frogs they had discovered hopping through the tall grass.

For More Information

St. Mary's Division of Tourism. P.O. Box 653, Governmental Center, 23115 Leonard Hall Dr., Leonardtown 20650; (800) 327-9023, www.saintmaryscounty.com/decd.

Annual Events

Maritime Heritage Festival. Historic St. Mary's City; www.stmaryscity.org. A radio-controlled model regatta, arts projects, and barbecue are on tap during this day of colonial-themed fun in June.

North Beach Bayfest. North Beach; (301) 855-6681, (410) 257-9618. This event, held the third weekend in August each year, features live entertainment, children's activities, and craft and food vendors.

Artsfest. Annmarie Garden on St. John; Solomons. In September, a juried fine art show, as well as performing arts, food, and a hands-on "discovery tent" for children. $, children twelve and under **free.**

Other Things to See and Do and See in Southern Maryland

- **African-American Heritage Society.** 7485 Crain Hwy (Route 301), La Plata; (301) 843-0371

- **American Indian Cultural Center/Piscataway Museum.** 16812 Country Lane, Waldorf; (301) 782-7622, (301) 372-1932

- **Cedarville State Forest.** Cedarville Road off Route 301, just before Waldorf; (301) 888-1410

- **Hollywood Swing and Swat.** Clarkes Landing Road (Route 235), Hollywood; (301) 737-1177

- **North Beach Public Beach.** Fifth Street and Bay Avenue, North Beach; (410) 257-9618

- **One-Room Schoolhouse.** Next to Christ Church on Broomes Island Road, Port Republic; (410) 586-0482

Christmas Doll and Train Exhibit. Potomac River Museum, St. Clement's Island. A December exhibit of antique dolls, miniature working trains, and other old-fashioned toys.

The Eastern Shore

A bird hovers, almost motionless, over the water, then suddenly plunges into the Chesapeake Bay, only to emerge moments later with a small silver fish in its beak. A sailboat glides silently across the sun-dappled water. These are some of the quiet pleasures of the Eastern Shore.

Separated from the rest of the state by the Chesapeake Bay, this craggy-shoreline chunk of land is defined by water, with the Atlantic on one side and the Chesapeake on the other. The Eastern Shore is a great place for boating, bike riding, bird-watching, and just plain relaxing.

But it's not all beaches and sunsets. The Eastern Shore boasts several cities, including St. Michaels, Easton, Salisbury, and Cambridge, with plenty of activities for the whole family. And of course, there's Ocean City, a waterfront playground for kids of all ages, with its amusement parks, miniature-golf courses, beaches, and outdoor sports.

This chapter takes you through the Eastern Shore from north to south, from the town of Rising Sun to the north to Crisfield on the southern tip of the state. We'll start by taking Route 1 over the Susquehanna River, then following Route 213 south all the way to the town of Wye Mills. At this point, Route 213 meets up with Route 50, which can be taken south to Cambridge and then east to Salisbury and Ocean City. Finally, we'll head even farther south on Route 413 to the small seaside community of Crisfield.

For visitors not starting at the northern part of the region, the major route to the Eastern Shore is the Bay Bridge, a 4-mile span across the Chesapeake Bay that's part of Route 50. The bridge is to the east of Annapolis, in Anne Arundel County, and it can get congested, especially on summer weekends.

Cecil County

Captain John Smith, the same man who sailed to Jamestown, Virginia, in 1608, was the first white person to explore the region that is now Cecil County. Though the county has

THE EASTERN SHORE

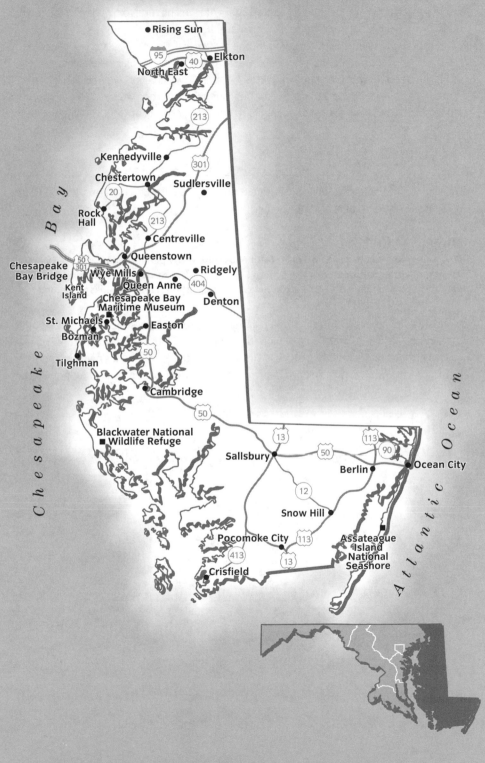

Rising Sun

95 40 Elkton
North East

213

Kennedyville
Chestertown   Sudlersville
20   301

Rock
Hall   213

Centreville

Queenstown
Chesapeake   50
Bay Bridge   301   Wye Mills   Ridgely
Kent   Queen Anne   404
Island   Chesapeake Bay   Denton
Maritime Museum

St. Michaels
Bozman   Easton

Tilghman   50

Cambridge
50

Blackwater National   13   113
Wildlife Refuge   Sallsbury   50   90
Berlin   Ocean City

12
Snow Hill

Pocomoke City   113
413
13   Assateague
Island
Crisfield   National
Seashore

Chesapeake Bay

Atlantic Ocean

been settled for more than three hundred years, it remains rural to this day. Small towns, farms, and residential neighborhoods dominate the landscape.

Located in the northeastern corner of the state, Cecil County is just south of the Mason-Dixon Line and Pennsylvania, and west of Delaware. The main east–west routes at the northern end of the state are Routes 1 and 273, which continue to Fair Hill Nature Center. At Fair Hill, Route 213 heads south through Elkton. Then we head east on Route 40 to North East. Rising Sun also connects to North East by taking Route 274 south.

Rising Sun

The small town of Rising Sun is the business hub for the surrounding farms. It is on Route 273, in the northern part of Cecil County.

Plumpton Park Zoo (all ages)

416 Telegraph Rd., Rising Sun 21911; (410) 658-6850, www.plumptonparkzoo.org. March through September, open daily 10 a.m. to 5 p.m.; October through February, open Thursday through Monday 10 a.m. to 4 p.m., weather permitting. Closed Thanksgiving and Christmas. $–$$, children under 2 free.

Your kids won't believe you when you tell them they're going to see a bearded dragon. Actually, it's a kind of lizard, one of more than 250 animals at the Plumpton Park Zoo. At just over one hundred acres, the zoo is small enough to navigate in a single afternoon, even for toddlers, yet it has plenty of animals and activities to keep your young ones

Karen's
TopPicks for fun on the Eastern Shore

1. Plumpton Park Zoo, Rising Sun

2. Elk Neck State Park and Forest, North East

3. Rock Hall Waterman's Museum, Rock Hall

4. Cross Island Trail, Chester

5. Chesapeake Bay Maritime Museum, St. Michaels

6. Salisbury City Park and Zoo, Salisbury

7. Ward Museum of Wildfowl Art, Salisbury

8. Boardwalk, Ocean City

9. Ocean City Life-Saving Station Museum, Ocean City

10. Assateague State Park, Assateague Island

Amazing
Maryland Facts

Rising Sun was named for a popular tavern, built in 1720, which provided a rest stop for travelers between Philadelphia and Baltimore.

amused. Potbellied pigs, miniature horses, lynx, and llamas are among the creatures on display. Kids will also enjoy the playground with swings by the entrance. You can bring your own goodies to eat in the designated picnic area.

Elkton

Elkton is at the intersection of Routes 213 and 40 and near the northernmost waters of the Chesapeake Bay.

Fair Hill Nature Center and
Resource Management Center (all ages)

630 Tawes Dr., Elkton 21921; (410) 398-1246, www.fairhillnature.org. Open weekdays mid-March to mid-June and late August through November, 9 a.m. to 3 p.m.; weekdays from mid-June through July, 8:30 a.m. to 2:30 p.m. Closed the week of July 4. $.

Many kid-friendly events are held at this nature center, including summer camps and educational programs such as hayrides and classes that teach kids how to identify animal tracks. The 5,600-acre property along the northeast border of the county has trails for hiking, biking, and horseback riding.

Milburn Orchards (ages 3 and up)

1495 Appleton Rd., Elkton 21921; (410) 398-1349, 800-684-3000, www.milburnorchards .com. Open July through January.

There's a lot for your family to do at this family-owned and operated farm. Pick fruits and vegetables in season, go on a hayride, feed the barnyard animals, ride a pony. In the fall, enjoy activities like face painting, scarecrow making, and exploring a corn maze. Locally made ice cream and baked goods are for sale.

Walnut Springs Farm (ages 2 and up)

3910 Blue Ball Rd., Elkton 21921; (410) 398-9150, www.strawberryfarm.com. By appointment only. Call or check the Web site for picking information.

Pick your own strawberries in the spring and pumpkins in the fall. Feed the bunnies and pet the goats. Sign up for a hayride, or slide down the strawberry slide at the playground. Inside the "mystery barn," explore the Labyrinth of Learning, with its hands-on education stations. You can even go vegetable bowling or play tomato basketball.

Where to Eat

Elkton Diner. 110 Big Elk Mall, Route 40, Elkton; (410) 620-0500, www.elktondiner.com. Old-fashioned diner, open twenty-four hours a day. $

Where to Stay

Days Inn Elkton. 311 Belle Hill Rd., Elkton; (410) 392-5010. Within walking distance of a Cracker Barrel restaurant. $$

Hampton Inn. 2 Warner Rd., Elkton; (410) 398-7777, (800) HAMPTON. Suites are available at this hotel with an indoor pool, complimentary breakfast, Internet access, and fitness room. $$$

North East

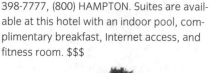

North East is not, as you might expect, in the northeast corner of the state. Rather, it is in the northeast portion of the Cheapeake Bay, on the Northeast River. The town is easy to reach by taking Route 40 from Elkton or by taking Route 100 south off I-95. Main Street, with its antiques stores, craft shops, and locally owned, casual restaurants, is popular with tourists and is a nice place to visit with children.

Elk Neck State Park and Forest (all ages)
4395 Turkey Point Rd., North East 21901; (410) 287-5333. Open daily 9 a.m. to sunset. $ on spring and fall weekends and during the summer, other times free.

With more than 400,000 visitors a year, this state park is the top family attraction in Cecil County. One reason is that there's so much to do here. You and your children can swim in the Northeast River or play on the sandy beach, which also has a snack bar, tire playground, and picnic areas. (No lifeguards, though.) Boats can be rented or launched from the Rogues' Harbor Boat Area.

There are many hiking trails, including an easy walk to the Turkey Point Lighthouse, which sits on a bluff 100 feet above the Chesapeake Bay, providing a wonderful view of the Elk River and Chesapeake Bay. If you want to make the park a vacation destination, there are nine four-person cabins that can be rented in summer, as well as sites for camping. Call ahead for details.

Tailwinds Farm (ages 8 and up)
41 Tailwinds Lane, North East 21901; (410) 658-8187, www.fairwindsstables.com. Open daily 9:30 a.m. to 5:30 p.m. $$$$.

Tailwinds can be visited for a couple of hours or it can be an overnight (or longer!) destination for your family. A combination bed-and-breakfast ($$) and stable, Tailwinds offers summer camps, hayrides, horseback-riding lessons, and trail rides. About half the guests at the bed-and-breakfast bring their horses, which can be boarded at the farm.

Amazing
Maryland Facts

Fanny Salter, who took over the Turkey Point Lighthouse after her husband died in 1925 and operated it until 1947, was the last female lighthouse keeper on the Chesapeake Bay.

If you simply want to make an afternoon of it, Tailwinds offers shorter options: Guided pony rides are available for younger children. Hayrides, which are offered year-round, include a one-hour ride followed by an hour-long bonfire, over which hot dogs and marshmallows can be roasted. Trail rides are one hour.

Upper Bay Museum (ages 3 and up)

End of Walnut Street, North East Town Park, North East 21901; (410) 287-2675; Open May through October, Sunday 10 a.m. to 4 p.m., or by appointment. $, children 12 and under free.

Local families have donated many of the materials that make up this informative museum, which overlooks the Chesapeake Bay. The region's heritage, especially as it relates to hunting and fishing, is explored in a kid-friendly way. One exhibit demonstrates how decoys are made, and another shows the different kinds of geese in the area. A fishing house on a sled is also on display. The Upper Bay Decoy Show, held the first weekend of each October, features activities for kids, food, carving competitions, and more.

Where to Eat

Pier 1. 1 South Main St., North East; (410) 287-6599. Popular, casual family restaurant. $

Woody's Crab House. 29 South Main St., North East; (410) 287-3541, www.woodys crabhouse.com. Soups, salads, sandwiches, and of course crabs and other seafood. There's a children's menu. $$

Where to Stay

Chesapeake Lodge at Sandy Cove. 60 Sandy Cove Rd., North East; (410) 287-5433, (800) 234-COVE (2683). This bed-and-breakfast at a nondenominational Christian conference center has many activities, including miniature golf (in season), an outdoor swimming pool, hiking trails, tennis courts, and a marina. All 153 rooms have private baths, and many are suites that can easily accommodate children. $$

Comfort Inn & Suites. 1 Center Dr., North East; (410) 287-7100, www.comfort inn.com/hotel-north_east-maryland-MD191? promo=gglocal. Suite hotel with kitchenettes and sitting areas in every room. Other amenities include an indoor heated pool and hot tub, exercise center, Internet access, complimentary breakfast, and guest laundry. $$–$$$

For More Information

Cecil County Tourism Bureau. 1 Seahawk Dr., North East 21901; (800) CECIL95, www .seececil.org.

North East Chamber of Commerce. 111 South Main St., Suite 210, North East 21901; (410) 287-2658, www.northeastchamber.org.

Town of North East. 106 South Main St., North East 21901; (410) 287-5801, www .northeastmd.org.

Kent County

This county, on a peninsula where the Sassafras and Chester Rivers meet, has all the small-town charms that make the Eastern Shore famous. The two main communities here, Rock Hall and Chestertown, have kid-friendly museums with boats and other tools of the waterman's trade. But in the summer, the water is the main attraction.

Kennedyville

The village of Kennedyville is on Route 213.

Kent County Farm Museum (ages 3 and up)

13689 Turners Creek Rd., Kennedyville 21645; (410) 348-5239, www.kentcounty.com/farm museum. Open April through November, first and third Saturday of the month, 10 a.m. to 4 p.m. **Free,** but donations appreciated. Heading south on Route 213 in Kennedyville, take a right onto Kennedyville Road. Cross Route 298 at the stop sign and continue on Turners Creek Road. The museum will be on your right before you reach Turners Creek.

The museum gives youngsters a glimpse of rural living in the nineteenth century by showing them household and farm items from the past. More than two hundred items are on display, such as antique tractors, horse-drawn carriages, and even a corn sheller. The museum's 163 scenic acres include nature trails, a servant's house, and a granary. Annual events include an antique tractor pull in July with more than ninety tractors, and a cider-pressing demonstration in October. Bring your own apples and take home your own cider!

Chestertown

The historic town of Chestertown is located on the Chester River, where it intersects with Route 213. The downtown area, partially closed to vehicle traffic, is wonderful for strolling. The kids will want to check out the toys and the real, live resident cat at Twigs and Teacups (111 South Cross St.; 410-778-1708) as well as the toys at Cornucopia (110 Cross St.; 410-810-2952).

Tolchester Beach Revisited Museum (ages 3 and up)

21341 Virginia Ave., Chestertown 21620; (410) 778-5347, www.rockhallmd.com/tolchester/ index.htm. Open 11 a.m. to 3 p.m. weekends March through December; group visits by appointment. **Free.**

The Tolchester Beach Amusement Park began rather inauspiciously in 1877 as a somewhat rustic attraction on ten acres near the shore, featuring picnic tables, some concessions, a bathhouse and a merry-go-round. But it soon grew to a 155-acre extravaganza, complete with a dance hall, carousel, roller coaster, bowling alley, and track for harness racing. At its peak, it attracted as many as 20,000 visitors a weekend, but the park closed in 1962.

Now, your children can get a peek at the fun of those sandy, sunny days at the Tolchester Beach Revisited Museum, which features memorabilia, posters, and more than three hundred photos from the amusement park.

Where to Eat

Play It Again Sam. 108 South Cross St., Chestertown; (410) 778-2688. Coffee shop with some light fare. $

Where to Stay

Comfort Suites. 160 Scheeler Rd., Chestertown; (410) 810-0555, www.comfortsuites.com. Complimentary breakfast buffet, heated indoor pool, wireless Internet, guest laundry. $$$, kids eighteen and under stay **free** with parents.

Rock Hall

Rock Hall, located on the Chesapeake Bay, has a small-town, relaxed charm. Its many family-friendly amenities include a beautiful beach, several kid-friendly restaurants, and a quaint Main Street that even has a candy shop that makes fudge and other sweets on the premises (Sweet Rick's, 5797 Main St.; 410-639-7700)!

Eastern Neck National Wildlife Refuge (all ages)

1730 Eastern Neck Rd., Rock Hall 21661; (410) 639-7056, www.easternneck.fws.gov. Open daily 7:30 a.m. to one half hour after sunset; office and bookstore open Monday through Friday 7:30 a.m. to 4 p.m., most Saturdays 8:30 a.m. to 4:30 p.m., and most Sundays 12:30 to 4:30 p.m. Free.

Look for bald eagles, Delmarva fox squirrels, and other forms of wildlife while hiking on some 6 miles of trails, or bring a trailered boat to the Bogle's Wharf landing on the east side of the refuge. Fishing and crabbing are allowed.

Rock Hall Waterman's Museum (ages 3 and up)

20880 Rock Hall Ave., Rock Hall 21661; (410) 778-6697, www.havenharbour.com/hhwatmus .htm. Open daily from 8 a.m. to 5 p.m. May through September, 10 a.m. to 4 p.m. October through April. Free, but donations accepted.

This small museum, in three rooms of the Haven Harbour Marina, showcases the lives of the watermen who make their living harvesting the edible sea creatures of the Chesapeake Bay. One room has photographs of watermen at work in the 1930s and 1940s, the second room has boats and equipment used by watermen, and the third has a

Take the **Trolley**

For a small price ($3 for adults, $1 for children) you can take a bright green old-fashioned-looking trolley from Rock Hall to Chestertown and then back again. The trolley makes a complete loop every hour and stops at all the restaurants, marinas, and shops—and of course the beach. Go to www.rockhall trolleys.com for more information.

reproduction of an oyster-shucking house and a shanty like the ones used by watermen during extended harvesting expeditions.

Where to Eat

Chessie's. New Yarmouth Plaza, Rock Hall; (410) 639-7727, www.rockhallmd.com/chess ies. Pizzas, steaks, subs, soups, and salads to eat in or take out. Children's menu. $

Durding's Store. 5742 Main St., Rock Hall; (410) 778-7957. Old-fashioned soda fountain in an 1872 building. Sit on the round stools at the counter, as patrons have been doing for more than sixty years, and enjoy a milk shake, sundae, or ice-cream soda. $

Pruitt's Swan Point Inn. Coleman Road and Rock Hall Avenue, Rock Hall; (410) 639-2500. Lots of seafood, which can be enjoyed on the outdoor deck overlooking the harbor. Children's menu. $$

Where to Stay

Tallulah's On Main. 5750 Main St., Rock Hall; (410) 639-2596, www.tallulahsonmain .com. This centrally located establishment has five suites equipped with kitchens, color televisions, and air-conditioning; several suites have a futon or fold-out couch. A second-floor deck is nice for relaxing in the sun. Or check out the nearby Beach Place, at 5783 Beach Rd., which has two bedrooms, plus a washer and dryer. $$$

For More Information

Kent County Office of Tourism. 400 High St., Chestertown 21620; (410) 778-0416, www.kentcounty.com.

Queen Anne's County

This county was officially established in 1706 and named for Queen Anne, the ruler of Great Britain and Ireland from 1702 to 1714. By that time, there were already more

Amazing
Maryland Facts

The Chesapeake Bay is the largest tributary in the United States.

than 3,000 European settlers in the county, as well as African Americans, both free and enslaved.

The county's long agricultural history can be seen in museums and historic sites, and its rural character is still strong. Queen Anne's County is easily reached from Annapolis by taking Route 50 over the Bay Bridge, or by traveling south from Kent County along Route 213.

Kent Island

Once across the Bay Bridge, you'll be on a spit of land known as Kent Island, home to the small towns of Chester and Stevensville.

Chesapeake Exploration Center (all ages)

425 Piney Narrows Rd., Chester 21619; (410) 604-2100. Open Monday through Friday 8:30 a.m. to 4:30 p.m. and Saturday and Sunday 10 a.m. to 4 p.m. Free.

You and your family can pick up free guides to the area and check out the new interactive exhibits in the center—a fun way to learn about the region's historic, natural, and cultural charms. Photographs and items from the island's past are mixed with displays of bay history and facts. The Exploration Center is also one of the starting points for the Cross Island Trail.

Cross Island Trail (all ages)

425 Piney Narrows Rd., Chester 21619; (410) 604-2100. Open daily sunrise to sunset.

This flat, paved 5-mile path is ideal for biking or walking. Since it's short, the trail is a nice length for families with young children who can travel in bike carriers, or for older youngsters who can make the ride themselves. The trail travels west through canopied forests, across creeks, and past beautiful views of the Chesapeake. At the end, you and your family will be rewarded when you reach the Terrapin Nature Park, which has a 1-mile nature trail, sandy beaches, tidal ponds, wildflower meadows, and a boardwalk leading to the bay.

Grasonville

As you head off Kent Island onto the mainland, you will come to Grasonville on Route 50.

Chesapeake Bay Environmental Center (all ages)

600 Discovery Lane, Grasonville 21638; (410) 827-6694, (800) CANVASBACK, www.bay restoration.org. Open daily 9 a.m. to 5 p.m. Closed major holidays. $, children 4 and under free.

Children will be enchanted by the butterfly and hummingbird garden at the visitor center of this habitat, a mecca for bird lovers of all ages. The five-hundred-acre property has six

Amazing
Maryland Facts

Kent Island, founded in 1631, was the first English settlement in Maryland. Only the settlements at Plymouth Rock in Massachusetts and Jamestown in Virginia are older.

waterfowl ponds and an enclosed aviary. A boardwalk makes walking through the marsh easy for all ages, and blinds and two observation towers provide better viewing of the herons, egrets, and other birds. Educational programs are offered for children and adults throughout the year.

Where to Eat

Holly's. 108 Jackson Creek Rd., Grasonville; (410) 827-8711. Fried chicken, homemade ice cream, and more. $

The Narrows. 3023 Kent Narrows Way South, Grasonville; (410) 827-8113, www .thenarrowsrestaurant.com. Steaks, crab cakes, and much more in a dining room with beautiful views of the water. $$$.

Where to Stay

Sleep Inn. 101 VFW Ave., Grasonville; (410) 827-5555, www.sleepinn.com. Outdoor pool, in-room refrigerators, and free ice cream.

Comfort Inn. 3101 Main St., Grasonville; (800) 828-3361. Indoor heated pool and sauna, complimentary continental breakfast, water views from some rooms, kitchenettes with stove and full-size refrigerator, free continental breakfast. $$$

Queenstown

As you drive off Kent Island, your next stop on Route 50 is Queenstown, at the split where Route 50 heads south and Route 18 heads north.

Make the Car Ride **More Fun**

When crossing the Bay Bridge from Annapolis to Stevensville, ask the toll taker for a copy or two of the state's *Bay Game*, a **free** activity book for children that holds stickers, interesting facts about the bay, and information about points of interest along the way. You can also get it online at http://dnr. maryland.gov/baygame. Your kids will thank you!

Wye Island Natural Resources Management Area (all ages) 🚶 🚲 🐘

632 Wye Island Rd., Queenstown 21658; (410) 827-7577. Open sunrise to sunset. **Free.** From the Bay Bridge, go 12.5 miles eastbound on Route 50 and turn right onto Carmichael Road. After about 5 miles, you'll cross the Wye Island Bridge. From there, travel south on Wye Island Road for about 4.2 miles, then look for a spot in the public parking areas along Wye Island Road.

On those winter days when you just have to get out of the house, why not take a trip to Wye Island so your children can see some wildlife that hasn't gone south for the winter? Located in the tidal recesses of the Chesapeake Bay, this 2,400-acre sanctuary is an important home to wintering waterfowl.

Of course, there are creatures to see in all seasons. The best way to see the animals is to take your children on some of the 6 miles of flat hiking trails. Though the trails are not difficult, they can get muddy in winter and early spring. The two most popular routes are the Ferry Point Trail, a 1.1-mile walk to a sandy beach with a picnic area, and the Schoolhouse Woods Nature Trail, which is 1.2 miles long and takes you and your children through old-growth forest.

Keep your eyes open for such creatures as bald eagles and the endangered Delmarva fox squirrel. As always, pack water and snacks.

Centreville

Once you're off of Kent Island, you can take Route 18 north and east to Centreville, the county seat.

Museum of Eastern Shore Life (ages 3 and up)

126 Dulin Clark Rd., Centreville 21617; (410) 758-1419, www.mesl.us. Open April to October, Saturday and Sunday 1 to 4 p.m., or by appointment anytime. **Free,** but donations suggested.

See a reconstructed blacksmith shop, antique farm tools, a 1913 Peerless tractor, watermen's tools, and other artifacts of Eastern Shore life. Special events include a spring festival and a holiday-season train show.

Where to Eat

Colosseum Pizza. 112 North Commerce St., Centreville; (410) 758-1800. Pizza and other Italian favorites. $

Here's the Scoop. 635 Railroad Ave., Centreville, (410) 758-4006. Ice cream. $

For More Information

Town of Centreville. 101 Lawyer's Row, Centreville 21617; (410) 758-1180, www .townofcentreville.org

Sudlersville

To get to tiny Sudlersville from Centreville, take Route 213 north to Route 300 east.

Sudlersville Train Station Museum (ages 3 and up)

101 Linden St., Sudlersville 21668; (410) 438-3501. Open by appointment. **Free.**

If your children like baseball or train stations, consider a detour to this 1885 train station, which is now a museum with memorabilia from Baseball Hall of Famer Jimmy Fo, born in Sudlersville in 1907. You'll also find exhibits relating to Sudlersville history.

Wye Mills

The small town of Wye Mills is south of Queenstown on Route 50.

Wye Grist Mill and Museum (ages 4 and up)

14296 Old Wye Mills Rd. (Route 662), Wye Mills 21679; (410) 827-6909. Open April through October, Monday through Thursday 10 a.m. to 1 p.m., Friday through Sunday 10 a.m. to 4 p.m. **Free,** but donation suggested.

The museum at this real working mill tells the story of its boom years, 1790 to 1830. Kids will enjoy watching the water-powered mill grind corn and wheat, which it does the first and third Saturday of each month. The picturesque spot is also nice for a picnic or freshwater fishing. Wye Mills Day, in October, features wagon rides, living history, crafts, music, and milling demonstrations.

Queen Anne and Ridgely

From Wye Mills, head west on Route 404 to get to the village of Queen Anne and its main attraction, Tuckahoe State Park, which extends into the town of Ridgely.

Adkins Arboretum (all ages)

12610 Eveland Rd., P.O. Box 100, Ridgely 21660; (410) 634-2847, www.adkinsarboretum .org. Arboretum open daily year-round; visitor center, gift shop, book store, and art gallery open Monday through Saturday 9 a.m. to 5 p.m. **Free,** $–$$ for programs.

Located in Tuckahoe State Park, this four-hundred-acre preserve has 4 miles of easy-to-walk trails that take children through wetlands, forests, and meadows. The arboretum staff periodically offers children's programs that combine stories, nature walks, and crafts. Children might learn how mother birds take care of their babies, or how to take care of a flower garden. These programs have a small fee. Call for details.

Tuckahoe State Park (all ages)

13070 Crouse Mill Rd., Queen Anne 21657; (410) 820-1668, www.dnr.state.md.us/public lands/eastern/tuckahoe.html. Open year-round, with camping from the end of April to the beginning of November. Free.

Young children will enjoy the playground of recycled tires, while older ones may be more interested in the hiking trails through this beautiful 3,800-acre park. A sixty-acre lake and the Tuckahoe Creek, which runs the length of the park, offer fishing and boating opportunities.

Canoes, kayaks, paddleboats, and mountain bikes can be rented between April and October, and guided canoe trips are offered throughout the year. Campsites and cabins are available, as are picnic areas. See if you and your children can spot bald eagles, beavers, ospreys, and blue herons.

Annual activities include a massive Easter egg hunt (more than 3,500 eggs) held in spring, and "outlaw days" in September, with wagon rides, gold panning, and an all-horse parade. Day camps are offered for children as young as age five.

For More Information

Queen Anne's County Chamber of Commerce. 1561 Postal Rd., P.O. Box 511, Chester 21619; (410) 643-8530, www.qacchamber .com.

Queen Anne's County Department of Business and Tourism. 425 Piney Narrows Rd., Chester 21619; (410) 604-2100, (888) 400-RSVP, www.qac.org.

Talbot County

From the swank, boat-crazy town of St. Michaels to the artsy little shops of Easton, Talbot County has something for everyone. Route 50 is the major artery. It will take you right into Easton. From there, you'll head west on Route 33 to get to St. Michaels.

Easton

Easton, with its many galleries and antiques shops, is considered a top destination for art lovers. It has plenty of fun shops for kids to explore, as well as a few attractions that will appeal to youngsters.

Academy Art Museum (ages 4 and up)

106 South St., Easton 21601; (410) 822-ARTS, www.art-academy.org. Open Monday and Friday 10 a.m. to 4 p.m., Tuesday,Wednesday, and Thursday 10 a.m. to 8 p.m. and Saturday 10 a.m. to 3 p.m. $, free on Wednesdays.

A recent exhibit on "the art of the toy" shows why this museum is wonderful for both children and adults. Because it is small, children can explore several exhibits without feeling overwhelmed. The building, about 150 years old, was once a schoolhouse.

Classes in dance, voice, ceramics, photography, and more are offered for children at all skill levels throughout the year.

Avalon Theatre (ages 7 and up)
40 East Dover St., Easton 21601; (410) 822-0345, www.avalontheatre.com.

This theater, a popular destination for concerts and performances, hosts summer drama camps for kids seven to fifteen, as well as summer workshops for kids seven to twelve.

Pickering Creek Audubon Center (all ages)
11450 Audubon Lane, Easton 21601; (410) 822-4903, www.pickeringcreek.org. Trails open daily, dawn to dusk; office with some exhibits open Monday through Friday 9 a.m. to 5 p.m., Saturday 10 a.m. to 4 p.m. Free.

From the Children's Imagination Garden to the deep-water pier, freshwater pond, and classrooms with live reptiles, Pickering Creek is a natural wonderland designed with children in mind.

In the herb garden, kids can pull out herbs and smell and taste them. In the imagination garden, they can see flowers and plants that represent every letter of the alphabet. In the prehistoric garden, they can explore a pond in the shape of a dinosaur's footprint, surrounded by plants believed to be growing in prehistoric times.

At the office, you can pick up a guide to the kids' hiking trail, which is just under a mile long, and see the live animals on display. At the waterman's shanty, kids can touch tongs and other tools of the trade and see crabs in season. Other attractions include goats, honeybees, and a picnic area.

Summer "ecocamps" are offered for children in second through eighth grades, and programs are offered year-round for children as young as age two.

Where to Eat

Old Towne Creamery. 9B Goldsborough St., Easton; (410) 820-5223. Great ice cream with homemade whipped cream. $

Washington Street Pub. 20 North Washington St., Easton; (410) 822-9011. Pubby atmosphere with burgers, noshes, and a kids' menu. $

Amazing Maryland Facts

The blue crab became the state's official crustacean in 1989.

Where to Stay

Comfort Inn. 8523 Ocean Gateway, Easton; (410) 820-8333. Complimentary breakfast and an outdoor pool and hot tub are among the amenities. $$, Children eighteen and under stay free with parents.

St. Michaels

St. Michaels, situated on the broad Miles River, is famous as a boating destination. It's crowded with interesting shops, restaurants, and ice-cream parlors. For children, there is the Maritime Museum in St. Michaels, plus plenty of beaches and parks. Get there by taking Route 33 west from Easton.

When my family is in St. Michaels, we like simply to walk around town, checking out the boats that are docked in the marinas, browsing in a store or two, stopping for an ice cream at Justine's (101 Talbot St.; 410-745-5416). The kids enjoy the shady playground in Hollis Park, a short walk from the Maritime Museum. It's shaped like a boat, of course.

Chesapeake Bay Maritime Museum (ages 2 and up)

Mill Street, Navy Point, St. Michaels 21663; (410) 745-2916, www.cbmm.org. Open daily year-round, 10 a.m. to 5 p.m. in spring and fall, 10 a.m. to 6 p.m. in summer, 10 a.m. to 4 p.m. Friday through Monday January 15 through April 3. $–$$, kids 6 and under free.

Ships, decoys, and an aquarium are among the exhibits at this interactive, kid-friendly museum, which also teaches youngsters about oystering and about the life cycle of Maryland's famed blue crab. In all, there are nine buildings arrayed along the waterfront in St. Michaels, including the Hooper Strait Lighthouse, which you can climb. Miniature versions of a skipjack and workboat, complete with instrument panels and masts, are made for small hands to touch and explore.

Where to Eat

Chesapeake Cove. 204 South Talbot St., St. Michaels; (410) 745-3300. Fresh seafood, sandwiches, fried chicken, and other good, basic fare in one of the more casual restaurants to be found in the heart of St. Michaels. Kids' menu. $

St. Michaels Crab and Steak House. 305 Mulberry St., St. Michaels; (410) 745-3737, www.stmichaelscrabhouse.com. As the name implies, crabs and steaks take up plenty of space on the menu, but there are also sandwiches, salads, and a kids' menu. $$

Amazing
Maryland Facts

St. Michaels, settled in the 1670s, became known as "the town that fooled the British" during the War of 1812. As British warships massed for an attack, locals extinguished the lights in their homes and hung their lanterns on trees and masts, so that the British from the water would miscalculate the town's location.

Where to Stay

Best Western. St. Michaels Motor Inn, 1228 South Talbot St., St. Michaels; (410) 745-3333, (800) 466-0100, www.bestwestern.com. Located 1 mile from downtown, this hotel has two outdoor pools and offers a complimentary continental breakfast and Internet access. Suites, cribs, and rollaway beds are available. $$, children seventeen and under stay **free** with parents.

The Inn at Perry Cabin. 308 Watkins Lane, St. Michaels, (410) 745-2200, www.perry cabin.com/web/omic/inn_at_perry_cabin. jsp. An indulgence for the whole family, this fabulous inn and spa boasts amazing views of the bay, incredible restaurants, and on-site pampering at the Linden Spa. Spacious suites provide plenty of elbow room for kids and adults. $$$$.

Tilghman

Continuing past St. Michaels on Route 33 will take you to Tilghman, a narrow finger of land pointing into the Chesapeake.

What Is a Skipjack?

Skipjacks are sailboats, but they are very special sailboats, ones that were created specifically for dredging oysters from the Chesapeake Bay. First constructed in the late 1800s, the boats were designed to maneuver in all parts of the Chesapeake, even in water as shallow as 3 feet. They were built with thick timbers, which made them sturdy but slow. It is believed that skipjacks got their name from a type of fish called a skipjack, better known these days as a bluefish. Like their namesake boats, these fish can skim the surface of the water.

In the 1890s, the Chesapeake's fleet of skipjacks numbered in the hundreds. Today, the few skipjacks that remain are used mostly for educational tours.

A Ferry Nice Way to Travel

Consider taking the **Oxford–Bellevue Ferry** from Oxford to Bellevue. Even though the seven- to ten-minute boat ride is not necessary (you can easily drive by car), it is fun for the children, who can watch birds hover overhead and feel the spray of the water on their faces. Established in 1683, it is considered the oldest privately operated ferry service in the United States. You can put your car on the ferry, or do what many people do: Take your bike. St. Michaels is 7 miles away from Bellevue. The ferry departs from a wharf next to the Robert Morris Inn. For a schedule, go to www.oxfordbellevueferry.com or call (410) 745-9023.

Chesapeake Bay Skipjack (ages 3 and up)

21308 Phillips Rd., Tilghman 21671, docked at the Dogwood Harbor on Tilghman Island; (410) 829-3976, (410) 886-2176, www.skipjack.org. Boat leaves at 11 a.m. and 5:30 p.m. daily, plus 1 and 3 p.m. on Saturday. $$$–$$$$.

Ever hear of the Oyster Wars? These took place in the late nineteenth century, when arguments over oyster-dredging rights between Maryland and Virginia got so ugly that sometimes actual shots were fired. You can hear about these battles, as well as other nautical adventures and discussions of the environment, from Capt. Wade H. Murphy Jr. during a two-hour ride aboard his 1886 skipjack, the *Rebecca T. Ruark.*

Bring a picnic or snacks, as well as cameras and questions. Murphy, a third-generation waterman, is renowned for his knowledge of the region. He'll even let you dredge for oysters, now that the Oyster Wars are over.

Bozman

From St. Michaels, get to Bozman by taking Route 579 (Bozman Leavitt Road) south along a narrow spit of land surrounded by Harris Creek on one side and Broad Creek on the other.

Jean Ellen duPont Shehan Audubon Sanctuary (all ages)

23000 Wells Point Rd., Bozman 21612; (410) 745-9283, www.audubonmddc.org. Open every Monday 9 a.m. to 4 p.m., and the last Sunday of the month from noon to 4 p.m. Free, but some programs charge a small fee.

Monarch butterflies, red fox, wild turkey, and wood ducks are among the animals that call this 950-acre sanctuary home. Run by the National Audubon Society, it has more than 10 miles of trails for hiking and biking and a freshwater pond for exploring. Summer camps are offered for kids in kindergarten through ninth grade. One called Sanctuary Sleuths lets kindergardeners and first graders "solve animal mysteries" by looking for tracks and clues.

For More Information

Talbot County Chamber of Commerce. Easton Plaza Shopping Center, 101 Marlboro Ave., Suite 53, Easton 21601-1366; (410) 822-4606, www.tourtalbot.org.

Caroline County

Caroline County, created in 1773 from Dorchester and Queen Anne's counties, was named for Lady Caroline Eden, the daughter of Charles Calvert and wife of Maryland's last colonial governor.

Though the county is the only one on the Eastern Shore without shoreline on the Atlantic or Chesapeake, it still boasts many water activities, thanks to the Choptank and Tuckahoe rivers. The main towns here are Denton and Ridgely. Denton, incorporated in 1802, is the county seat, and Ridgely was established as a planned community in the rail-roading boom that followed the Civil War.

We'll focus on Denton, the largest town in this rural county.

Denton

Denton, a small town along the Choptank River in the heart of Caroline County, is easily reached by taking Route 313 south from Queen Anne's County, or by taking Route 50 to Wye Mills, then heading east on Route 404 for about 15 miles. The downtown business district is a hub of commerce for the surrounding rural areas.

Choptank River Heritage Center and Joppa Wharf Museum (ages 3 and up)

10215 River Landing Rd., Denton 21629; (410) 479-4950, www.riverheritage.org. Open May through September, Friday and Saturday, 11 a.m. to 3 p.m.; specific programs for children held on request. Free, $ for programs.

This museum is designed as a replica of an 1883 steamboat terminal and wharf along the Choptank River. There is one skipjack along the wharf and another that serves as a land-based exhibit. Children can explore the boats, look at old photographs, and look at the re-created warehouse space and offices.

Martinak State Park (all ages)

137 Deep Shore Rd., Denton 21629; (410) 820-1668, www.dnr.state.md.us. Open daily year-round. Free.

Fishing and boating on the Choptank River and Watts Creek are popular activities at this park, but you and your kids will have fun even if you don't go near the water. A picnic area with tables, playground, and restrooms overlooks the Choptank, and there are cabins and campsites for overnight stays. Programs offered throughout the year include Park Pals activities (craft, game, snack, story, etc.) for children ages four to six, and Junior Ranger programs for children ages seven to twelve. Some activities have a fee.

Museum of Rural Life (ages 3 and up)

16 North Second St., Denton 21629; (410) 479-2055, www.tourcaroline.com/pdfs/museum_ rack_card_2006.pdf. Call for museum hours or to arrange a tour. Free, donations accepted.

This small museum tells the unique story of Caroline County, one of the very few counties in the entire United States to develop with no industry other than agriculture for more than three centuries. For children, guides often tell what life was like for youngsters of yore in Caroline County. Don't miss the stuffed chicken. In its prime, this winged wonder was a second-place egg-laying champ for the region.

Where to Eat

Colosseum Pizza and Subs. 146 Denton Plaza, Denton; (410) 479-4600. Pizza and other Italian food to eat in or take out. $

Market Street Public House. 200 Market St., Denton; (410) 479-4720, www.public houseonline.com. Breakfast, lunch, and dinner to carry out or eat in. Everything from sandwiches and salads to prime rib, rockfish, and crab cakes. $–$$

Where to Stay

Holiday Park. Drapers Mill Road, Greensboro; (410) 482-6797. This two-hundred-site campground has lots of activities for children, including a large swimming pool, a game room, four playgrounds, a miniature-golf course, a basketball court, and more. It borders the Choptank River and has trails for hiking and biking. Planned activities, such

as hayrides or Gospel music concerts, are offered on weekends. $

Riverside Hotel. 204 North Main St., Greensboro; (410) 482-7100, www.anywhere gourmet.com/GreensboroMD/RiversideHotel. aspx. The rooms are spacious, and the hotel is happy to add cots to accommodate family members. The hotel's charms include a nice location on the Choptank River and two on-site restaurants that serve breakfast, lunch, and dinner, plus Sunday brunch. $$–$$$

For More Information

Caroline County Office of Tourism. 317 Carter Ave., Denton 21629; (410) 479-0655, www.tourcaroline.com.

Town of Denton. 13 North Third St., Denton 21629; (410) 479-2050, www.denton maryland.com.

Dorchester County

Bounded by the Chesapeake Bay and Choptank River, Dorchester County is a rural place with one major hub: Cambridge. For the most part, the county consists of small towns and wide-open spaces, great for families to explore by bicycle or boat.

Cambridge

Cambridge, the county seat and largest city in Dorchester, is right on Route 50, about 50 miles south of the Bay Bridge. It's on the south side of the Choptank River, just over the Senator Malkus Jr. Bridge.

Blackwater National Wildlife Refuge (all ages)

2145 Key Wallace Dr., Cambridge 21613; (410) 228-2677, www.friendsofblackwater.org, www.blackwaterfws.gov. Visitor center open 8 a.m. to 4 p.m. Monday through Friday, 9 a.m. to 5 p.m. weekends. $.

This 23,000-acre refuge, located 12 miles south of Cambridge, is home to more than one hundred eagles, the endangered Delmarva fox squirrel, ducks, and shorebirds. One way to look for them is to take the 6½-mile loop drive through the park. Walking and bicycling are allowed on the road. Other walking trails go on an 80-foot boardwalk into the marsh and through woods and fields. Interpretive trail leaflets are available at the visitor center, which also has nature exhibits and films. Boating is permitted April 1 to October 30.

Harriet Tubman

Born a slave in Dorchester County, Harriet Tubman became one of the most important figures in American history. She escaped slavery when she was thirty, then put her life at risk again and again to return south and free hundreds of other slaves. She helped create the Underground Railroad, a system of save havens for slaves fleeing north. Her achievements are even more remarkable because she suffered from narcolepsy caused by a blow to the head when she was still a slave. This meant she would fall asleep without warning—certainly a handicap for someone who freed the enslaved.

The Harriet Tubman Organization at 424 Race St. in Cambridge (410-228-0401) provides tours of places connected to Tubman and presents videos about her life. It also operates a gift shop.

A stretch of Route 50 that runs through Cambridge is dedicated to Tubman.

The Harriet Tubman Memorial Garden near the intersection of Route 50 and Washington Street has interpretive signs and a mural.

Her birthplace is noted by a marker on Bucktown Road (also known as Route 397), 8 miles south of Cambridge and Route 50.

The Annie Oakley **House**

Annie Oakley, who lived from 1860 to 1926, is remembered as a woman of the American West, a champion shooter, and the star of Buffalo Bill's Wild West show. Her only surviving residence is in Cambridge, Maryland. She and her husband, Frank Butler, lived there from 1913 to 1917. The house at 28 Bellevue Ave. is a private residence and is *not* open to the public. But you're welcome to look at it from the street.

James B. Richardson Maritime Museum (ages 3 and up)

401 High St., Cambridge 21613; (410) 221-1871, www.richardsonmuseum.org. Open Wednesday and Sunday 1 to 4 p.m.; Saturday 10 a.m. to 4 p.m. or by appointment. **Free,** donations accepted.

Models of actual boats used to harvest oysters and crabs make this a fun museum for both kids and adults. The museum, located in an eighteenth-century bank building in the heart of town, is named for a boatbuilder who died in 1991. In addition to the ships, there are photographs, tools, and a model-building shop, where youngsters can watch models being made.

Sailwinds Park (all ages)

200 Byrn St., Cambridge 21613; (410) 228-SAIL, www.sailwinds.org. Open Monday through Friday, 9 a.m. to 5:30 p.m. **Free.**

From waterfront fireworks on the Fourth of July to concerts to the Delmarva Chicken Festival (a celebration of the local poultry industry), it seems like there's always an event or activity at Sailwinds Park, a 14,000-square-foot facility overlooking the Choptank River. There's also a playground here where kids can work off some energy after a long drive. Call or visit the Web site for details about events.

Where to Eat

Cambridge Diner and Restaurant. 2924 Old Rd. 50, Cambridge; (410) 228-8898. Very pleasant diner with an extensive, inexpensive menu. Children's menu. $

Millie's at the Point. 1-A Sunburst Hwy, Cambridge; 410-228-9873. Home cooking. $.

Where to Stay

Holiday Inn Express. 2715 Ocean Gateway, Cambridge; (410) 221-9900. Indoor pool and hot tub, complimentary breakfast, rooms with cable television, and free morning newspapers. Suites and rooms with two beds are available. $$$

Hyatt Regency Chesapeake Bay. 100 Heron Blvd., Cambridge; (410) 901-1234. A destination that is a vacation in itself, this new four-hundred-room resort has a golf course, marina, spa, and an indoor-outdoor pool with a two-story waterslide. There's even a day camp for kids four to twelve, and an outdoor playground. $$$$

For More Information

Dorchester County Department of Tourism. 2 Rose Hill Place, Cambridge 21613; (410) 228-1000, (800) 522-TOUR, www.tourdorchester.com.

Wicomico County

The name of this county comes from Native-American words meaning "place where houses are built" because English and Scottish settlers came in the 1600s to build homes and start farms. Today, much of the county outside of Salisbury remains rural.

Salisbury

Salisbury, the largest town on the Eastern Shore, is the focal point of Wicomico County and home to many kid-friendly attractions, including the Salisbury Zoo and the Ward Museum of Wildfowl Art. The historic downtown has a pedestrian-only area with fun shops and several family restaurants. Salisbury can be reached by car by taking Route 50 south from Dorchester County.

Salisbury City Park (all ages)

755 South Park Dr., Salisbury 21802; (410) 548-3188, www.salisburyzoo.org. Open daily dawn to dusk. Free.

The forty-one-acre park is home to the Salisbury Zoo, and it also has two play structures, six tennis courts, a lake, and about 6 miles of walking trails—plenty to keep your gang happily occupied for hours. In the summer, concerts are often held at the park's bandstand, and a tree-lighting celebration is held in early December.

Salisbury Zoo (all ages)

755 South Park Dr., Salisbury 21802; (410) 548-3188, www.salisburyzoo.org. Open daily 8 a.m. to 7:30 p.m. Memorial Day through Labor Day; 8 a.m. to 4:30 p.m. the rest of the year. Closed Christmas Day and Thanksgiving. Free.

From the sleek jaguar to the pair of playful otters, the animals at this cozy zoo will delight children of all ages. The zoo has more than four hundred specials of animals, but it is small, so you can explore the whole thing in a single afternoon, even with small children. Programs include story times appropriate for preschoolers and one-week camps for kids entering kindergarten through fifth grade.

Ward Museum of Wildfowl Art (ages 5 and up)

909 South Schumaker Dr., Salisbury 21804; (410) 742-4988, www.wardmuseum.org. Open Monday through Saturday 10 a.m. to 5 p.m., Sunday noon to 5 p.m. Closed Easter, Thanksgiving, and Christmas. $–$$, preschoolers free.

For a form of art that kids can readily understand, visit this museum. Duck decoys were once created for the simple purpose of luring ducks. No more. Now, thanks in part to brothers Lem and Steve Ward of Crisfield, decoy making is serious art. The Ward Museum, named for the brothers, showcases decoys from the Eastern Shore and explores the history of decoy making and other wildfowl art. The museum is considered the premier place for wildfowl art. After kids get their fill of the fake birds, they can watch real ones on the man-made pond.

Where to Eat

Adam's Rib. 219 North Fruitland Blvd., Salisbury; (410) 749-6161. All-American fare including ribs and burgers. Children's menu. $–$$

Pizza City. 301 East Carroll St., Salisbury; (410) 546-3800. Pizza and other Italian favorites in a pleasant and casual setting. $–$$

Where to Stay

Best Value Inn. 2625 North Salisbury Blvd., Salisbury; (410) 742-7194, (888) 315-BEST, www.bestvalueinn.com. Outdoor pool, complimentary breakfast and newspaper, on-site Indian restaurant. $$$

Microtel Inn and Suites. 3050 Merritt Mill Rd., Salisbury; (410) 742-2628, (888) 771-7171. Amenities here include a continental breakfast, guest laundry, and cribs upon request. Suites sleep four and have a kitchenette. $$, children under sixteen stay free.

For More Information

Wicomico County Convention and Visitors Bureau. P.O. Box 2333, Salisbury, 21802; (410) 548-4914, www.wicomicotourism.org.

Worcester County

Located to the south and west of the Eastern Shore, Worcester County is easily reached by taking Route 50 east from Salisbury. The county, of course, is best known for Ocean City, but other small towns have attractions for children, too.

Once you leave the razzmatazz of Ocean City, things get quiet in a hurry. Consider spending an afternoon fishing, bike riding, or just splashing in the surf. See the wild ponies at Assateague Island, or look for tiny treasures in the surf.

And when you want a break from all that nature, visit the towns of Berlin, Snow Hill, and Pocomoke City. The movies *Tuck Everlasting* and *Runaway Bride* were both filmed in Berlin's picturesque downtown. Snow Hill has more than one hundred houses that are over a century old. Pocomoke City, on the banks of the Pocomoke River, was once an important shipbuilding community and is still defined by the river.

Ocean City

Ocean City, basically a barrier island sandwiched between the Chesapeake and Atlantic, was a small fishing village when it was incorporated in 1875. Today it's one of the smaller cities in the state, with an off-season population of only 8,000. But this small community is a wonderful family destination, featuring block after block of fun things to do. In the summer, the population swells to about 300,000. In addition to the beach and boardwalk, "OC" is loaded with amusement parks, waterslides, miniature-golf courses, ice-cream stands, and playgrounds.

This is the place to go fishing for a day, rent a bicycle, take a nature boat cruise, or just fly a kite. More adventurous families can rent Jet Skis or go parasailing. When the hustle and bustle of the boardwalk gets tiring, escape to Assateague, where wild ponies roam the beaches.

Though Ocean City is primarily a sunny-day resort, there are things to do when it rains or even when it's cold out. Visit the Ocean City Life-Saving Station Museum to learn the fascinating history of this resort town, or take in the sights at Ripley's Believe It or Not on Boardwalk.

One caveat, however. Though Ocean City is popular with families, it is also a play-ground for young adults. Be advised that in the summer months you'll see celebrations of alcohol and scanty clothing, on everything from T-shirts to the contests that are held at local bars. You can't escape them entirely, but if you avoid the bar scene you'll miss the worst of it.

Getting around Ocean City is easy. The main driving road is Coastal Highway, and the main walking road is the Boardwalk. Ocean City is bordered to the north by the Delaware border at 146th Street and continues south, with numbers going down, to the inlet and South Division Street. Boardwalk starts at Twenty-seventh Street.

Buses take passengers up and down Coastal Highway for a small daily charge, and trams take tired walkers to their Boardwalk destinations. The tram operates Easter through September.

Amazing
Maryland Facts

On August 23, 1933, a massive four-day storm literally changed the shape of Ocean City by separating it from what is now Assateague Island. This act of nature was incredibly destructive, but it made Ocean City what it is today by creating a direct link to the ocean and opening the market for both commercial and sport fishing.

Assateague Island Nature Cruise with Discovery Cruises
(ages 2 and up)

First Street on Bay at BJ's South Bayfront Bar and Restaurant, Ocean City; (410) 289-2700. Cruises depart at 8:30 a.m., 10 a.m., noon, 2 p.m., and 4 p.m. from late June to early September; in May and June and in fall (weather permitting), cruises depart at 10 a.m., noon, and 2 p.m. $$–$$$, children under 5 **free.**

This ninety-minute boat ride is ideal for children because it has so many hands-on activities. Parents will enjoy it, too, because the knowledgeable naturalists who conduct the tours provide lots of history and information about Ocean City and the waters surrounding it. After the boat cruises around Assateague so its passengers can search for wild ponies, the boat docks on Assateague Island. Everyone goes ashore and is given a net so they can search for sea creatures in the damp sand. On the way back, the naturalist discusses what was found and passes around starfish and sea urchins for the kids to touch. The creatures are then returned to the water. Restrooms are on board.

Assateague Adventure/OC Rocket (ages 4 and up)

311 Talbot St., Ocean City 21842; (410) 289-3500, www.talbotstreetpier.com/boatrides. Open May through October, schedule varies. $$$, children under 4 **free.**

During the ninety-minute narrated Assateague Adventure cruise, you and your family will see ponies, birds, and maybe even dolphins as you ride to Assateague Island and get off the boat to explore. Kids can pull a crab pot out of the water and touch the live animals in the touch tank on board.

To satisfy your thrill seekers, this company also hosts fifty-minute OC Rocket tours aboard superfast powerboats that provide an exhilarating wind-in-the-face water tour.

Boardwalk (all ages)

Starts at the inlet and stretches 3 miles to Twenty-seventh Street, along the ocean. Open all the time, though most of the businesses and attractions are seasonal. **Free.**

The boardwalk was first built in 1910 and still has all the over-the-top charm of an old-fashioned carnival. There are rides, games, retail shops, and of course lots of food. The boardwalk is anchored at the inlet side by Trimper's Rides and Amusements (Boardwalk and South First Street, 410-289-8617), which has been in business since 1890. Trimper's has around fifty rides and is best known for its roller coaster, Ferris wheels, and restored 1902 carousel. Trimper's is open noon to midnight weekends, 1 p.m. to midnight during the week. Outdoor rides open as early as mid-April and don't close until mid-November.

Indoor rides, including a kiddie carousel and bumper cars, are open year-round.

Next to Trimper's is Marty's Playland (410-289-7271, open year-round) with more than 250 arcade and video games.

Don't miss the two Fisher's Popcorn stands at Seventh Street and Talbot Street. The Fisher family has been selling warm, caramel-covered popcorn since 1937. Another favorite is Thrasher's French Fries (between Wicomico and Worcester Streets), which sells what some consider the best fries anywhere.

A Good Guide

Pick up a copy of the *Ocean City Visitors Guide*, available at many restaurants and hotels, for discounts on a wide range of restaurants, attractions, and stores.

Finally, stop by the Kite Loft at Fifth Street (as well as other locations in Ocean City) to see the beautiful, multicolored creations flutter in the wind.

Grand Prix Family Amusements (ages 3 and up)

12639 Ocean Gateway, West Ocean City 21842; (410) 213-1278, www.grandprixoc.com. Open 9 a.m. to 11 p.m. May through September; hours vary in spring and fall. $ per 3 minutes of riding.

This park boasts seven go-kart tracks, plus bumper-boat rides and a play area for toddlers. Kids eight and older can ride the go-karts by themselves, and younger ones can go with a paying adult. There's also a snack bar selling reasonably priced kid-friendly food.

Jolly Roger Amusement Park (ages 2 and up)

Thirtieth Street and Coastal Highway, Ocean City 21843; (410) 289-9100, www.jollyroger park.com. Open Memorial Day weekend to Labor Day, 2 p.m. to midnight. No charge to enter, pay for the rides, $$$$.

This large family entertainment center is a favorite with my family because so many of the rides are appropriate for young children. The amusement park has a kid-size Ferris wheel, a train ride, a carousel, and other rides that range from the slightly scary Wild Mouse roller coaster to the totally mild bumper boats.

The park also has two miniature-golf courses, plus an enormous water park called Splash Mountain (open 10 a.m. to 8 p.m.), which has water-tube rides and enormous slides for older kids, plus a 2-foot-deep splash pool and a watery playground for the not-able-to-swim-yet crowd.

Speed World (open noon to midnight Memorial Day weekend to Labor Day, noon to 6 p.m. April, May, and September, plus October weekends) is also part of the same park. It features cars and boats, ranging from the very tame bumper boats to the challenging bullet cars on the speed track. A "kiddie track" is somewhere in between. Pay by the ride.

Ocean City Life-Saving Station Museum (ages 3 and up)

Boardwalk at the Inlet, P.O. Box 603, Ocean City 21843; (410) 289-4991, www.ocmuseum .org. Open daily June through September, 11 a.m. to 10 p.m.; open daily May and October 11 a.m. to 4 p.m.; open winter weekends 11 a.m. to 4 p.m. $.

Even if the sun never stops shining during your visit to Ocean City, take some time away from the beaches and amusement parks to visit this cool museum. The fun starts with the large taxidermy-ized shark in a glass case by the entrance (1,210 pounds, caught in 1983), and continues with exhibits of turtles, starfish, and other sea creatures. Go up the stairs for exhibits about the heroism of the U.S. Lifesaving Service and about the storms that literally shaped Ocean City by altering the shoreline.

Other exhibits include a doll-house-scale model of Ocean City in 1935, displays about Victorian-era bathing suits, mermaids, and artifacts recovered from shipwrecks, and vials of sand from all over the world. Free educational programs are offered in July and August.

Old Pro Golf (ages 4 and up)

Several locations in Ocean City; (888) OLD-PRO1, (410) 524-2645, www.oldprogolf.com. Open 9 a.m. to 1 a.m. in season, Sixty-eighth Street location open year-round. $, children 2 and under free.

Several themed courses, including an indoor one for rainy days, make Old Pro a logical destination for miniature golf in Ocean City. Check out Temple of Dragons at Twenty-third Street, Renaissance Castle at Twenty-eighth Street, Prehistoric Dinosaurs and Undersea Adventure at Sixty-eighth Street, or Pirate Ship, African Safari, and Polynesian Garden at 136th Street. The Undersea Adventure is indoors, heated, and open year-round. Arcades can be found at Sixty-eighth Street and 136th Street.

Planet Maze & Laser Storm (ages 2 and up)

Thirty-third Street and Coastal Highway, Ocean City 21842; (410) 524-4FUN, www.planet maze.com. Open 9 a.m. to midnight year-round. $$ per attraction.

This park is actually three attractions. Children must be eight or older for Laser Storm, a game in which players put on special suits and battle for points in a laser-beam shoot-out played in an indoor arena. Planet Maze, for children ages two to ten, has giant slides, crawl-through tubes, and foam forests to explore. Children must wear socks to play at Planet Maze. An alien-theme eighteen-hole miniature-golf course, called Lost Galaxy Golf, is at the same site. There's also a snack bar, called the Comet Café, as well as a video arcade.

Ripley's Believe It or Not (ages 5 and up)

401 Atlantic Ave., Ocean City 21842; (410) 289-5600, www.ripleys.com/oceancity.html. Open daily Memorial Day weekend to Labor Day, 9 a.m. to midnight; weekends in October, November, March, and April; closed December through February. $$, children 6 and under free.

Even before you go inside, Ripley's is a boardwalk attraction because of the large wiggling false shark that looks like it escaped through the roof. Inside, there are more than five

Save Money

With many Ocean City attractions, you can save a few dollars by checking the Web sites for coupons.

Ocean City Playgrounds

For all the activities and attractions at Ocean City, my kids, at ages three and six, may have liked the simple wooden play structures on the beach best of all. Shaped like a castle, an airplane, a tank, and other structures, these playgrounds in the sand along Boardwalk provide hours of entertainment, particularly in the cooler hours of the evening. And judging from the crowds of kids climbing and swinging on the structures each day, my children weren't the only ones who loved them.

Here are a couple of other favorite playgrounds:

- **Northside Park,** 125th Street and the bay, is the largest park, with sports fields, a fishing lagoon, two playground stuctures, two piers, and a concession stand. My family likes to walk along the pier and watch people catch crabs and fish.

- **Third Street Park** is also home to the Ocean Bowl Skate Park, a 17,000-square-foot concrete utopia of ramps and bowls. Skaters must wear protective gear, and they must be registered. Legal guardians must be present at registration for children under age eighteen. The skate park is open in the summer from 9 a.m. to dark, and in the fall and spring from 11:30 a.m. to dark weekdays and 9:30 a.m. to dark weekends. In the winter, it is open weekdays except Wednesday from 1:30 p.m. to dark, and weekends and no-school days from 9:30 a.m. to dark. Beginner hours are 9:30 to 11 a.m. daily in the summer. The cost is $$.

hundred freaky exhibits and strange sights, including some, such as shrunken heads, that may be a little too gross or scary for the very young or easily frightened.

65th Street Slide and Ride (ages 3 and up)

Sixty-fifth Street near the Bay, Ocean City; (410) 524-5270, www.slidenride.com. Open daily 10 a.m. Memorial Day to Labor Day. $ per attraction or half-hour waterslide pass.

The main attraction here is a triple-flume waterslide, but there are other waterslides, too, including a kiddie slide. Other attractions include miniature golf, bumper boats, batting cages, backshot basketball, a moon bounce, and a snack bar. To ride the King Kiddie slide, you must be "almost three years and almost 35 inches tall."

For all three of the slides, you must be "almost six years old and almost 46 inches tall."

Wheels of Yesterday Antique and Classic Cars Museum
(ages 3 and up)

12708 Ocean Gateway (Route 50), Ocean City 21842; (410) 213-7329, www.wheelsofyesterday .com. Open October through May 9 a.m. to 5 p.m., and June through September 9 a.m. to 9 p.m. $.

If members of your family like old cars, take them to this museum, which features about thirty of them, including a 1904 Oldsmobile, a 1957 Chevy, and a 1928 seven-passenger Lincoln. There's even a replica of a ca. 1950 service station. A gift shop sells car-related posters, books, and of course toy cars.

Where to Eat

Pizza joints, sub shops, ice-cream stands, and burger shacks seem to fill every square inch of Ocean City. In this supercasual beach town, nearly every spot is good for the family.

But here are a few popular options.

The Dough Roller (five Ocean City locations). South Division Street and Boardwalk, Third Street and Boardwalk, and Coastal Highway at Forty-first Street, Seventieth Street, and 124th Street. The Dough Roller serves hearty, inexpensive meals all day long. For breakfast, there are pancakes, French toast, omelets, and egg sandwiches. Later in the day, feast on pizzas, salads, and subs. At several locations, kids can pick out a small toy. Boardwalk stores don't take credit cards. $

Dumser's. 4901 Coastal Hwy (410-524-1588) and 12305 Coastal Highway (410-250-5543); Ocean City. A favorite in my family, this ice-cream stand, which dates from 1939, serves burgers, chicken tenders, and other kid-friendly fare as well as fantastic ice cream. On nice days, grab one of the picnic tables on the wooden deck. $

Mackey's. 5311 Coastal Hwy, Ocean City; (410) 723-5565. Like many Ocean City eateries, Mackey's is as much bar as restaurant, but its location on the bay and its efficient, friendly service make it a popular option for families tired of fast food. Kids can eat the usual chicken tenders and burgers if they don't like the adult menu of seafood, salads, and pasta. $$

Paul Revere Smorgasboard. Boardwalk and Second Street, Ocean City; (410) 524-1776. An enormous array of food, including seafood, barbecue, a salad bar, and desserts. $, kids four and under eat free.

Where to Stay

Ocean City has more than 10,000 hotel rooms and suites, but they fill up quickly during the height of the summertime season.

They also get pretty expensive, with rooms costing in excess of $250 the norm. Book your room early, and if you are planning to stay a week, you may want to rent an apartment or condominium. Realtors in town who can help with this include **Moore, Warfield and Glick** (877-RENTMWG, www .mwgbeach.com) and **Prudential Carruthers Realty** (800-638-3242, www.ocean cityresortproperties.com).

Carousel Resort Hotel. 118th Street and the ocean, Ocean City; (800) 641-0011, www .carouselhotel.com. This oceanfront hotel has it all, including an indoor pool, sauna, and whirlpool, a video arcade, and an ice-skating rink with ice shows. Options include condos of two or three bedrooms, hotel rooms, and deluxe hotel rooms. All have microwaves and refrigerators. A deli and restaurant are on the premises. $$$$

Comfort Inn Gold Coast. 112th Street and Coastal Highway, Ocean City; (410) 524-3000, (800) 228-5150; www.comfortgoldcoast.com. The hotel has an indoor pool and whirlpool as well as a restaurant and a convenience store in the lobby. Internet access. $$$$

Days Inn Oceanfront. Boardwalk at Twenty-third Street, Ocean City; (410) 289-7161, www.daysinnboardwalk.com. Outdoor pools including a kiddie pool, free daily newspaper. Rooms with refrigerators, microwaves, cable television. $$$$

For More Information

Ocean City Convention and Visitors Bureau. 4001 Coastal Hwy, Ocean City 21842; (410) 289-8181, www.ococean.com.

Ocean City Hotel–Motel–Restaurant Association. (410) 289-6733, (800) OC-OCEAN, www.ocvisitor.com.

Worcester County Tourism. P.O. Box 208, Snow Hill 21863; (800) 852-0335, www.visit worcester.org.

Berlin

To the west of Ocean City along Route 707 is the town of Berlin. The downtown, which has forty-seven structures on the National Register of Historic Places, is definitely worth a look.

Assateague State Park and Assateague Island National Seashore (all ages)

7303 Stephen Decatur Hwy, Berlin 21811; (410) 641-2120, www.nps.gov/asis/home.htm. Open daily 9 a.m. to 5 p.m. except Thanksgiving and Christmas. $.

What could be more enchanting to children than seeing wild ponies?

Assateague is run by the National Park Service in cooperation with Assateague State Park and the Chincoteague National Wildlife Refuge in Virginia. Maryland's only ocean park has 37 miles of beach and facilities for camping, hiking, fishing, swimming, biking, and kayaking, but the real attraction is the famous wild ponies that wander all over the place.

Legend has it these ponies swam to shore in the 1600s from a shipwrecked Spanish galleon, but they might also be descendants of domestic horses brought to the barrier island in the 1700s. No matter where they came from, these ponies are now wild and must be treated with respect. Feeding or touching the horses is forbidden. Park rangers roam the beaches, keeping the ponies away from people and their food.

Seasonal activities include a Junior Ranger program for kids six to fourteen and a Mini-Ranger Program for kids four and five. Kids can earn certificates by going on ranger-guided programs and completing activities in a book they pick up at the Barrier Island Visitor Center or the Toms Cove center in Virginia. A concession stand at the entrance to the Maryland state park sells ice cream, hamburgers, and the like. The Barrier Island Visitor Center has many exhibits, including an aquarium and touch tank.

A Nitkin Family **Adventure**

On a recent weeklong trip to Ocean City, my husband and I took the kids to Assateague for the day. I was one of those horse-crazy girls who read *Misty of Chincoteague*, the award-winning 1947 Marguerite Henry book about the wild ponies, a thousand times when I was thirteen, so seeing the shaggy, sturdy wild ponies on the beach was like a childhood fantasy come to life. My kids were too young to know about the book, and they weren't quite sure why mommy was getting all nostalgic, but they had a great time, too.

The beach itself was wonderful, sandy and soft, with just the right amount of surf for Ronnie and Sammy, who were five and two at the time. The wind was perfect for flying the kite that we purchased at the camping store.

Another youngster was collecting butterfly clams in a net and invited my daughter to join in the fun. They scooped up tiny sea creatures for a long time, glancing up every now and then when a wild pony appeared on the beach. At one point, a small group of the ponies even trampled the kids' sand castle.

We returned to Ocean City as the sun began to set. We were sandy, salty, tired, and very happy.

Frontier Town Western Theme Park (ages 3 and up)
8430 Stephen Decatur Highway, Berlin 21811; (410) 641-0057, www.frontiertown.com. Open daily 10 a.m. to 7 p.m. mid-June through Labor Day; Frontier Town Campground is open April to mid-October. $–$$, children 3 and under free.

Here's a Western-theme amusement park where children can pan for gold and watch live Wild West shows, as well as enjoy the traditional attractions of waterslides, pool, miniature golf, arcades, and more.

The Golf and Water Park in the same complex has waterslides and other wet attractions, plus an eighteen-hole miniature-golf course. Though there is separate admission to each park, combination tickets are available.

For More Information
Town of Berlin Chamber of Commerce.
10 William St., Berlin 21811; (410) 641-2770, www.berlinMdCC.org.

Snow Hill

The small town of Snow Hill can be reached by taking Route 113 south from Berlin.

Furnace Town Living Heritage Museum (ages 3 and up)

3816 Old Furnace Rd., Snow Hill 21863; (410) 632-2032, www.furnacetown.com. Open daily
April through October 10 a.m. to 5 p.m. $, children 2 and under **free.**

Every day, two or more artisans in nineteenth-century clothes perform such activities
as woodworking, gardening or broom making to show what life was like in this iron-
manufacturing village of three hundred. The twelve-acre site has twelve historic structures, including a church, a blacksmith shop, and a woodworker's shop that children
can go inside. There are picnic areas and walking trails that take children over bridges
that cross a cypress swamp. If they're quiet, youngsters might see turtles, deer, rac-
coons, woodpeckers, and other animals.

Julia A. Purnell Museum (ages 6 and up)

208 West Market St., Snow Hill 21863; (410) 632-0515, www.purnellmuseum.com. Open
April through October, Tuesday through Saturday 10 a.m. to 4 p.m., Sunday 1 to 4 p.m. $.

This museum, housed in an 1892 church, was named for a local artist and includes her
collection of needle art among its more than 10,000 pieces. Artifacts, exhibits, and programs tell you the story of the Eastern Shore, from the first Native Americans to the present day.

Mt. Zion One Room School (ages 3 and up)

Ironshire Street, Snow Hill 21863; (410) 632-1265, www.octhebeach.com/museum/Zion
.html. Open mid-June through August, Thursday through Saturday 1 to 4 p.m. $.

Moved in 1959 from rural Worcester County, this school is filled with donated artifacts like
a teacher's desk, a potbellied stove, and early textbooks—all of which will help kids see
how a typical schoolroom has changed over time.

Pocomoke River State Park (all ages)

3461 Worcester Hwy, Snow Hill 21863; (410) 632-2566. Office open 8 a.m. to sunset; closed
major holidays. **Free.**

Famous for its stand of loblolly pine and its cypress swamp, this park is also a nice place
to take kids out on a canoe, rowboat, or kayak. You can launch your own vessel at the
Shad Landing or Milburn Landing areas in the park, or rent a rowboat or canoe at the
Shad Landing Marina. The park has playgrounds, campsites, bike trails, a visitor center,
and a swimming pool. The pool ranges in depth from 3 to 12 feet, and is open on the
weekends starting Memorial Day and daily starting in mid-June. There is also a wading
pool for small children. There is no charge to use the pools. The concession stand operates May through September.

For More Information

Snow Hill Area Chamber of Commerce.
P.O. Box 176, Snow Hill 21863; (410) 632-0809, www.snowhillmd.com.

Pocomoke City

Pocomoke City can be reached by continuing south on Route 113 past Snow Hill.

Sturgis One Room School (ages 3 and up)

209 Willow St., Pocomoke City 21851; (410) 957-1913, www.octhebeach.com/museum/Sturgis.html. Open May to October, Wednesday and Saturday 1 to 4 p.m., or by appointment.

Artifacts in this restored century-old school showcase the history of the area as well as explain what African-American life was like here. It is the only African-American one-room schoolhouse in Worcester County that is intact as it was.

Somerset County

Beautiful Somerset County, on the southwestern tip of the Eastern Shore, is a watery, craggy place, almost a step back in time. Crabbing is the main engine that drives the economy here. In the town of Crisfield, on the water's edge, a painting of a crab adorns the water tower and the signs welcoming visitors to town. Why fight it? The best thing to do here is grab a table at one of the wharfside restaurants, order a mess of crabs, grab a mallet, and dig in.

Like other Eastern Shore counties, Somerset is mostly rural, with one major town. In this case, the town is Crisfield, on the very southwestern edge of the state.

Crisfield

The town of Crisfield is built on oysters—literally. Even before it was officially founded in 1872, many of the homes were built on piles of oyster shells that were used to fill in the swampy land. Today, billions of these shells form the base for much of the downtown area.

The centerpiece of Crisfield is the city dock, where boats loaded with crabs and other treasures of the sea still arrive. Naturally, seafood is the thing to eat here, and there are several casual restaurants where your kids can pound crabs with mallets to their hearts' content.

To get to Crisfield, follow Route 413 south until you see water and the dock in front of you and you can't go any farther.

J. Millard Tawes Historical Museum, Visitor's Center, and Gift Shop (ages 3 and up)

3 Ninth St. and the Somers Cove Marina, Crisfield 21817; (410) 968-2501, www.visitsomer set.com. Memorial Day through October, open Monday through Friday 9 a.m. to 4:30 p.m., weekends 10 a.m. to 3 p.m.; November through Memorial Day, open Monday through Friday 9 a.m. to 4:30 p.m. $, children 12 and under free.

The history of Crisfield and the Lower Shore are explored at this museum, which has exhibits on such prominent locals as the late Governor J. Millard Tawes and Curly Byrd, founder of the modern University of Maryland. The two great local arts—decoy carving and seafood harvesting—are also depicted. Kids will probably like the working crab shanty, a live demonstration of the soft-shell crab industry.

Janes Island State Park (ages 3 and up)

26280 Alfred Lawson Dr., Crisfield 21817; (410) 968-1565, www.dnr.state.md.us/public lands/eastern/janesisland.html. Open 8 a.m. to dusk in the summer, 8 a.m. to 4 p.m. in the winter; campgrounds available April to October, cabins open year-round. Closed major holidays. Free.

In the summer, the best way to experience Janes Island State Park is from the seat of a canoe or kayak, with plenty of bug spray and sunscreen slathered on. The park is mostly

Smith Island

Maryland's only inhabited offshore island is actually a group of islands that form three communities: Ewell, Tylerton, and Rhodes Point. The entire island has about three hundred residents, who must travel about an hour by boat to reach the mainland at Crisfield.

There is no hospital here, no movie theater, no police station. People get around on bicycles and golf carts, and nearly everyone relies on crabbing for a living. In Ewell, the largest town, the **Smith Island Visitor's Center Cultural Museum and Gift Shop** (20846 Caleb Jones Rd., 410-425-3351, 410-651-2292) provides insights into the long history of the island, first settled in 1657. The museum has exhibits on the role of women in island life and the distinctive speech patterns that are found on Smith Island. It is open daily April through October, noon to 4 p.m., and from November to April on Wednesday and Saturday, noon to 4 p.m.

To get to Smith Island, take one of several boats that depart from the Crisfield wharf at the end of Route 413. All cost approximately $20 round-trip.

The **Captain Jason II** (410-425-4471) goes to both Ewell and Tylerton.

Smith Island Day Cruises (410-425-2771) has boats that leave from Crisfield and from Point Lookout in Southern Maryland.

marshes with several water trails through them. There are trails that take you to sandy beaches, or you can go out in a canoe and enjoy the serenity of the still water and the open sky. Boats can be rented at the camping store during camping season. Day-use amenities include a picnic area, playground, volleyball court, and nature center with reptiles and some toys.

Tangier Island Cruises (ages 3 and up)

1001 West Main St., Crisfield 21817; (410) 968-2338, www.tangierisland-va.com/steven thomas. Departs daily mid-May through mid-October from the dock at Tangier Island Cruises. $$$.

Kids can learn about the floating and flying creatures of the Chesapeake Bay aboard a three-hundred-passenger boat.

Where to Eat

Captain's Galley Restaurant. Main Street and City Dock, Crisfield; (410) 968-3313. Great crabs, crab cakes, fried chicken, and more make this restaurant a local landmark. $–$$$

Ice Cream Gallery, Inc. 5 Goodsell Alley, Crisfield; (410) 968-0809. All things cold and sweet, from milkshakes to floats to Italian ices, in a location that overlooks the water. $

Where to Stay

Econo Lodge. 10936 Market Lane (Route 13), Princess Anne; (410) 651-9400, www .choicehotels.com. Outdoor pool, complimentary continental breakfast. $$, kids eighteen and younger stay **free** with parents Somers Cove Motel. 700 Robert Norris Dr., Crisfield; (410) 968-1900. Within walking distance of the boat ramp, restaurants and shops, this motel has an outdoor swimming pool and rooms with microwaves, refrigerators, air-conditioning, telephones, and televisions. $$

For More Information

Somerset County Tourism Office. P.O. Box 243, 11440 Ocean Hwy, Princess Anne 21853, or 3 Ninth St., Crisfield 21817; (410) 651-2968, (410) 968-2501, (800) 521-9189, www.skipjack.net/le_shore/visitsomerset.

Annual Events

Kite Festival. Ocean City; (800) OC-OCEAN, www.ococean.com. World-class fliers compete on the beach in April.

Oxford Day. Oxford; (410) 226-5730, www .oxfordmd.com/oba. Family fun day in April with pancake breakfast, dog show, historic reenactments, crab races, and more.

Soft Shell Spring Fair. City Dock, Crisfield; (410) 968-2500. Children's activites, crafts, and crabs galore at this popular May event.

Strawberry Festival. Ridgely. Sunday before Memorial Day. In addition to featuring lots and lots of strawberries, this festival includes games, a parade, and dancing, plus other kinds of food.

Chestertown Tea Party. Chestertown. A festival celebrating the events of May 23, 1774, when local residents supported the actions of the Boston Tea Party by dumping tea from a boat anchored in the Chester River. Held on Memorial Day weekend.

Cypress Festival. Cypress Park, Pocomoke City. Music, a duck derby, craft show, rides, food, and a tug-of-war competition, held in June.

Other Things to See and Do on the Eastern Shore

- **Action Watercraft Rentals.** 142nd Street Marina, Ocean City; (301) 537-6500, (888) 2-GET-WET, www.actionmarine.org

- **Adkins Museum and Historical Complex.** 1010 Camden Ave., Salisbury; (410) 749-4871

- **Baja Amusements.** 12639 Ocean Gateway, West Ocean City; (410) 213-BAJA (2252), www.bajaoc.com

- **Bicycle Rentals and Atlantic Bike Company.** Eighth Street on the Boardwalk, Ocean City; (410) 289-3305

- **Carousel Ice Rink.** Inside Carousel Beachfront Hotel, 11700 Coastal Hwy, Ocean City; (410) 524-1000

- **Cecil County Dragway.** 1916 Theodore Rd., Rising Sun; (410) 287-6280, (410) 287-9105, www.cecilcountydragway.com

- **Chester River Kayak Adventures.** 5758 Main St., Rock Hall; (410) 639-2001, www.crkayakadventures.com

- **Country Comfort Farm.** 23720 St. Michaels Rd., St. Michaels; (410) 745-3160

- **Dockside Express.** St. Michaels Harbor, St. Michaels; (410) 886-2643, www.docksidexpress.com

- **Drag-N-Fly Go-Karts.** Sixty-eighth Street on Bay, Ocean City; (410) 723-2234

- **Island Water Sports.** First Street and Bay, Ocean City; (410) 289-2896

- **Historic Chestertown New Yarmouth Tours.** P.O. Box 632, Chestertown; (410) 778-3221

- **Liquid Fun, Locust Point Marina.** 145 River Rd., Elkton; (866) LQID-FUN

- **Miss Clare Cruises.** Chesapeake City; (410) 885-5088, www.missclare-cruises.com

- ***Nathan of Dorchester* Chesapeake Bay Skipjack.** 526 Poplar St., Cambridge; (410) 228-7141; www.skipjack-nathan.org/Default.htm

- **OC Bayside Rentals.** 307 Dorchester St., Ocean City; (410) 289-7112, www.ocbaysiderentals.com

- **Paw Paw Heritage Museum.** 98 North Main St., Port Deposit, (410) 378-3086, www.portdeposit.com/History/pawpaw.htm

- **Perdue Stadium.** 6400 Hobbs Rd., Salisbury; (410) 546-4444, www.theshore birds.com

- **Sport Crabber.** Twenty-second Street Bayside, Bahia Marina, Ocean City; (410) 726-8223, www.sportcrabber.com

- **Spring Valley Farm.** 724 Conowingo Rd., Conowingo; (410) 378-3280, www .springvalleyfarm.com

- **Tangier Island Cruises.** 1001 West Main St., Crisfield; (410) 968-2338, 800-863-2338, www.tangiercruise.com

- **Tangier Sound Outfitters.** 27582 Farm Market Rd., Marion; (410) 968-1803, http://tsokayaking.tripod.com

Queen Anne's County Waterman's Heritage Festival. Wells Cove Road, Grasonville; (410) 643-8530. A June celebration of local seafood and the people who catch it, with children's activities.

Live Music in Fountain Park. Chestertown. Held on Saturdays in June, July, and August. Music starts at 7 p.m.

July Fourth Fireworks and Parade. Rock Hall. An old-fashioned parade plus live music, craft vendors, horseshoe tournaments, turtle races, and more. The fireworks are the most extravagant on the Eastern Shore.

Concerts on the Beach. Ocean City; (410) 250-0125 or visit www.ococean.com. Every Wednesday in July and August starting at 8 p.m. **Free.**

Sundaes in the Park. Northside Park, Ocean City; (410) 250-0125, www.ococean .com. A free family concert is held every Sunday in July and August from 6 p.m. to 8 p.m. Make your own ice-cream sundaes for a small fee and participate in children's activities while watching the sun set over the bay.

Berlin Summer Celebration. Main Street, Berlin; (410) 641-4775. Children's activities, food, live music, and sidewalk sales in August.

Caroline Summerfest. Denton; (888) SUN-FEST, www.carolinesummerfest.com. A twoday arts and entertainment festival located in the heart of town, held on the third Friday and Saturday in August. Plenty of food.

Great Pocomoke Fair. Pocomoke Fairgrounds, Pocomoke. Carnival rides, horse shows, tractor pull, and other country fun in August.

National Hard Crab Derby. Crisfield. Crab races, crab-cooking contests, crab-picking contests and crabs to eat, plus a parade, boat races, entertainment, and crafts in August.

Sunfest. Inlet Parking Lot, Ocean City. Live music, arts and crafts, food, and more kick off what is known as the "second season" in Ocean City in September.

Chesapeake Celtic Festival. Furnace Town Historic Site, Snow Hill; (410) 632-2032. In October, celebrate the region's Celtic heritage with sheepherding, a medieval encampment, music, dancing, and more.

Downtown Halloween Funfest. Salisbury; 704-638-5297. Haunted trolley rides, clowns, food, hayrides, costume contests, live music, trick-or-treating with local merchants, and other seasonal fun.

Oysterfest. Chesapeake Bay Maritime Museum, St. Michaels; (410) 745-2916, www.cbmm.org. Live music, kid activities, shucking, and plenty of oysters for eating in November.

Waterfowl Festival. Easton; (410) 822-4567, www.waterfowlfestival.org. Top wildlife artists from around the country gather in November to offer their works for sale. Also, kid activities, food, music, and craft demonstrations.

Christmas Parade. Ocean City, (800) OC-OCEAN. A holiday-season tradition with marching bands, colorful floats and more.

First Night Talbot. Several locations in Easton; (410) 820-8822, www.easternshore.com/firstnighttalbot. Family-oriented alcoholfree celebration with lots of entertainment to ring in the New Year.

New Year's Eve Celebration. Ocean City Convention Center, Ocean City; (410) 798-6304, www.ococean.com. Live entertainment, children's activities, and a huge beach ball that drops at midnight.

Index

About the Author

Karen Nitkin is a freelance writer and editor. She lives in Ellicott City, Maryland, with her husband, David, and their two children, Veronica and Samuel. She writes frequently for the *Baltimore Sun,* and her work has appeared in *Cooking Light, Baltimore* magazine, and many other publications.